THE WATERY GRAVE

The Life and Death of HMS Manchester

THE WATERY GRAVE

The Life and Death of HMS Manchester

Richard Osborne

Frontline Books

THE WATERY GRAVE
The Life and Death of HMS Manchester

This edition published in 2015 by Frontline Books,
an imprint of Pen & Sword Books Ltd,
47 Church Street, Barnsley, S. Yorkshire, S70 2AS

ISBN: 978-1-47384-585-5

CIP data records for this title are available from the British Library

Printed and bound by CPI Group (UK) Ltd, Croydon, CR0 4YY
Typeset in 10/12 point Palatino

For more information on our books, please email: info@frontline-books.com, write to us at the above address, or visit
www.frontline-books.com

Contents

List of Maps

Foreword

Igrew up in Portsmouth and from 1956 went to school in Southsea. My bus journey took me past the Portsmouth Naval Base where, until 1958, I could see the cruiser HMS *Liverpool* laid up in Reserve. *Liverpool* was the name-ship of a sub-class of three ships belonging to the Town-class and had been badly damaged by torpedoes in the Mediterranean in both 1940 and 1942. The latter incident occurred during a Malta convoy code-named Operation *Harpoon* and the torpedo damage was so severe that *Liverpool* was not returned to service until after VE day. *Gloucester*, one of her two sisters, was sunk off Crete during May 1941 having run out of anti-aircraft ammunition. Her other sister, *Manchester*, was a Portsmouth-based ship and was lost during the Malta convoy code-named Operation *Pedestal*.

By the early 1960s I had read Volume II of Captain Stephen Roskill's official history *The War at Sea* 1939 – 1945, and noted that he had recorded *Manchester* as being scuttled prematurely. Many of my school friends' fathers had served in the Royal Navy during the Second World War but I could never persuade them to comment on the loss of *Manchester*. Eventually, one former Royal Navy officer who had served in the Mediterranean during 1941–1943 expressed the opinion that the loss of *Manchester* was 'not the Royal Navy's finest moment' but would not elaborate further.

In due course I became a University Lecturer in Pharmacology at the University of the West of England but continued to develop my interest in the Royal Navy and its ships as a hobby. From 1979 onwards I organised an annual meeting in Bristol for World Ship Society warship enthusiasts and, during the 2010 event, Dr Chris Simons, a university colleague of mine, gave an illustrated presentation about his dive on the wreck of *Manchester* the year before. This rekindled my interest in the loss of the cruiser and resulted in several visits to the National Archives at Kew where I was able to view the Minutes of the court martial convened to consider the loss of *Manchester*. These Minutes were written up in three volumes (with the National Archives references: ADM 156/209–211), the last being ship plans, totalling 600 pages of questions and answers plus the apportionment of blame.

This book charts the origins and career of the Town-class cruiser *Manchester* from the date she was ordered until 13 August 1942 when she scuttled off Kelibia. I have drawn extensively upon the material in the Minutes of the court martial in an attempt to explain what happened that night in August 1942. However, to understand why *Manchester* was scuttled it is also necessary to consider 'her experience' and that of her Captain during another Malta convoy, code-named Operation *Substance*, in July 1941. There is no doubt that the scuttling of *Manchester* triggered a robust response from the higher echelons in the Admiralty, not least because during 1941 and 1942 several British cruisers had been fought until they were sunk. The tame scuttling of a large cruiser therefore did not go down well with Their Lordships. In this book I have attempted to address the problems facing *Manchester*'s commanding officer, the alternative actions he could have taken and the possible consequences for his ship and the convoy operation in which he was involved.

Richard Osborne
Nailsea, August 2015

Glossary
of Technical Terms and Abbreviations

AA	Anti-Aircraft.
AB	Able Seaman.
Abaft	A relative term used to describe the location of one object in relation to another in which the object described is farther aft than the other.
Abeam	The bearing of an object 90 degrees from ahead (in a line with the middle of the ship).
'A' bracket	A bracket supporting the after end of the propeller shaft and propeller in twin or multiple screwed ships having propellers fitted off the centreline.
ABU	Auxiliary Back Up.
ACNS	Assistant Chief of the Naval Staff.
AFO	Admiralty Fleet Order.
ADO	Assistant Divisional Officer.
AMC	Armed Merchant Cruiser.
AR.RDF	Aerial Ranging Radio Direction Finding.
A/S	Anti-Submarine.
ASDIC	Usually claimed to stand for Anti-Submarine Detection Investigating Committee but Willem Hackman (*Seek & Strike: Sonar, Anti-Submarine Warfare and the Royal Navy 1914-54*, HMSO 1984) could find no evidence for the existence of such a committee. He believed that the acronym stood for 'Anti-Submarine Division-ics' – the Department that initiated research into underwater detection during 1914-1918. Today ASDIC is known as SONAR.
Athwartships	Across the ship, at right angles to the centreline.
AW. RDF	Air Warning Radio Direction Finding.
Barbettes	Structures upon which gun turrets rotate. Shells and propellants are passed up to the guns from the shellrooms and magazines
Beam	The registered breadth of a vessel measured at the outside of the hull amidships, or at its greatest breadth.

Bearing	The direction of an object with reference to you, your ship or another object.
Bilge	Lowest points within hull compartments where liquids may accumulate.
Bilge keel	Non-retractable elongated longitudinal fins protruding from the bilge and used to reduce rolling.
BR	Book of Reference.
Bulkhead	A vertical structural partition in a vessel's interior dividing it into various compartments for strength and safety purposes.
Bulkhead gland	Gland which allows bulkhead penetration by cables etc. without compromising the bulkheads watertight integrity.
Bulwark	Barrier of stiffened plating at the outboard edge of the main or upper deck to prevent or inhibit the entry of the sea.
Cable (length)	100 fathoms or 600 feet.
CAFO	Confidential Admiralty Fleet Order.
Capstan	Steel warping drum rotating on a vertical axis for the handling of mooring lines and, optionally, anchor cable.
CERA	Chief Engine Room Artificer.
C-in-C	Commander-in-Chief.
CO	Commanding Officer.
Coaming	Any vertical surface on a ship designed to deflect or prevent entry of water.
Cdr (E)	Engineer Commander.
Cdr (N)	Navigator Commander.
Compartment	A subdivision of space or room in a ship.
Condenser	Heat exchanger which converts gaseous steam into liquid water.
Controller	Third Sea Lord.
CPO	Chief Petty Officer.
CS	Cruiser Squadron.
Deck	A platform or horizontal floor which extends from side to side of a vessel.
Displacement	The weight of the water displaced by a ship. This weight is the same as the weight of the ship when afloat. Standard displacement is the displacement of a warship complete, fully manned and equipped ready for sea including all ammunition, equipment, provisions, miscellaneous stores and fresh water for the crew but without fuel or reserved boiler water on board. Full load is standard displacement plus fuel and reserve boiler water on board.
DCT	Director Control Tower.
DCNS	Deputy Chief of Naval Staff.
DNC	Director of Naval Construction.
DF	Destroyer Flotilla.
DG	Degaussing, the process of decreasing/eliminating the magnetic field of a ship.

DNI	Director of Naval Intelligence.
DNO	Director of Naval Ordnance.
Draft (draught)	The depth of a vessel below the waterline measured vertically to the lowest part of the hull, propellers or other reference point.
DSC	Distinguished Service Cross.
DSM	Distinguished Service Medal.
Engine Room	Space where the main engines of a ship are located.
ERA	Engine Room Artificer.
FAA	Fleet Air Arm.
Fathom	A seagoing unit of measure equivalent to six feet.
FD	Fighter Direction.
FDO	Fighter Direction officer.
Flat	A small partial deck, built level, without curvature (e.g. keyboard flat, midshipman's chest flat, 'X' flat etc.)
Flare	Outward curvature or widening of the hull above the waterline present in the bow section.
FO	Flag Officer.
Forecastle	A structure at the forward end of a vessel formed by carrying up the ship's shell plating a deck height above the level of the uppermost complete deck and fitting a deck over the length of this structure.
Forecastle deck	A deck over the main deck.
Forefoot	The forward end of a vessel's stem which is stepped on the keel.
Forepeak	The narrow extremity of a vessel's bow. Also the space within it.
Foul	Jammed, not clear.
Frames	The ribs of a ship.
Freeboard	Vertical measurement from the vessel's side amidships from the load waterline to the upperside of the freeboard deck.
Gunner	Warrant Officer given training as a gunnery instructor with particular emphasis on Direction. Their skills and training also helped to ensure high levels of availability.
Gunner (T)	Warrant Officer trained as a gunnery instructor but with the emphasis on torpedoes.
Gunnery Control Tables	Mechanical computers used for fire control of, for example, the 6-inch and 4-inch guns in HMS *Manchester*.
HA	High Angle (gunnery).
HACP	High Angle Control (or Calculating) Position (analogous to TS).
HA.DCT	High Angle Director Control Tower.
Halliards or Halyards	Ropes used for hoisting gaffs, sails and signal flags.
Hawse	The part of a ship's bow in which are the hawse holes for the anchor chains.
Heel	Inclination of a vessel to one side.

HF/DF	High Frequency Direction Finding.
HMAS	His Majesty's Australian Ship.
HMS	His Majesty's Ship.
IFF	Interrogator Friend or Foe.
Inboard	Towards the centreline of a ship.
Knuckle	Abrupt change in direction of hull surface or structure.
LA	Low Angle (gunnery).
LA.DCT	Low Angle Director Control Tower.
LS	Leading Seaman.
Lt	Lieutenant.
Lt Cdr	Lieutenant Commander.
Lt Cdr (G)	Gunnery Lieutenant Commander.
List	To lean to one side.
Main circulator	Pumps which circulate seawater around he condenser tubes.
Main deck	The main continuous deck or principal deck of a vessel.
MAS	*Motoscafo Armato Silurente.*
Mechanician	Not a current Royal Navy rank, the Mechanician (machinist) was skilled in making machinery and tools.
Mile	Where 'mile' is used in this book as a distance at sea, the nautical mile or sea mile should be assumed – one minute of latitude, equivalent to 6,080 feet (usually rounded off to 2,000 yards in naval practice and 1.8532 kilometres. The English land mile is 1,760 yards (5,280 feet).
MT	Motoscafo Turismo.
MTB	Motor Torpedo Boat.
MTL	*Motoscafo Turismo Lenta.*
MTS	*Motoscafo Turismo Silurente.*
nm	nautical mile.
oa	Length measured from the foremost point of the stem to the aftermost part of the stern.
Outboard	In a direction towards the side of the ship.
OS	Ordinary Seaman.
NOIC	Naval Officer In Charge.
Panting	The pulsation in and out of the bow and stern plating as the ship alternately rises and plunges deep into the water.
Paravane	A type of water kite which is towed with wire rope from a fitting on the forefoot of a vessel, operates to ride out from the ship's side and deflect mines which were moored in the path of the vessel and to cut them adrift so that they rose to the surface where they could be seen and destroyed.
Pintle	A metal pin secured to the rudder, which is hooked downwards into gudgeon on the stern post, and affords an axis of oscillation or the rudder is moved from side to side for steering in a seaway.
Pitching	The oscillatory vertical motion of a vessel forward and aft.

Platform	A partial deck and which does not contribute to the overall longitudinal strength of the vessel.
Plummer block	A plummer block is a pedestal used to provide support for a rotating shaft.
Plot clock	Used in navigation in conjunction with nautical charts in the chart house or plotting room.
PO	Petty Officer.
Port side	The left hand side of the ship looking forward.
pp	Length between the perpendiculars from the forward side of the stem to the aft side of the stern part of the designed waterline.
Quarter	A side of a ship between the main midship frames and the stern.
Quarterdeck	The after portion of the weather deck and allotted for the use of officers.
RADAR	RAdio Detection and Ranging.
RAF	Royal Air Force.
RCNVR	Royal Canadian Navy Volunteer Reserve.
RDF	Radio Direction Finding (Radar).
Ring Main	An electrical wiring technique used in electricity supply.
RM	Royal Marine.
RN	Royal Navy.
RNR	Royal Navy Reserve.
RNVR	Royal Navy Volunteer Reserve.
Roll	Motion of a ship from side to side, alternatively raising and lowering each side of the deck.
RPC	Remote Power Control.
Shaft	Long, round, heavy forging connecting engine and propeller.
Shaft alley	Covered tunnels within a ship through which the tail shafts pass.
Schoolmaster	Instructor, e.g. Instructor Lieutenant.
SHP	Shaft Horse Power.
Shore(s)	Wooden props by which ribs or frames of a vessel are externally supported while the ship is held upright on the ways. Timber used to shore up damaged and/or vulnerable bulkheads.
SLC	*Siluri Lenta Corsa.*
Slop room	A utility room typically used for laundry.
SNOIC	Senior Naval Officer In Charge.
SPO	Stoker Petty Officer.
SONAR	SOund Navigation and Ranging.
SR.RDF	Surface Ranging Radio Direction Finding.
SS	Steam Ship.
Starboard side	The right hand side of the ship looking forward.
Stern post	The after post to which the rudder is hinged and placed on the skeg with sufficient clearance for the propeller to revolve.
Stern tube	The bearing which supports the propeller shaft where it emerges from the ship. A cast iron or steel cylinder, fitted with brass, which

are lined with lignum vitae or white metal bearing surfaces upon which the propeller shaft, enclosed in brass sleeve, rotates.

Strakes
A continuous line of plates on a vessel's side, reaching from stem to stern.

S/Lt
Sub Lieutenant.

SW.RDF
Surface Warning Radio Direction Finding.

Telemotor
A mechanical, electrical, or hydraulic system by which power is applied at or controlled from a distant point, especially such a system actuating a ship's rudder.

Trim
To modify the angle of a vessel to the water by shifting cargo or ballast; to adjust for sailing; to assume, or cause a vessel to assume, a certain position, or trim, in the water.

TS
Transmitting Station – A compartment between decks which housed the fire-control predictors. They were fed target information (range, bearing, elevation) from optical instruments (sights and rangefinders) and/or radar equipment trained on the target; they calculated the future position of the target; and they transmitted to the gun mountings the predicted ranges, bearings and elevations for the guns to hit the target. In larger ships the TS was concerned with LA (surface) fire control only, the HA equivalent being the HACP.

TSDS
Two Speed Destroyer Sweep. TSDS comprised a pair of davits on the quarters to hoist out paravanes, stowed on the quarterdeck, and winches to haul and veer on the wires, plus stowages for said wires, and for the other minesweeping apparatus (kites, otters). The equipment was designed to sweep moored mines.

Turbine Relief Valve
Limits pressure in the system.

Turrets
Structures designed for the mounting and handling of guns of a warship constructed so as to revolve (usually on barbettes) about a vertical axis usually by means of electrical or hydraulic machinery.

Type 273
Surface warning radar.

Type 279
Long range air warning radar.

Type 284
LA gunnery control radar.

Type 285
HA gunnery control (HA/LA gunnery control in destroyers) radar.

Ultra
Code-name and message prefix for Special Intelligence from codes and cyphers.

USS
United States Ship.

Valve pintle
A short extension of the needle-valve tip to facilitate control of fluid through the valve.

WO
Warrant Officer.

Working up
A period spent in exercises working up the efficiency of a ships'

	company of ships newly commissioned after building or refit.
W/T	Wireless Telegraphy.
'Y' work	The interception of enemy signals including direction finding.
Zig zag patterns	Strict navigational evolutions involving changes of courses at pre-determined intervals so as to make submarine attacks more difficult. Each ship in the group was given precise instructions prior to the commencement of an operation and specific zig zag patterns would be initiated in response to a signal from the group commander. Zig Zag Plan 10, 110 would mean base course 110 degrees with a 15 degree turn to port after 20 minutes, a 20 degree turn to starboard after 30 minutes, a 25 degree turn to port 15 minutes later and then a 10 degree turn to after 25 minutes … Repeat *ad nauseum* until ordered to stop.

Acknowledgements

My thanks go to the following people for the help that they have given me in the four years of research that led to the publication of this work:

Dr Chris Simons whose presentation on diving the wreck of HMS *Manchester* reawakened my interest in the fate of this ship. I am also grateful for his permission to use his superb underwater photographs to illustrate this volume. Andrew Smith whose linguistic skills have enabled him to delve into and translate Italian sources, provided information on Axis forces involved in the assault on the *Pedestal* convoy. Rear Admiral Roger Morris RN Retired provided valuable insight into the problems of leadership and, in particular the form of dynamic leadership required to recover ships that had 'got into difficulties'.

I am indebted to Professor Andrew Lambert for his encouragement and advice which shaped my thoughts with regard to the context in which *Manchester*'s loss occurred. My gratitude also goes to Dave Sowdon, Geirr Haarr and Mike McAloon for their advice and support as this project developed. I am especially grateful to David Goodey for the many hours spent reading my manuscript and his constructive criticism with regard to content and direction. I thank John Grehan and Martin Mace of Frontline Books for giving me the opportunity to explore a controversial subject.

Finally, I thank my wife Chris for her patience and support throughout the many months of research and writing.

Introduction

'NOT THE ROYAL NAVY'S FINEST HOUR'

In August 1942 the Town-class cruiser HMS *Manchester* formed part of the escort to a convoy, code-named Operation *Pedestal*, of fourteen merchant ships carrying desperately needed supplies to the besieged island of Malta. The cruiser was a constituent of Force X which was tasked with providing close escort to the merchant ships as they fought their way eastward to Malta in the face of relentless air attacks and the possible intervention by Italian light and heavy naval units.

At about 01.10 hours on 13 August 1942, HMS *Manchester* was torpedoed on the starboard side abreast the after engine room when in a position approximately two miles east of Kelibia Light, Tunisia. The explosion put three of the four engines out of action and the crippled ship was brought to a stop a few minutes later. By 02.40 hours that morning *Manchester* was ready to proceed using the port outer engine and power steering restored. However, the controversial decision to scuttle the ship had been made already and at 06.47 hours *Manchester* sank stern first.

The majority of her crew then endured several months in captivity at the hands of the Vichy French in Laghouat internment camp in Algeria before being returned to the United Kingdom and participating in the Royal Navy's longest ever court martial. The outcome of the latter was summarised succinctly by Captain S.W. Roskill in Volume II of his *Official History of the Second World War, The War at Sea 1939–1945*: 'The loss of the *Manchester* led to the trial by court martial of certain of her officers and men after they had been released from internment in French North Africa. The findings of the court were to the effect that the decision to scuttle the ship had been premature.'[1]

Captain Drew was dismissed from his ship and never again employed afloat. It was, and remains, a contentious punishment because many of *Manchester*'s survivors felt that they owed their lives to his decision to scuttle which, they believed, had been taken to avoid an unnecessary loss of life. Thus, his abandonment of the crippled ship was applauded by many of his crew, who saw that *Manchester* was adrift in waters dominated by enemy aircraft, torpedo boats and submarines, and believed she was destined to be sunk in any subsequent attack. In their minds, the sentence was unfair, and represented a slur on their integrity. They argued that Captain Drew was the victim of a miscarriage of justice. There the matter would have remained but for advances in diving technology and the eventual release of the court martial papers.

The issue was reignited by a British diving expedition, led by Simon Bennett, which found *Manchester*'s wreck in 2002 and examined it in the hope that they could determine whether or not Captain Drew was right to scuttle his ship after she had been torpedoed.[2] Film taken by the divers was used in a TV documentary, entitled *Running the Gauntlet*, produced by Crispin Sadler.[3] Two veterans from HMS *Manchester*, Stoker First Class Eddie Pykett and Leading Steward Allan Walker, accompanied the expedition to observe the diving and view video footage from each dive. They recounted how *Manchester* survived three days of relentless air attacks only to be torpedoed in the after engine room by an Italian MS (*Motoscafo Silurante*) torpedo boat. They told of how Captain Drew had 400 men taken off by an Allied ship, ordered the remaining 500 to abandon ship and set scuttling charges to ensure that *Manchester* sank rather than fall into enemy hands. Allan Walker observed that 'he had no choice. All of the ship's engines were out of action, we were drifting and we had no power – we couldn't fire the guns. The ship was sinking.'

The two veterans reminisced about standing on *Manchester*'s deck and being told to abandon ship and head for the faint lights visible on the nearby Tunisian coast. Eddie Pykett clearly remembered Captain Drew telling the assembled crew on the cruiser's flight deck that 'your lives are now more valuable than the ship'.

In his documentary Crispin Sadler reported that he had seen an enormous hole in *Manchester*'s side around the aft engine compartment, and the shattered remains of the two propeller shafts. He went to say that 'there was, I believe, some talk that *Manchester* might have been able to make anywhere between two and twelve knots. Well, there was not a chance in a million that she could have made twelve knots. You could have driven a car through that hole.'

This sounds impressive until it is remembered that on 23 July 1941 *Manchester* was damaged by an Italian aerial torpedo while escorting an earlier Malta convoy. The torpedo, which exploded on the port side abreast the after engine room, blew a hole eight feet in diameter in the outer bottom. A hole of that size would accommodate a BMW Series 3 estate car, and yes, *Manchester* did manage to make twelve knots during the difficult journey back to Gibraltar.

At about the same time the wreck was being dived, Neil Tweedie, in an article for the *Telegraph* newspaper which was published on 15 August 2002, recounted the basic facts about the loss of *Manchester* and then went on to consider the court martial, writing:

'But the Admiralty insisted on a court martial which was held *in camera* and concluded that Drew had scuttled the ship prematurely. He was never given another command at sea, and died at the age of ninety-two in 1987, the stain still on his character.

'The evidence against Drew was rumoured to have been aided by one or more of his officers, rescued by British ships, who said that the ship might have been able to limp to a friendly port. Drew was unable to defend himself immediately, having been interned by the Vichy French. His court martial followed his return to Britain months later.'[4]

One implication of the article is that Captain Drew was the victim of a miscarriage of justice because the court martial was *in camera*. However, courts martial are always closed proceedings which are only open to those who have reason to be present and it is little more than inflammatory rhetoric to describe the process in such a manner.

The second implication is that Drew was the victim of a conspiracy by some of his officers who disagreed with his decision to scuttle his ship. Evidence given during the court martial did indeed reveal that many officers and men, and particular those in the Engineering Department, were most aggrieved by the decision to scuttle, which was made before attempting to get the ship underway.

Like so many contentious events, the loss of *Manchester* has spawned its own set of 'urban myths' constructed using the usual suspects of factual inaccuracy, half-truth, fading memory and, of course, conspiracy theory. Examples of such erroneous stories about *Manchester* include the following:

'Explosive charges proved ineffective and as the ship remained afloat its hulk was sunk by torpedo fired from HMS *Pathfinder*.'[5]

'The ship was completely disabled with no power and developed a twelve degree list.'[6]

'Efforts to control the flooding and enable the ship to return to Gibraltar proved unsuccessful and scuttling charges were placed. After the remainder of the ship's company had abandoned ship the charges were detonated – a torpedo from *Pathfinder* is reported to have assisted in the sinking.

'We were down to 10-15% ammunition, listing at nearly 45 degrees, with one engine destroyed and not much hope of getting the other working. The Captain decided that his choices were to wait until dawn and get blown to buggery, or to save the men.'[7]

The latter is a particularly egregious example of an urban myth because the statement about the ammunition supply is at best simplistic, the list never exceeded twelve degrees initially (and had been largely corrected at the time of scuttling), and, finally, *Manchester* actually had four engines, one of which remained operational until the end.

Ordinary Seaman Ronald Hindmarsh's recollections are of an altogether much higher calibre even though he erroneously stated that the list to starboard was gradually increasing. More intuitively, he observed the absence of all communication which he found to be unnerving. He went on to ask 'what had gone wrong with the TS [Transmitting Station]? Perhaps it was the TS that had been hit: that might explain the failure of all communications.' Later, Hindmarsh went to the flight deck and 'a minute later the Captain spoke to officers and men. He told us that we had been holed in the after engine room, and that the water was coming in through a hole too large to repair with canvas. Also the turbines have been thrown out of line and the port ones could only give us about five knots. Oh, and that we had almost run out of ammo for the Oerlikons and four-inch, so we wouldn't be able to defend ourselves. So he had decided to scuttle his valuable ship to save its falling into the hands of the enemy, and that we were to abandon ship before dawn.'[8]

To be fair to Captain Drew he was in a particularly difficult situation which would require him to choose a course of action from two extremely unpleasant options. It is also true that whatever decision he made would be subjected to criticism. That being the case, the question remains, why was the loss of HMS *Manchester* so controversial? Any attempt to explain this controversy will have to address six issues: (1) why did the combination of enemy action and the decisions made on board after the ship had been torpedoed reduce a hitherto effective fighting unit into little more than a helpless hulk; (2) was *Manchester* as helpless as actually claimed; (3) what options did Captain Drew have to choose from; (4) why did he choose to scuttle his ship; (5) why did the Admiralty decide not to employ him afloat again; and, (6), was the court martial fair? Let us investigate.

Chapter 1

The Watery Grave

On 9 July 2009, Chris Simons was one of the photographers in a nine-man dive team that visited the wreck of HMS *Manchester* which lies off Kelibia in eighty-five metres of water. His interest in the ship had been triggered in 2003 during a diving trip to Narvik, Norway where he had met Crispin Sadler. About a year earlier the latter had produced a TV programme, entitled *Running the Gauntlet*, which told the story of Operation *Pedestal* and, in particular, the circumstances surrounding the loss of the cruiser.

Chris heard that *Manchester* had been rediscovered in 2002 by Simon Bennett and that it was rumoured to be the most intact British light cruiser wreck anywhere in the world. He was intrigued to learn that the 12,300 ton, thirty-two-knot cruiser had been part of the convoy's close escort and had been the victim of an ambush by Italian motor torpedo boats lying in wait off Cape Bon, Tunisia, early in the morning of 13 August 1942. Crispin Sadler then related how one torpedo struck the ship's starboard side aft causing very serious damage and leaving the ship lying drifting and helpless a mere two miles from a shoreline with sandbanks to one side and a Vichy French minefield on the other. Placed in this difficult situation Captain Drew decided to scuttle his ship rather than risk secrets including her radar equipment, falling into enemy hands courtesy of the Vichy authorities in Tunisia. Just as dawn broke, *Manchester* slipped under the waves and settled on the bottom on her starboard side on the bed of the Mediterranean.

The nine-man expedition, led by Matt Outram[1], arrived at Tunis airport to be transported to Kelibia along with half-a-ton of rebreather diving equipment. Once in Kelibia their host diving operation, Odysea Diving, dropped a bombshell: 'Our permit is suspended, there will be no diving on *Manchester* this week.' The suspension of their permit had been caused by an unauthorised dive the previous week and the dive team now faced an anxious wait.

'Thankfully, with enormous relief,' recalled Chris Simons, 'we were permitted to dive HMS *Manchester* a few days later.' Chris continued: 'We had the use of Odysea's boat, compressor and cylinders, and our nine-man dive team planned to use closed-circuit rebreathers with a mixture of air and helium as diluent breathing gas to prevent narcosis at depth. On our way to the dive site, I remember that we politely asked the skipper if he could put us on the bow or the stern of the wreck. After wiping a momentary smile from his face, he told us that his mark was for amidships, but that it might just be possible to drop a lead-weighted rope ('shot-line') down to the bow area. Our two support divers set up decompression stations at 9m, 6m and 4.5m and made cylinders available of air/diluent and oxygen. Jumping into the big blue Mediterranean water is always stunning: we immediately appreciated the clarity of the water and felt huge thermoclines as we descended seventy-eighty metres from the surface water with a temperature of 24°C on the surface to the 14°C water surrounding the wreck. Diving to depths of eighty metres (260 feet) meant that time spent on the bottom exploring the wreck would realistically be limited to just thirty minutes which only added to our sense of anticipation. There was no way in the time available that we could explore the whole of a 600 foot-long wreck and, as we descended, we wondered what we would see after many years of planning this dive.

'It was hugely exciting; the wreck which suddenly came into view as we descended past sixty meters in depth and, incredibly, the skipper's line-shot was dropping to the seabed beyond the keel and very close to the bow – at that moment, I thanked the skipper for the perfect shot-line deployment. As we got closer I could see *Manchester* lying on her starboard side. Usually decay in salt water alters the shape of a wreck beyond recognition but, unbelievably, here was *Manchester* looking like she'd just landed on the seabed. The shape of the port hull was obvious and so we finned over the gunwales and headed aft for 'A' Turret. We observed that, while the foredeck and anchor chains were *in situ*, the tip of the bow section seemed to have broken off. Once on the foredeck, our brains automatically corrected for the list to starboard and our attention quickly switched to the 6-inch guns pointing straight ahead. Even at a depth in excess of seventy metres the water was incredibly clear and, consequently, everything was immediately recognisable in the sunlight that shone over the portside gunwales. Moving aft, the three 6-inch guns of 'B' Turret pointed majestically forwards above 'A' Turret, but were also pointing a little to port and almost skywards. 'B' Turret and its guns appeared massive and we were fascinated by the detail in the armour plating and the fixtures remaining on the decking. However, much as we may have wanted to linger, the bridge was beckoning.

'Then *Manchester* revealed her port bridge superstructure and at the top were the remains of the Director Control Tower (DCT) and rangefinders for the 6-inch gun main armament. The tripod foremast that should have been

2

aft of the main DCT appeared to be missing. Forward of the DCT was the open bridge area where Captain Drew and his officers would have stood to command the ship. One deck below, the rectangular windows with their sliding glass panes were intact. A porthole lay open, presumably as it had been when the cruiser was scuttled. The well-preserved port High-Angle Director Control Tower (HA.DCT) was clearly visible abaft the bridge as were the twin 4-inch gun mountings that constituted the ship's secondary armament. I inspected a 20mm gun that lay forward of the port HA.DCT before observing a skyward pointing Bofors 40mm gun lying near to the twin 4-inch guns. Was this one of the two Bofors 40mm guns fitted on the cruiser's flight deck? Examination of the forward section of the open bridge showed that some of the glass-panelled spray and windscreens were still intact.'

This was an unusual occurrence in Chris Simons' experience. One of the divers decided to inspect the front of the bridge more closely and later reported seeing the telegraph and telemotor intact.

Chris Simons recalled that, 'twenty minutes had now flashed by and it was now time to return to the shotline and begin the ascent, although not before pausing to take one last look at 'B' Turret's gun barrels pointing skywards and note the absence of a Bofors 40mm gun that had been on top of the turret when *Manchester* disappeared below the waves. Gentle finning brought me back to the port bow section and I used the remaining few minutes of bottom time to photograph some resident damselfish that had made their home on the port-side hull.'

Resurfacing after diving in excess of seventy metres and remaining at that depth for twenty minutes is a slow business requiring ninety minutes to achieve full decompression. Chris Simons remembers that, 'as I slowly ascended the line towards other divers ahead of me on the decompression trapeze I had plenty of time to reflect on what I had seen in this truly amazing dive. This was indeed the most intact Second World War light cruiser wreck I had ever visited. I sensed it was an incredibly vivid snapshot of a hugely significant moment in time. After the dive I was all the more determined to find out much more about *Manchester* and, in particular, what had happened aboard the doomed ship in the hours between being torpedoed and hitting the bottom shortly after dawn on 13 August 1942.'

Chapter 2

A Ship is Born

HMS *Manchester* was a 6-inch gun armed cruiser of the Southampton or Town-class as it was known later. The class was conceived in 1933 when it became known that the Japanese were building the Mogami-class of warships. At that time, the only information available about these ships was that they would be armed with fifteen 6.1-inch guns and would have 5-inch-thick side armour, all on a standard displacement of just 8,500 tons. By comparison, the Leander-class cruisers then being constructed for the Royal Navy had a standard displacement of approximately 7,000 tons, were armed with just eight 6-inch guns and protected by 2 to 4-inch side armour[1].

The obvious inferiority of the British design led to demands for the construction of a matching class with a similar armament and displacement for the Royal Navy. Consequently, the Admiralty asked Sir Arthur W. Johns, the Director of Naval Construction (DNC), to consider the possibility of constructing similar ships to counter the Mogami-class. The DNC reported back that it was virtually impossible to produce a realistic design for adequately armoured cruisers armed with fifteen 6-inch guns and with a speed well in excess of thirty knots on a standard displacement of just 8,500 tons. One can well imagine that, in private, Sir Arthur must have informed members of the Admiralty Board that either the Japanese had managed to change the laws of physics or they were cheating on their Treaty obligations.

The Admiralty response in September 1933 was to issue a revised set of requirements for a 6-inch gun cruiser armed with twelve 6-inch guns in four triple turrets, six 4-inch AA guns in three mountings, three quadruple 0.5-inch machine-gun mountings and two triple tubes for 21-inch torpedoes. The sides of the machinery spaces and magazines were to be immune to 6-inch gunfire, the decks above the machinery spaces were to be immune to 6-inch gunfire under 16,000 yards and the magazine crowns were to be immune to 6-inch gunfire under 21,000 yards. The ship was to have a range of 7,000 miles at sixteen knots, a speed of thirty knots at standard displacement and to be able to carry up to five aircraft. The DNC produced four initial sketch designs A, B, C and D developed from the preceding Amphion-class:[2]

	A	B	C	D
Length waterline (feet)	570	600	600	600
Beam upper deck (feet)	58	61	62	62
Standard displacement (tons)	7,800	8,640	8,530	8,835
Shaft Horse Power (SHP)	50,000	65,000	50,000	72,000
Speed (knots)	30	31.75	30	32
Complement (as flagship)	757	781	781	796
Aircraft	3	3	5	5

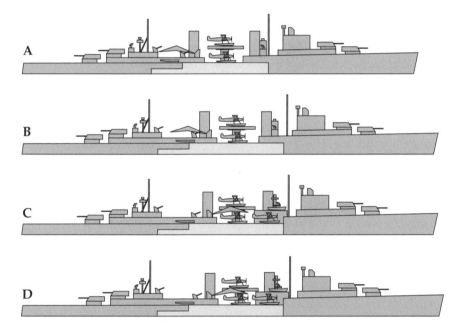

A

B

C

D

All four designs had four triple 6-inch turrets with stowage for 200 rounds per gun, three twin 4-inch HA mountings with 200 rounds per gun, three quadruple 0.5-inch machine-guns with 2,500 rounds per barrel and two sets of triple tubes for 21-inch torpedoes. The third 4-inch gun mounting was on the centreline just forward of the mainmast and it was therefore impossible to get the all-round fire requested. The sides had 5-inch armour protecting the machinery spaces, the magazines were armoured with 3-inch sides and ends plus 2-inch crowns and the deck armour over the engine and boiler room was 1.25-inch.

Designs A, B and D all had the short forward boiler room and long after boiler room arrangement of the Amphion-class with the forward engine room between the two boiler rooms. In design C, to facilitate aircraft handling the forward boiler was longer than the after boiler room. Designs A and B were criticised for their lack of hangars to protect fragile aircraft from damage in heavy weather. Experience with the Leander-class had shown the inadvisability of carrying fragile aircraft and boats in unprotected upper deck positions and this had led to the inclusion of hangars in designs C and D. However, even in these two designs, with five aircraft embarked, two would have to be stowed in the open and, should they have become unserviceable, they would block access to and from the hangar. Under those circumstances, the only way of resuming flying operations would be to jettison damaged machines.

Of the four sketches, Design C was the nearest to meeting the staff requirement but, the Third Sea Lord and Controller of the Royal Navy, Vice Admiral Sir Reginald Henderson, ruled that design D should be adopted because of its thirty-two knot speed. Furthermore, he ruled that no aircraft should be carried on the open deck thereby reducing the number embarked to three. During discussion of protection, it was argued that although the machinery spaces were well protected against 6-inch gunfire the unarmoured sides fore and aft were vulnerable along the waterline. Consequently it was suggested that the side armour should be extended along the waterline. The close range AA fire was also considered to be weak and therefore two quadruple 2-pounder gun mountings were added to the design. The overall length of the design was another concern because of the limited number of docks which could accommodate ships of that size.

By the middle of October 1933, the DNC had produced a modified design D with a waterline length of 584 feet and the side armour and armoured deck extended forward by forty-five feet. The armoured belt now covered forty per cent of the ship's waterline length and, in order to reduce weight, the side armour and magazine sides were reduced in thickness by half-an-inch. Weight was also saved by reducing the shell allowance for each 6-inch and 4-inch gun from 200 to 150. A fixed-transverse catapult was fitted amidships with its trolley at forecastle deck level. Consequently, to facilitate aircraft handling, the floor of the hangar was raised to the same level and the forecastle deck extended aft in the form of a platform running aft from the hangar doors to the after funnel. These changes meant that aircraft could be manhandled from the hangar, across the flight deck and onto the catapult without needing to be hoisted from the deck.[3]

At this time it was decided that the class would be named after mythical beasts and that the first of the class would be called *Minotaur*. Consequently, the modified design D became design A of the M-class. Further modifications to the design resulted in the elimination of the centreline twin 4-inch gun mounting and the addition of twin 4-inch guns to port and starboard some thirty-six feet aft of the original pair. The original centreline High Angle Director Control Tower (HA.DCT) on the bridge was removed and HA.DCTs sited to port and starboard on the hangar roof. The Controller decided that the funnels should be raked, ostensibly to get smoke away from the bridge but probably mainly for aesthetic reasons and the end was a particularly handsome design.[4] By this time, the standard designed displacement had risen to 9,100 tons and 11,500 tons at full load.

Two ships, named *Polyphemus* and *Minotaur*, were ordered under the 1933 Defence Estimates but soon afterwards it was decided to name the class after towns, and the ships became *Newcastle* and *Southampton* respectively. Three more ships, to become *Birmingham*, *Glasgow* and *Sheffield*, were ordered to the same design under the 1934 Estimates. A further trio, to become *Gloucester*, *Liverpool* and *Manchester*, was ordered under the 1935 Estimates but their design was modified to incorporate a second 6-inch DCT and a third HA.DCT on the centreline on the after superstructure. A shelter for gun crews was added between the twin 4-inch gun mountings to port and starboard and the bridge front rounded as an anti-inclination measure. The beam was increased by eight inches at the waterline to provide for heavier armour to the 6-inch gun turrets.[5] These alterations raised the designed standard displacement to 9,400 tons and 11,900 at full load and consequently their Shaft Horse Power (SHP) had to be increased from 72,000 to 82,500 in order to achieve thirty-two knots.[6]

The order for the future HMS *Manchester* was placed with R. & W. Hawthorn Leslie & Co. Ltd., of Hebburn-on-Tyne, on 23 October 1935. Her keel was laid on 28 March 1936, and the following January the first naval personnel, commanded by Commander (E) G.C. Ross, travelled to Hebburn to stand by the ship in the run-up to her launch. *Manchester* was launched by Mrs J. Toole, the Lady Mayoress of Manchester, on 12 April 1937. Fitting out proceeded apace and just nine months later, on 17 January 1937, Captain H.H. Bousfield became the cruiser's first commanding officer and he travelled north to stand by the ship. The first major draft of 424 ratings joined *Manchester* in her builder's yard on 3 August 1938. The following day she left Tyneside to commence her acceptance trials in the North Sea, during which she experienced engine room defects which took several hours to rectify. Gunnery trials were carried out in the afternoon, after which she anchored off South Shields at 20.42 hours that day. About thirty minutes later Captain Bousfield formally accepted *Manchester* from Hawthorn Leslie & Co. Ltd. and at 22.30 hours the ship weighed anchor and sailed for her home port of Portsmouth, arriving on 6 August.

Once in Portsmouth her complement was brought up to full strength and preparations made for her sea trials which began on 31 August and were completed on 9 September. During the next fourteen days *Manchester* was commissioned at Portsmouth and prepared to replace the cruiser *Enterprise* in the 4th Cruiser Squadron on the East Indies Station based on Trincomalee. On 24 September *Manchester* left Portsmouth en route for

Gibraltar, Malta and Alexandria, where she remained for four days before sailing for Port Said on 7 October prior to transiting the Suez Canal. The cruiser arrived at Aden on 12 October where she officially became a unit of the East Indies Station sailing the next day, in company with the cruiser *Norfolk*, which was flying the flag of the Commander-in-Chief (C-in-C) Vice Admiral James Somerville, en route for Bombay. By the end of the month *Manchester* had arrived in Trincomalee and subsequently spent much of November working up, often in company with the 8-inch gun cruiser *Norfolk*.

On 1 December *Manchester* and *Norfolk* left Trincomalee to fly the flag at Indian ports visiting Karachi (7–13 December), Goa (15–19 December), Cochin (20–25 December) and Trivandrum (27–30 December) before arriving Colombo on 31 December for a ten-day-long maintenance period. *Manchester* spent the rest of January exercising out of Trincomalee in preparation for another round of flag flying in company with *Norfolk*, this time in the Bay of Bengal. After visiting Madras (22–24 February), Calcutta (27 February–3 March) and Rangoon (6–9 March) the two cruisers arrived in Singapore on 13 March for a ten-day visit which included exercises with four destroyers. *Norfolk* and *Manchester* left Singapore on 21 March for exercises off the east coast of Malaya with the aircraft carrier *Eagle*, the heavy cruiser *Kent* and the submarine depot ship *Medway*. Thereafter, *Manchester* sailed through the Strait of Malacca en route for the rarely visited Nicobar and Andaman Islands while at the same time observing Japanese fishing vessels in the area.

After visiting Port Blair (28 March–2 April) *Manchester* headed for Trincomalee to prepare for a short refit in Colombo. However, the deteriorating situation in Europe meant that on 9 April the cruiser was ordered to remain at short notice for steam in Trincomalee. The crisis ended a week later and *Manchester* arrived at Colombo for her delayed assisted maintenance period, which was completed in early June. She returned to Trincomalee on 3 June, sailing again three days later to start her last peacetime cruise to East African and Indian Ocean ports. Subsequently, *Manchester* arrived at Diego Garcia on 9 June where she provided fuel and stores to a flying boat which was undertaking an Anglo-Australian survey of the Indian Ocean to determine the best air routes between the United Kingdom, East Africa and Australia. Having left Diego Garcia on 14 June, *Manchester* arrived at Zanzibar six days later for a week-long visit. Leaving Zanzibar on 27 June the cruiser proceeded up the East African coast visiting Dar-es-Salaam (7 July), Tanga (8–10 July) and Mkoani Island (11–13 July) before anchoring in Kilindini on 14 July where she joined her sister ship *Gloucester*. The latter was flying the flag of Rear Admiral Ralph Leatham, the newly appointed C-in-C East Indies, who had relieved Vice Admiral Somerville when the latter had been diagnosed with tuberculosis and placed on the retired list.

Throughout the summer the international situation in Europe continued to deteriorate and it was obvious to all that the outbreak of war was but a matter of weeks away. At that time the Italian colony of Abyssinia, with its 400 nautical mile-long coastline at the southern end of the Red Sea, posed a potentially serious threat to British shipping sailing between the eastern Mediterranean and the Indian Ocean. Abyssinia was garrisoned by about 250,000 Italian troops supported by aircraft, while the small force of destroyers and submarines based at Massawa was ideally situated to interdict British shipping in the Red Sea. On 25 July, *Manchester* and *Gloucester* left Mombasa for Aden where they were joined by the sloops *Egret* and *Fleetwood*. Unsurprisingly, in view of the burgeoning international crisis, the four ships undertook a series of convoy escort exercises in the Red Sea along the 700 nautical miles between Aden and Port Sudan.

An example of this took place on 10 August when *Manchester*, in company with *Gloucester*, *Fleetwood* and *Egret*, left Aden to escort a six-ship troop convoy which was travelling from Bombay to Egypt. On completion of this exercise *Manchester* entered Port Sudan on 14 August, where she remained for two days before sailing onto Aden. Seven days later she left Aden to rendezvous with the troopship *Dilwara*, which was sailing from Bombay to Alexandria, and escorted her past the potentially hostile coast of Abyssinia as far as Port Sudan. The cruiser was back in Aden on 31 August leaving the next day to patrol in the southern Red Sea and the Gulf of Aden.

War was by now imminent and the ship's company was at defence stations with the ship darkened at night. *Manchester* arrived back at Aden on Sunday, 3 September at approximately 10.30 hours local time, some two and half hours before war was declared. After refuelling she sailed for Colombo in company with her sister *Gloucester*.

On 9 September 1939, *Manchester* departed Colombo for a five-day patrol in local waters. A few days later the cruiser sailed for Bombay, arriving on 21 September. She left the same day to continue her patrol duties in the Arabian Sea. On 25 September *Manchester* joined the sloop *Rochester* as escort to the troopships *Indora* and *Rohna* which were transporting Indian soldiers from Bombay to Suez. After covering the passage of the two ships north of the Sudan border, *Manchester* returned to Aden to await an Anglo-French convoy. The latter was escorted from Aden to just south of the Gulf of Suez where the cruiser rendezvoused with the 21,000-ton *Empress of Australia*, which had been requisitioned as a troopship, and conveyed her to Colombo via Aden. Soon thereafter *Manchester* was detailed to return to the United Kingdom to act as flagship of the 18th Cruiser Squadron of the Home Fleet based on Scapa Flow.

Consequently, on 10 November, *Manchester* left Colombo for the United Kingdom via Aden and Port Said, arriving at Malta on 18 November. At Malta, Vice Admiral Geoffrey Layton hoisted his flag on *Manchester* on assuming command of the 18th Cruiser Squadron. Layton has been described as a 'tough sailor whose phraseology was reminiscent of language usually heard in the fo'c'sle of a dreadnought and who did not hesitate to use the whiplash of his tongue when he felt people were not pulling their weight'.[7] Sadly, his relationship with the ship and her complement got off to a bad start because after leaving Malta on 20 November *Manchester* ran into heavy weather which caused superficial damage forward as well as flooding various parts of the cruiser including the Admiral's quarters aft.[8] The Vice Admiral was unimpressed and made his displeasure known to all and sundry using the most colourful language.

During her homeward dash, *Manchester* called briefly at Gibraltar on 22 November and arrived at Portsmouth three days later. Soon after her arrival the cruiser was docked for a short refit during which a range of defects were corrected and storm damaged stanchions replaced as the ship was prepared for war in northern waters.

Chapter 3

War

On 22 December 1939, *Manchester* left Portsmouth, steaming north via the Irish Sea for Scapa Flow to join the Home Fleet. While on passage the opportunity was taken to carry out some post-refit trials. The cruiser arrived at Scapa Flow during a blizzard on Christmas Eve, joining the 18th Cruiser Squadron as the flagship of Vice Admiral Geoffrey Layton. At that time of year, ships involved in the Northern Patrol had to endure what seemed to be endless days and weeks roaming the cold and inhospitable waters in the Denmark Strait and the Iceland–United Kingdom gap enforcing the blockade of German imports and exports. This gloomy prospect must have percolated into the Vice Admiral's subconscious because when he addressed *Manchester*'s company on Christmas Day he told them 'that they would be spending at least twenty-five days a month at sea in the worst possible conditions' and enjoined them 'to try not to let the ship be flooded again in a slight blow'.[1] Having told them not to distribute tea and cigarettes to any Germans that they captured, Layton finished his cheery Christmas address by informing the assembled company that they would be sailing to their assigned patrol position early the next day.

On Boxing Day, *Manchester* sailed from Scapa Flow to relieve *Sheffield* on patrol north of the Shetland Islands. The Swedish SS *Virginia* was intercepted and boarded for inspection during the afternoon of 28 December. Her cargo appeared to have a neutral destination and consequently *Virginia* was allowed to proceed. *Manchester* was back in Scapa Flow on 2 January sailing a day later, after refuelling, for a twenty-four-hour patrol. After a ten-day rest period in the bleak northern base, *Manchester* left Scapa for a twelve-day patrol during which she intercepted the Norwegian SS *Lisa* on 20 January and sent her into Kirkwall for examination. The cruiser returned to Scapa Flow on 27 January for a much-needed boiler clean before sailing again on 2 February. On the evening of 5 February *Manchester* intercepted the Norwegian SS *Cetus* but was unable to put a boarding party on board because of the heavy seas. The cruiser stayed with the merchant ship until she was able to hand the Norwegian over to an armed trawler which then escorted *Cetus* to Kirkwall where her cargo was checked for contraband. The patrol ended with *Manchester*'s arrival at Scapa Flow on 12 February.

Although *Manchester*'s next patrol ended with her return to Scapa on 25 February, Vice Admiral Layton's War Diary for the 18th Cruiser Squadron reveals that there was little respite from this monotonous and punishing routine during the following month.[2] *Manchester* left Scapa at 07.30 hours on 2 March and proceeded to take up patrol position NP 54. At 10.30 hours a patrol aircraft reported Swedish vessel SS *Lagaholm* on fire and sinking in position 59° 34'N 5° 10'W and a submarine submerging nearby in the vicinity. A lifeboat with survivors was also reported. *Manchester* sighted *Lagaholm* at 11.45 hours, when there was no fire, but the ship had a big list. The cruiser signalled aircraft to obtain assistance from a trawler while at the same time altering course to northeast to move away from the suspected submarine at nineteen knots. The weather was fresh with a strong westerly and the sea moderate becoming rough.

At 16.20 hours on 3 March *Manchester* sighted the Norwegian SS *Hallinodal* bound for Oslo from Cardenas with a cargo of sugar. The weather was unsuitable for boarding and *Manchester* escorted her to the West Faeroes trawler rendezvous. The wind was recorded as a strong westerly with the sea rough, the sky overcast but with good visibility. *Manchester* turned *Hallinodal* over to the trawler *Northern Gem* at 17.30 hours on 4 March. The weather was atrocious with a north-westerly gale veering north by northwest, the sky being overcast with good visibility. The cruiser shaped to course 290 degrees to return to the eastern end of patrol position NP 54 but excessive rolling, thirty-five degrees either way, made it necessary to heave to on course 330 degrees with an approximate speed of four knots. By 18.00 hours the wind was north by west Force 10, with the sea state moderate to rough and it was snowing heavily. The gale moderated during the night and the following morning, at 09.00 hours, course was altered to take up a new position on NP 54. By noon the wind had backed to westerly, Force 2–3, the sea now being slight with good visibility.[3]

By 11.30 hours on 5 March *Manchester* arrived back on her patrol line having been absent for forty-three hours because of bad weather, and at 15.45 hours she carried out a range and inclination exercise with the 8-inch gun armed cruiser *York*. An hour and ten minutes later she sighted the Danish SS *Venus* with an armed guard from the armed merchant cruiser *Derbyshire* on board.

At 20.25 hours, when in position 62° 39'N 15° 40'W, *Manchester* sighted the Swedish SS *John* from Buenos Aires to Landskrona with general cargo. The ship was boarded and it was found that the whole cargo was covered by Navicerts[4] except for 200 tons of Ground Nut Expeller. SS *John* was therefore sent to Kirkwall for inspection. On 6 March the weather remained quite good with a Force 3–4 south-south-westerly wind, a slight swell and good visibility. But it was too good to last and the following morning brought strong south-south-westerly winds veering to the west which reached gale force by the afternoon. At 11.10 hours on 7 March, when in position 63° 30'N 12° 10'W, *Manchester* sighted Swedish SS *Inger* eastbound, but the latter was allowed to proceed in accordance with an earlier Admiralty message. At 19.30 hours the Belgian trawler *Van Oost*, steering south-south-east, was sighted in position 62° 42'W 15° 30'W but was also allowed to proceed.[5]

The Swedish *Hammaren*, westbound from Gothenburg to New York, was sighted at 01.15 hours on 8 March in position 63° 12'N 13° 22'W but she was allowed to proceed in accordance with Admiralty instructions. At 05.00 hours that morning the wind suddenly veered to the north and the temperature fell from 37°F to 28°F with considerable snow in the afternoon. *Nordstjernan*, another Swedish ship, was sighted at 14.35 hours that day in position 63° 9'N 13° 22'W but was allowed to proceed in accordance with an earlier Admiralty message.

Some eight hours later, at 22.30 hours when in position 68° 48'N 14° 32'W, *Manchester* sighted a darkened ship bearing 200 degrees at a range of about ten miles. *Manchester* challenged the vessel twice with a box lamp and five times with Aldis without reply and consequently increased speed to thirty knots to intercept. Shortly afterwards at 23.00 hours the cruiser fired four rounds of star shell over the darkened ship which proved to be the armed merchant cruiser *Carinthia*. The latter then challenged by signalling VF and *Manchester* identified by replying VC. *Carinthia* then made the first private identification signal several times. Meanwhile, at 23.01 hours, a flashing light on the port quarter was reported and this proved to be a challenge from the armed merchant cruiser *Cilicia* in patrol position NP 55. *Manchester* made her identification signal several times. *Carinthia* should have arrived on NP 57 at 16.00 hours on 8 March and was some fifty miles too far to the northward of her proper position when first sighted, and keeping a very poor lookout. Clearly this series of events could have resulted in a very serious incident and potential loss of ship and life.

After these alarums and excursions, the remainder of the patrol became a matter of enduring the weather. The morning of 9 March started with a westerly to north-westerly wind with fine weather and extreme visibility which in the afternoon deteriorated into a series of violent squalls of snow, rain and wind, the latter reaching fifty knots in gusts. At dark, the weather cleared and the wind moderated. The following day brought little respite with fresh to strong squally westerly winds veering to the north with snow and rain squalls, visibility being good except in rain and snow. The weather improved on 11 March with moderate to fresh west-north-west winds, wintry showers and slight seas. *Manchester* arrived at Scapa at 08.30 hours on 12 March to refuel and re-provision, but even then could not escape the weather because on 15 March there was a violent north-westerly gale with gusts up to sixty-five knots.[6]

Manchester was still in Scapa Flow on 16 March when, at 19.52 hours, an enemy air attack on the fleet anchorage began at dusk. The cruiser was the only ship of the 18th Cruiser Squadron present and was also the designated anti-aircraft (AA) guardship but a delay in opening fire occurred because the pom-pom and 0.5-in machine-gun crews had been fallen out prematurely. Consequently, the first wave of attackers was not engaged at all and only one of the second wave when retiring. The first wave scored a direct hit on the 8-inch gun cruiser *Norfolk*. *Manchester* fired sixty rounds of 4-inch and 140 rounds of 2-pounder ammunition in subsequent attacks but was not herself attacked. The all-clear was given at 21.15 hours.[7] No doubt there were some interesting communications between ships and staffs relating to this incident.

At 07.00 hours on 18 March Vice Admiral Layton, in *Manchester*, left Scapa to relieve *Southampton* on Northern Patrol and the following day met *Southampton* and *Derbyshire* leaving the patrol area to refuel and re-provision. At 16.30 hours, when in position 62° 33′N 16° 15′W, *Manchester* sighted the Fleetwood trawler *Dhoon* and Grimsby trawler *Evelyn Rose*, steering 120 degrees. Subsequently, on 20 March at 13.15 hours in position 62° 33′N 16° 33′W N she encountered the Belgian trawler *Freddy* of Ostend, steering 330 degrees. An unidentified Icelandic motor trawler steering 135 degrees was encountered at 22.20 hours in position 62° 12′N 17° 23′W. At 17.04 hours the following day, when in position 62° 03′N 17° 23′W, *Manchester* closed upon the Icelandic *Edda* which was travelling from Runcorn to Reykjavik, her last port of call being Troon. The wind during these four days was consistently moderate to fresh east-north-east with cloudy and bright periods, visibility good except during rain squalls. During the night of 22-23 March the wind increased to a fresh north-westerly.

The next day, 23 March, was busy with an Icelandic trawler being sighted at 01.12 hours, one armed and four unarmed Grimsby trawlers at 02.47 hours, a Belgian trawler at 05.18 hours, *Manchester*'s sister *Birmingham* at 08.00 hours, the armed merchant cruiser *Salopian* at 09.34 hours, an Icelandic trawler at 17.00 hours and the Dutch SS *Sloterdijk* at 17.15 hours. The following day the wind increased to gale force from the northeast with a rough sea and the weather showery and significantly colder. Fortunately, conditions improved somewhat the day after as the wind decreased and visibility remained good except during rain squalls. At 04.50 hours on 25 March *Manchester* sighted an unidentified trawler, the Danish SS *Betty Maersk*, at 14.20 hours, the Finnish *Marienburg* at 16.12 hours, the Icelandic trawler *Ran* at 18.30 hours and the Icelandic trawler *Muginn* at 23.50 hours.[8] This patrol was proving to be much busier than earlier wintry sojourns.

The wind was moderate on 26 March but increased steadily from fresh to strong during the day with good visibility except in snow squalls. *Manchester* sighted some Grimsby trawlers at 02.17 hours, five trawlers at 04.30 hours, and the Norwegian ship *Mostun* at 13.01 hours. The latter was en route from New York to Bergen with general cargo which included a deck cargo of Ford cars. The weather was unsuitable for boarding and *Mostun* was escorted towards the West Faeroes trawler rendezvous. While undertaking this task, *Manchester* encountered a group of Hull trawlers at 16.00 hours, identifying *Lady Shirley* (armed), *St Helena*, *Lady Rosemary* and *Stella Carina* (armed). The wind increased to gale force with a rough sea during the night of 26-27 March and at 03.10 hours *Manchester* intercepted the Norwegian *Haarfagre* which was allowed to proceed.

At 08.15 hours she turned *Mostun* over to the armed trawler *Kingston Topaz* at the West Faeroes rendezvous from where she was taken for examination. Later that morning scheduled gunnery practices with *Birmingham* were abandoned because of the weather which had become Force 8, with rough seas and frequent heavy snow showers. *Manchester* shaped course for Scapa and soon afterwards, at 11.35 hours in position 61° 50′N 8° 30′W, she intercepted the Finnish ship *Nina* from Genoa to Bergen and ordered her to proceed for examination.[9] The strong north-westerly winds were still blowing when *Manchester* arrived at Scapa Flow at 08.00 hours on 28 March.[10] This period of rest and recuperation was interrupted by an ineffectual German air raid on the base which started at 20.40 hours on 2 April, just a few hours before the cruiser was scheduled to sail on patrol again.[11]

However, the decision to undertake minelaying operations in Norwegian waters led Admiral Forbes, the C-in-C Home Fleet, to withdraw all supporting cruisers from the Northern Patrol and consequently the 18th Cruiser Squadron was re-deployed to convoy duties. *Manchester*, *Southampton* and *Sheffield* provided cover for ON and HN convoys en route to Norway, with two out of the three deployed on each convoy.[12]

The Norwegian Campaign
During the period from January to March 1940, German fears that the Allies were planning to invade Norway and Sweden, so as to interdict the flow of iron ore to the Third Reich, coincided with ill-thought-out British and French ambitions to aid the Finns in their fight with the Russians. The Germans decided to eliminate this potential threat by launching Operation *Weserübung* – the invasion of Norway and Denmark. This began with ships leaving German and Baltic ports on 7 April and radically altered the strategic situation in the area.

It was the audacity and scale of Operation *Weserübung* that surprised the British who were slow to react and made a number of serious mistakes early on. The Allies also had plans to deny Norwegian territorial waters to German ships by mining the approaches to Narvik (Operation *Wilfred*).[13]

To counter any German retaliation against Norway, an expeditionary force was being held aboard a force of cruisers and destroyers at Rosyth (Operation *R4*).[14] On 7 April intelligence suggested that a major German naval operation was underway. The Admiralty assumed that this was another Atlantic breakout and consequently on the orders of the First Lord, Winston Churchill, Operation *R4* was abandoned and the Home Fleet sortied to cover the routes into the Atlantic. The cancellation of Operation *R4* and the disembarkation of troops destined for Norway was one such early mistake and resulted in series of poorly planned and executed military operations in Norway.

On 7 April *Manchester*, in company with the cruisers *Southampton* and *Calcutta*, and assisted by the destroyers *Eclipse*, *Grenade*, *Javelin* and *Juno*, was at sea providing close support to the forty-three-ship outward bound convoy ON25 which was on passage to Norway. That afternoon Vice Admiral Layton received orders to turn the convoy back towards Scotland and take *Manchester* and *Southampton* to join the Home Fleet under the command of Admiral Forbes in the Norwegian Sea. The two cruisers joined the fleet at 06.30 hours on 9 April. At 09.00 hours that morning German floatplanes started to shadow the Home Fleet which, in turn, had been ordered to conserve AA ammunition. The aircraft appeared to jettison bombs as they left their patrols but *Manchester* and *Southampton* avoided them by taking evasive action.[15]

It became known on the morning of 9 April that German forces were landing at several points on the Norwegian coast. At 11.30 hours on 9 April the 18th Cruiser Squadron (*Manchester*, *Southampton*, *Glasgow*, *Sheffield*) was detached from the Home Fleet off Norway to cover the Tribal-class destroyers *Afridi*, *Mohawk*, *Somali*, *Gurkha*, *Sikh*, *Mashona* and *Matabele* which had been ordered to attack Bergen where, it was believed, there was a German Köln-class cruiser in the harbour. The Admiralty cancelled the operation at 14.00 hours but while on the way back to rejoin the Home Fleet the ships were bombed by He 111s and Ju 87s which hit and sank the destroyer *Gurkha* as well as damaging *Southampton* and *Glasgow* with near misses.

During the night of 9–10 April, *Manchester*, *Southampton* and the 4th Destroyer Flotilla swept the Norwegian coast off Fejeosen in an attempt to prevent reinforcement of German forces in Bergen. There were no contacts during the night, although *Manchester* sighted a submarine on the surface on the starboard bow, crossing between *Southampton*, which was leading, and *Manchester*. The latter's wheel was put hard a starboard and the ship increased to full speed and attempted to ram, but passed over the submarine just as it submerged, only striking a glancing blow.[16] Soon afterwards, the cruiser was ordered back to Scapa Flow to refuel and replenish its ammunition, arriving on 10 April. However, there was no respite because throughout the following day the anchorage was subjected to regular German air raids.

On the afternoon of 12 April Captain H.G. Parker took over command of the cruiser from Captain Bousfield. At 15.30 hours *Manchester*, flying the flag of Vice Admiral Layton, sailed from Scapa Flow a mere fifteen minutes after Captain Bousfield had left his former command! Soon afterwards she rendezvoused with her sister *Birmingham*, the AA cruiser *Cairo*, the repair ship *Vindictive* and the destroyers *Acasta, Ardent* and *Codrington,* which had also sailed from Scapa Flow to join the escort of a military convoy. The latter consisted of the troopships *Empress of Australia, Reina Del Pacifico, Monarch of Bermuda, Batory* and *Chrobry* carrying the 146th Infantry Brigade to Norway. On 14 April *Manchester, Birmingham, Cairo* and the destroyers *Highlander, Vanoc* and *Whirlwind* were detached to escort *Empress of Australia* and *Chrobry* to Namsos while the rest of the convoy continued northwards. However, their destination was changed to Lillesjona because of a perceived air threat and poor harbour facilities at Namsos.

The convoy dropped anchor in Lillesjona just before dawn on 16 April. As it happened, repeated air attacks at Lillesjona rendered the port an unsuitable base for operations and Layton decided to transfer all the troops in *Empress of Australia* to the faster and more manoeuvrable *Chrobry* which would then make a dash for Namsos. The transfer completed, at dusk on the 17th *Chrobry*, escorted by the cruiser *Curlew* and six destroyers, sailed up the fjord to Namsos where the soldiers were disembarked. The troopship still had about 130 tons of equipment on board and, having spent most of the 18th offshore, returned to Namsos that evening to unload the rest of her cargo.

On 19 April *Manchester* sailed for Rosyth to prepare for Operation *Hammer* which would have involved an opposed landing on Trondheim with the main units of the Home Fleet under continuous threat of air attack. On 18 April the C-in-C Home Fleet had made it clear that it would be suicidal to take troops in transports to Trondheim but he was prepared to do so using warships. Fortunately, the Naval Staff were aware of the huge commitments for cruisers and destroyers at Andalsnes, Namsos and Narvik and must have advised the Chiefs of Staff of the impossibility of mounting yet another landing. Furthermore, the Royal Navy was so short of anti-aircraft ammunition that Admiral Forbes had already been advised of the need for strict economy. These factors must have weighed heavily upon the Chiefs of Staff and on 19 April Operation *Hammer* was cancelled.[17]

However, at 17.41 hours that day *Manchester* was ordered back to the Namsos area to cover Convoy F.P.1 until 13.00 hours on 21 April when she left the convoy and sailed for Scapa Flow at twenty-three knots so as to arrive before dark. She was immediately ordered to Rosyth where she joined *Birmingham* and *York* embarking troops for Andalsnes and Molde. Embarkation took twenty-four hours and it was not until 06.00 hours on 24 April that Vice Admiral Layton took the three cruisers to sea accompanied by the destroyers *Arrow, Acheron* and *Griffin*. At 16.00 hours on 25 April two German aircraft carried out a high level bombing attack dropping two sticks of eight bombs, four of which fell near *Manchester*. At 19.00 hours the force arrived off Bjornsund and entered the fjord with *Arrow* and *Acheron* carrying out an anti-submarine (A/S) sweep ahead followed by *Manchester, York* and *Birmingham*, in that order, with *Griffin* being stationed on the port quarter. *Manchester* went alongside the pier at Molde at 20.30 hours while the remainder of the force proceeded to Andalsnes. Disembarkation from *Manchester* commenced immediately with troops and guns being landed on the quay.

After successfully completing the operation all three cruisers were offshore by the following morning, when *York* and the destroyers were ordered home. *Manchester* and *Birmingham* remained offshore to support the destroyers *Ivanhoe, Icarus* and *Impulsive* which were laying mines in the approaches to Trondheim. Thereafter, on 27 April, the cruisers patrolled offshore between Namsos and Trondheim in support of destroyers operating in the lead. At 17.50 hours that day *Manchester* and *Birmingham* engaged a single twin-engine bomber after which, at dusk, they sailed to cover the entrance to Trondheimsfjord in the expectation of encountering German transports in the area but without success. The following morning *Manchester* and *Birmingham* were recalled to Scapa Flow, arriving at 05.00 hours on 29 April. There they refuelled and restocked with ammunition prior to participating in the evacuation of Andalsnes.[18]

At 19.00 hours on 1 May 1940, Vice Admiral Layton's 18th Cruiser Squadron with *Manchester* and *Birmingham*, plus the destroyers *Inglefield, Delight* and *Diana*, arrived off Romsdalfjorden where they were joined by the AA cruiser *Calcutta*, the sloop *Auckland* and the destroyers *Somali* and *Mashona*. The air attacks began as soon as the squadron entered the fjord at 14.25 hours with a series of enemy aircraft attacks on *Manchester* and *Birmingham*. The first attack was carried out by three Ju 88s diving from a great height to 2,500 feet, but there were no hits. Between 14.55 hours and 15.10 hours five more aircraft attempted high level attacks. At 20.25 hours, during another high level attack, a salvo of bombs fell about 500 yards off *Manchester*'s port quarter. The last attack of the day occurred at 21.45 hours when the cruiser was deep inside the fjords and a well-judged, unseen air attack on *Manchester* was delivered by a single aircraft from a considerable height. A salvo of three bombs burst close to *Manchester*'s port bow and threw many splinters on board. The shock of the explosion carried away the main and secondary W/T aerials but these were soon replaced by the ship's crew. Eventually, at about 23.00 hours *Manchester* and *Birmingham*, which were too big to use the quay, anchored off Andalsnes, while destroyers went in to ferry soldiers out to them. Some 860 British troops and eight German prisoners were taken out to *Manchester* by *Delight* before the ships sailed at 01.15 hours on 2 May. *Manchester* had cleared the fjords at 02.50 hours and by 08.00 hours was over 100 miles clear of the coast travelling at twenty-five knots heading for Scapa Flow where she arrived at 00.45 hours on 3 May in company with *Birmingham*, *Inglefield* and *Delight*. The evacuated troops were disembarked into tugs and drifters during the morning and thence to liners for passage to the Clyde.[19]

Structural Problems Identified

At 03.00 hours on 10 May, Vice Admiral Layton in *Manchester*, accompanied by *Sheffield*, left Scapa Flow to provide cover for the tow of Lord Louis Mountbatten's crippled destroyer *Kelly* which had been torpedoed by E-boats in the North Sea. At 06.21 hours Layton received news of the German invasion of the Netherlands and, a little later, that of Belgium and Luxemburg. The two cruisers made contact that afternoon and covered the tow for about twenty-four hours. Intermittent air cover was provided by RAF Hudsons and Blenheims which sometimes flew too directly towards the ships that they were escorting. During one such occasion on 10 May, *Sheffield* fired a few rounds of 2-pounder ammunition at an errant Hudson. Between 14.50 hours and 15.00 hours the following day, and in the presence of escorting RAF aircraft, the ships were attacked by three or four twin-engine bombers which dropped five salvoes of bombs from 6-8,000 feet. Two salvoes were aimed at *Manchester*, one at *Sheffield* and two at *Kelly* but none of the ships were hit. Reports of the presence of U-boats in the area resulted in a signal from C-in-C Home Fleet at 17.11 hours ordering the two cruisers to Rosyth where they arrived at 01.00 hours on 12 May.[20] *Kelly* eventually reached the Tyne at 17.30 on 13 May.

Unbeknownst to *Manchester*'s crew, only a few hours before the cruisers left Scapa to assist the severely damaged *Kelly*, the German Army had changed the strategic situation once again by launching its invasion of France when 137 German divisions began to roll across the western frontiers of Hitler's Reich. Five days later the Netherlands capitulated and the French front on the River Meuse had been destroyed. The poorly-trained French troops were out-generalled and out-manoeuvred while at the same time being harassed by a rampant Luftwaffe. Within a matter of days it was apparent to all that the French Army had been beaten. Each day thereafter, Hitler's panzers drew ever closer to the Channel ports as they forced the encircled Anglo-French troops towards Dunkirk. With the French in disarray an invasion of the United Kingdom became a distinct possibility and, on 12 May, *Manchester*, *Sheffield* and *York* were put at the disposal of C-in-C Nore Command, based at Sheerness, while at Rosyth on anti-invasion and evacuation duties.

During the afternoon of 12 May, Vice Admiral Layton visited C-in-C Rosyth with a view to arranging for the completion of degaussing work in *Manchester* and *Southampton* with all despatch. As *Manchester* had been nearly six months without granting its crew any night leave, the Vice Admiral telephoned the C-in-C Home Fleet and obtained approval from him to give one night's leave to each watch. Layton considered this to be most desirable before calling on the ship's company for further arduous service. On 13 May the work on running the first degaussing cables in *Manchester* was begun by the ship's company and completed by 17.00 hours. Earlier, at 11.03 hours that day, Vice Admiral Layton had impressed upon Admiral Forbes the desirability of considering an early refit for *Manchester* in spite of the grave military situation. He pointed out that the ship had in fact been running continuously for a longer period than had been achieved by any other cruiser of the 18th Cruiser Squadron and her many defects could not be allowed to go unattended for much longer. Fitting temporary degaussing to *Manchester* was completed on 21 May and a degaussing calibration trial subsequently carried out.

That day Layton received news that dockyard work on *Glasgow* at Liverpool could not be completed until 1 July because structural defects had been discovered, which, although they might have been secondary effects of bomb damage, seemed to indicate a weakness in design. He therefore asked C-in-C Home Fleet whether *Manchester* could be taken in hand for refit and repair on completion of work on her sister *Newcastle*.[21]

On 26 May *Manchester*, *Birmingham* and *Sheffield* were ordered to proceed to the Humber and come under the orders of C-in-C Nore. The 18th Cruiser Squadron sailed at 04.15 hours the following day and arrived off Immingham without incident at 17.00, anchoring in the stream, rather than coming alongside, at thirty minutes' notice. Vice Admiral Layton was informed by C-in-C Nore that the most probable function of his squadron would be to act in case of (a) an attack by enemy destroyers or larger ships on our shipping off Dunkirk or (b) an attack by enemy forces on the east coast of England. Layton was instructed to proceed without any further orders should there be any indication of either of these events, and to inform the C-in-C Nore and Admiralty of his intentions before sailing.

On 1 June Vice Admiral Layton had become unimpressed with the choice of Immingham as a base for his squadron and consequently, on that day, he wrote to the Flag Officer-in Charge (FOIC) Humber, the Admiralty and the C-in-C Home Fleet pointing out that his ships were very exposed to attack by Motor Torpedo Boats (MTBs) either alone or in conjunction with aircraft and that anti-MTB boom defence was an urgent requirement. He added that even a dummy boom would be of some value. The C-in-C Nore must have shared Layton's concerns because, on 9 June, he suggested to the Admiralty that the ships of the 18th Cruiser Squadron should be moved to Rosyth for a few days because their presence at Immingham must have become well-known to the enemy. The Admiralty agreed. However, reports of enemy activity in the North Sea resulted in C-in-C Nore ordering the three cruisers to raise steam for full speed. As it transpired nothing came of this scare and the ships sailed from the Humber at 04.30 hours on 10 June, arriving at Rosyth at 16.30 hours that day.

Five days later Layton was superseded as Flag Officer commanding the 18th Cruiser Squadron by Vice Admiral Sir George Edward Basset Edward-Collins who had been in command of the Home Fleet's 2nd Cruiser Squadron since 13 June 1938. This would be Edward-Collins' last sea-going command, but for Layton, who was Knighted at a personal investiture soon after he became C-in-C China Station on 10 July, it was the beginning of five demanding years in the Far East and South Asia.

Meanwhile, *Manchester*, *Birmingham* and *Sheffield* remained at Rosyth under the orders of C-in-C Nore at one hours' notice for steam. On 20 June C-in-C Home Fleet indicated that *Manchester* was to refit when *Birmingham*, which had developed seventy leaky rivets and required at least twenty-four hours docking, was again available. The following day, in response to reports that a squadron of German ships, including the battlecruiser *Scharnhorst*, had sailed from Trondheim for Germany, the 18th Cruiser Squadron, with *Manchester* as flagship, together with *Sheffield*, *Birmingham*, *York* and the destroyer *Gallant*, sailed from Rosyth to rendezvous with *Sussex* and *Newcastle*. The operation was cancelled when it was confirmed that the German vessels were safe in a German port and consequently the 18th Cruiser Squadron returned to Rosyth.

Birmingham's docking was delayed by bad weather and it was *Manchester*, *Newcastle* and *Sheffield* that left Rosyth at 05.00 hours on 1 July arriving at Immingham at 19.30 hours the same day. Edward-Collins informed the C-in-C Nore that he intended to transfer his flag to *Birmingham* after return of the squadron from patrol off Brown Ridge on 3 July. He then expected that *Manchester* would sail to Portsmouth for that much-needed refit.

Vice Admiral Edward-Collins was also unimpressed with Immingham as a home for his squadron and informed C-in-C Nore of his reasons for objecting to the Humber as an operational base:

'My dislike of the Humber as operational base for large cruisers is mainly on account of [a] long approach through water too shallow to admit use of paravanes or for degaussing to afford security with strong cross tide which makes close adherence to a narrow swept channel difficult at all times and virtually impossible in misty weather. Further objections are the danger entailed in leaving harbour on an ebb tide particularly at night and in the absence of any effective A/B or A/S obstructions.

'In view of restricted area available for patrol, its proximity to enemy coast and the likelihood of encountering "E" boats or aircraft which will entail maintenance of high speed at night, request arrangements may be made for fullest degree of air protection whilst on patrol.'[22]

Despite these objections it was made clear that the 18th Cruiser Squadron was needed to repel any invasion in the area south of the Wash and consequently would remain in the Humber. Edward-Collins duly transferred his flag from *Manchester* to *Birmingham* at 08.00 hours on 4 July, at Sheerness, following which *Manchester* then sailed to Portsmouth to refit.[23] Unfortunately congestion in the dockyard meant that the cruiser could not be taken in hand on arrival and she remained at eight hours' notice for steam.

On 19 July the Admiralty informed the C-in-C Home Fleet that *Manchester* would begin her refit after the new cruiser *Fiji*, which was scheduled to complete on 31 July, had been docked and was ready for service. Unfortunately, an Admiralty Telegram sent on 31 July said that it would not be possible to spare *Manchester* for refit before the autumn and it was proposed that she be prepared for sea by the end of the week and sailed to re-join the C-in-C Home Fleet.[24] However, the Admiralty was reminded that some 450 officers and men had not seen their homes since November or December 1939, that the majority of the officers and men had only had seven days leave in two years and that the ship was ten months out of dock. Consequently, the Admiralty relented and on 1 August approved that *Manchester* would be docked and give seven days leave in one batch while docking.[25]

On 6 August the Admiralty ordered *Manchester* to sail from Portsmouth on completion of leave and docking as required by C-in-C Home Fleet. The same day, C-in-C Nore informed Vice Admiral Edward-Collins that it seemed doubtful if the cruisers in the Nore Command were getting enough sea time or gunnery practices and suggested a continuous change round of ships in the Humber.[26]

On completion of docking, and having given leave to its weary crew, *Manchester* left Portsmouth on 20 August for Scapa. She arrived at 18.00 hours on 22 August having been unsuccessfully attacked by an aircraft in position 52° 05′N, 03° 41′W. Vice Admiral Edward-Collins immediately transferred his flag from *Birmingham* to *Manchester*. Later that day reports of a concentration of shipping at Den Helder caused the Admiralty to order *Manchester* and *Birmingham* to be sailed forthwith for Rosyth and to be placed, together with *Southampton*, under command of the C-in-C Nore. *Manchester* and *Birmingham* duly sailed from Scapa, arriving at Rosyth at 10.30 hours.

Soon after their return to Rosyth, *Manchester* and *Birmingham* were inspected by a Constructor Commander who was concerned about the cracks that had developed on the upper deck amidships. Consequently, on 24 August C-in-C Home Fleet informed the Admiralty that it was essential for stiffening to be carried out in *Manchester* and *Birmingham* before the ships experienced another season of winter gales. He added that *Manchester* was in the worst condition and that it was probable it would take two or three months to complete the work, while that required by *Birmingham* might be completed in six to eight weeks. The following day the Admiralty replied that they preferred to retain *Manchester* with the fleet until either of the new cruisers *Nigeria* or *Kenya* was worked up.

Meanwhile, there was no rest for the hard-worked *Manchester* which was patrolling the Pentland Skerries in company with her equally 'groggy'[27] sister *Birmingham* in late August. This was a period of frequent invasion scares and on 2 September *Manchester*, *Birmingham* and *Southampton* were at Rosyth preparing to go south to meet any emergency. At 12.30 hours the next day, the three cruisers sailed for Immingham, arriving at 23.45 hours and becoming part of the Humber Force. On 3 October *Manchester* left Immingham at 19.00 hours for overdue gunnery practice in Scapa, arriving on 4 October. Subsequently, *Manchester* left Scapa at 22.30 hours on 12 October and arrived at Rosyth at 07.00 hours the next morning, sailing for Immingham at 16.20 hours on 15 October. At 02.30 hours the following morning *Manchester* detonated a mine when in position 054° 21.3'N 000° 18'W. A double explosion was heard, and felt, but no apparent damage was sustained and the ship arrived at Immingham at 06.30 hours.

On 5 November information was received that *Manchester* and *Southampton* were to be fitted with Type 286 radar equipment at Rosyth and were to arrive there no later than the afternoon of the 7th and 08.00 hours on the 8th respectively. *Manchester* sailed from Humber at 07.45 hours the following day and arrived at Rosyth at 18.30 hours. A few days later, on 12 November, Vice Admiral Sir Edward-Collins was superseded as the flag officer commanding the 18th Cruiser Squadron by Vice Admiral Lancelot Holland. Two days later *Manchester* left Rosyth, arriving at Scapa the next day where she carried out 6-inch gun full calibre day firing and HA gun practices in preparation for a Mediterranean convoy operation code-named *Collar*.

Chapter 4

Captain Drew

At 13.00 hours on 15 November *Manchester* sailed from Scapa to rendezvous with the merchant ships *Clan Forbes, Clan Fraser* and *New Zealand Star*, the troop transport *Franconia* and HM Ships *Southampton, Furious, Dido,* and *Cairo* in position 55° 36'N 9° 36'W at 08.30 hours on 16 November. Soon afterwards the assembled ships set course for Gibraltar in the face of gale force winds and heavy seas. Bad conditions, admittedly, but all the better to keep the enemy at bay.

The weather abated during 20 November while off Portugal and *Manchester* was able to catapult her Walrus amphibians to carry out anti-submarine patrols. Sadly one aircraft capsized and sank during an attempted recovery operation at about 19.00 hours. A naval airman was thrown into the sea and despite a thorough search there was no trace of the missing man. *Manchester* arrived at Gibraltar in company with *Franconia* at 17.00 hours on 21 November and the Flag Officer Force H (Vice Admiral James Somerville) ordered that no leave was to be given to *Manchester* or *Franconia* and that no more than 200 troops were to be on the deck at any one time. Furthermore, no one on either ship was allowed to visit any other ship. *Southampton* arrived at Gibraltar on 23 November and came under the same leave restrictions.

The 20,175-ton liner *Franconia,* which had been converted to a troopship at Liverpool in 1939, was too large and too valuable to be risked in the Mediterranean and, therefore, the cruisers *Manchester* and *Southampton* had to act as personnel carriers. Consequently, on 24 November transfer of baggage from *Franconia* to *Manchester* and *Southampton* commenced at 20.00 hours. The following day the Admiralty directed that if Italian surface forces were sighted the action taken by warships carrying army and RAF personnel must be the same as if personnel were not aboard. The signal clearly bore the hallmarks of interference by Winston Churchill and there can be no doubt that neither Vice Admiral Holland nor Admiral Somerville considered that two cruisers carrying 1,400 passengers between them would be in a satisfactory condition to fight an action against surface forces.

Commencing at 04.00 hours on 25 November, *Manchester* and *Southampton* embarked 667 and 750 passengers from *Franconia*. These were mainly composed of RAF personnel but also some army details and railhead officers. *Southampton*'s figures also included thirty-nine naval personnel.

The convoy, designated Force F, consisted of the cruisers *Manchester* (Vice Admiral L.E. Holland), *Southampton*, the destroyers *Duncan*, *Hotspur* and *Vidette*, the corvettes *Peony*, *Salvia*, *Gloxinia* and *Hyacinth*, and the merchant ships *Clan Forbes*, *Clan Fraser* and *New Zealand Star*, which were all carrying tanks and heavy equipment.

At 07.30 hours *Manchester* and *Southampton* sailed with Force H, which was composed of *Renown*, *Sheffield*, *Ark Royal*, *Despatch* and the destroyers *Faulknor*, *Firedrake*, *Forester*, *Fury*, *Wishart*, *Encounter*, *Kelvin* and *Jaguar*. Course was set to pass south of Alboran Island and thence keeping about forty miles from the African coast. Meanwhile the three merchant ships *Clan Forbes*, *Clan Fraser* and *New Zealand Star*, which had passed Europa Point at 02.00 hours that day, escorted by *Duncan*, *Hotspur* and the four corvettes, were keeping close to the Spanish coast. During the night of 26 November the convoy crossed to the African coast and proceeded eastwards keeping thirty miles from it. At 08.15 hours, Force H was in position 37° 05'N 01° 13'E and the old D-class cruiser *Despatch* was detached to join the convoy. The remainder of Force H continued on course until 15.00 hours, making as though steering for northern Sardinia.

At 15.00 hours the course was altered to the southward and at 17.10 hours *Manchester* and three destroyers were detached to join the convoy which was sighted at 17.45 hours in position 37° 10' N 02° 42'E steering 085° at thirteen knots. Since it was necessary to steam fifteen knots to keep to the timetable, Vice Admiral Holland detached the corvettes to proceed to Malta via the Galita and Skerki Channels. The convoy proceeded at fifteen knots but at 20.25 hours this was reduced to fourteen and a half knots because, with paravanes streamed, *Clan Forbes* could not keep up. During the night, the remainder of Force H kept about thirty-five miles, and sixty-five degrees, from the convoy. At 09.30 hours on 27 November the three merchant ships were ordered to haul in their otters so that fifteen knots could be maintained. About this time, Force H closed the convoy and thus began the circumstances leading to the engagement south of Sardinia which became known as the Battle of Cape Spartivento (or Cape Teulada to the Italians).

Battle of Cape Spartivento
Vice Admiral Holland's account of this action was written on 2 December and provides the 18th Cruiser Squadron's perspective on the events that unfolded on 27 November (all times at Z minus two hours):

At 0900 on 27 November MANCHESTER, SOUTHAMPTON, DESPATCH and COVENTRY were in position 37° 39'N, 07° 11'E in company with a convoy comprising SS NEW ZEALAND STAR, SS CLAN FRASER and SS CLAN FORBES. The convoy was escorted by DUNCAN, WISHART, ENCOUNTER, FURY and FIREDRAKE. HOTSPUR without ASDIC and speed restricted to 16 knots was also in the convoy. RAF and Army reinforcements for the Middle East were embarked in MANCHESTER and SOUTHAMPTON, the total number being 667 in the former and 750 in the latter.

The mean line of advance of the convoy which was carrying out zig-zag number 11 was 081° making good 14 knots. HM ships were at 2nd degree of HA readiness and 4th degree of LA readiness with steam for full speed at 10 minutes' notice.

A covering force consisting of RENOWN, SHEFFIELD and ARK ROYAL screened by FAULKNOR, FORESTER, KELVIN and JAGUAR about 15 miles to the north eastward of MANCHESTER. The visibility was extreme, sea smooth, wind SE Force 3.

At 0948 a corrupt signal originated at 0931 was received from an aircraft reporting one battleship and seven destroyers which was amended shortly afterwards to two battleships. The position to which this reported was not received so the possibility of reporting Force D could not be ruled out. Force D consisted of RAMILLIES, BERWICK, NEWCASTLE screened by DEFENDER, HEREWARD, VAMPIRE, VENDETTA and VOYAGER was expected to be approaching from the eastward.

At 0957 an amplifying report from an aircraft was received giving the enemy's position course and speed as 38° 32'N, 08° 29'E, 15 knots.

At 1005 Flag Officer Force H ordered steam for full speed and in his signal 1008 which was received at 1024 he reported that 5 enemy cruisers and 5 destroyers had been reported in position 38° 25'N, 08° 27'E at 09.20 steering 255°.

Two aircraft reports both originated at 1010 were received at 1016 of six cruisers and eight destroyers in position 38° 28'N, 08° 34'E steering 250° and at 1021 of one battleship, one cruiser and five destroyers in position 38° 39'N, 08° 42'E also steering 250°.

At 1054 FO Force H reported at 0948 two battleships and seven destroyers were in position 38° 40'N, 08° 33'E.

At 1035 FO Force H ordered DESPATCH to keep well clear to southward with the convoy and for MANCHESTER and SOUTHAMPTON to join him. Thereupon the convoy was ordered to cease zig-zagging and was turned to course 120°. MANCHESTER and SOUTHAMPTON altered course to 050°, speed 24 knots, working up to 30 knots by 1101. This course was selected to take the cruisers to a position on the engaged bow of RENOWN consistent with instructions given by FO Force H in his preliminary orders. Various alterations of course were made to conform with these instructions and SHEFFIELD joined my flag taking station astern of SOUTHAMPTON.

At 1053 I signalled to DESPATCH and the destroyers in company, except HOTSPUR, to join me and at 1112 I instructed Captain (D) 8 to take up station 5 miles 040° from RENOWN.

At 1131 Force D was sighted distant 14 miles on a bearing 064° and at 1148, I received a signal to take all cruisers, except DESPATCH and COVENTRY, under my orders. At 1150, I signalled to NEWCASTLE and BERWICK to join me but at 1158 BERWICK signalled that his speed was limited to 27 knots and that he proposed to join RENOWN. I replied immediately 'join me' but BERWICK had turned already to the south west to implement his proposal. This was unfortunate as it prevented BERWICK from forming with the remaining cruisers which, from the original position, he could have done and resulted in the ship being at 2,000 to 4,000 yards greater range from the enemy than was necessary.

At 1123 I turned the cruisers in succession to 073° so as to dispose them roughly at right angles to the probable direction of the enemy. By 1210 NEWCASTLE had reached a position about 5 cables 240° from MANCHESTER. My original intention was that NEWCASTLE should be the fourth ship of the line but as it was apparent that she could not reach that position I ordered her to move up between MANCHESTER and SOUTHAMPTON, the latter ship being told to make room for this. BERWICK was given a bearing on which to form up on my squadron but was unable to reach that position.

At 1200 smoke was sighted from MANCHESTER on a bearing 360° and at 1207. I turned the cruisers together from 040° to 360°. Masts became visible within a minute or two of the smoke being sighted and a report was made at 1205.

At 1207 three cruisers, to be referred to as Group A [the 8-inch gun cruisers *Trieste*, *Trento* and *Bolzano* plus three destroyers], came into sight on a bearing 353° from MANCHESTER at a range of 15 miles. These cruisers either turned to the NW at about this time or else were steering in this direction when sighted, the right hand cruiser subsequently engaged by MANCHESTER, turning further to NE.

At 1213 MANCHESTER made an enemy report of three cruisers and two destroyers bearing 337° and 343° respectively at a range of 15 miles steering 300°.

At 1214 a further group of cruisers, referred to as Group B [the 8-inch gun cruisers POLA, GORIZIA and FIUME plus 4 destroyers] came into sight further to the eastward by MANCHESTER, at that time, as four cruisers bearing 003° 15 miles distant. At 1216, I received a signal from FO Force H saying that a Sunderland had reported that no enemy battleships were present.

At 1220 the enemy of Group A opened fire and at 1221 MANCHESTER engaged the right hand cruiser of this Group at a range of 21,000 yards and the action became general. The first enemy salvo fired at MANCHESTER was exact for range, all the splashes falling within the length of the ship but about 100 yards clear.

The ships of Group A started to make smoke which by 1235 had obscured them from view. At this time, the course of our cruisers was 020° and Group B was passing across the front from left to right.

At 1232 MANCHESTER gave a shudder which must have been caused by a very near miss, but at the time gave a first impression that the ship had been hit.

At 1234 I altered course to 360° with the object of separating the two enemy Groups so that our attention could be concentrated on half of this force. This worked out as desired and I considered which of the enemy Groups should be our future objective. It was reasonable to suppose that the smoke screens enveloping Force A was hiding some damage and this Group was believed to be the weaker of the two. By closing Group A, it seemed that some immediate tactical achievement might result. Against this, however, it had to be appreciated that the object of the whole enterprise was to pass a convoy through the Narrows and that if our cruisers sheered off to the NW the field would be left for Force B to turn SE and attack the convoy. I therefore decided that Force B should be our future target and at 1245 altered course to 090° to bring this Group to bear on the port bow.

At 1234 MANCHESTER checked fire on the right hand cruiser of Group [A] which had become obscured by smoke, the range being 20,000 yards. Fire was shifted to the left hand ship of Force B on the starboard bow at a range of 21,000 yards. This target was engaged from 1236 to 12.39, the range remaining constant. The ships of Group B were identified as being 8-inch gun cruisers probably of the Zara-class.

At 1236 ships of Group B observed firing their HA guns in response to attack by aircraft from ARK ROYAL.

At 1240 a destroyer on the port bow steering to the eastward and making smoke screen presented a favourable target and fire was opened on it at a range of 17,000 yards and continued until 1245 during which period the destroyer received several 12 gun straddles and was driven away under smoke. [The destroyer in question was *Lanciere* which was hit by two 6-inch shells from SOUTHAMPTON during this period].

At 1245, course was altered to 090° which brought the ships of Group B on the relative bearing of Red 40. Fire was opened on the nearest (i.e. left hand) ship at a range of 19,000 yards. On being engaged Group B turned at 1246 to the SE which gave them an advantage in regard to gun arcs, as they were crossing my T. I wished to prevent the enemy breaking away to the SE so turned the cruisers at 1250 to what I judged to be a parallel course. The enemy's reaction to this was to turn away to port and I altered to 090° at 1252, to 070° at 1256 and to 030° at 1258.

28

During this phase, the range of the enemy steadily increased from 19,000 at 1246 up to 22,500 at 1256. At 1252 the enemy being engaged was observed to be on fire aft and to haul away to port, resuming a course parallel to the other two cruisers of Group B about two minutes later. The range of the ship dropped to 21,000 at 1259 but started to open again until 1304 it had reached 21,500 yards. MANCHESTER ceased firing on this target at 1306 when extreme gun range was reached.

At 1301 the masts of a new enemy unit judged to be four ships was sighted at extreme visibility and right ahead (i.e. on bearing 045°). At 1301 MANCHESTER catapulted a Walrus aircraft to aid spotting. However, technical problems aboard the cruiser meant that the aircraft could not communicate with MANCHESTER. Furthermore as neither of the cruiser's cranes was in a fit state to receive aircraft at sea, the Walrus landed on ARK ROYAL.

At 1305, two battleships [*Vittorio Veneto* and *Giulio Cesare*] were identified in this unit and an enemy report was made.

The end-on approach of this unit resulted in the range decreasing very rapidly and it was evident to me that it would be necessary to take action to avoid our cruisers from running into effective gunfire of the heavy ships. At 1305 I turned the cruisers to 120° with the dual object of working round to the flank of the enemy battleships and also to close the gap to RENOWN. At this time, however, the enemy battleships altered course to the NE and presumably joined their 8-inch gun cruisers, whereupon, at 1308, I altered back to 090° and continued to turn until a course of 050° was reached.

The larger splashes seen falling around BERWICK and later near MANCHESTER corroborated that this new unit included capital ships.

At 1309 I received a signal from FO Force H asking 'Is there any chance of catching the cruisers?' To this I answered 'No', the experience during the run to the NE being that the enemy ships were able to increase the range and that this included the damaged ship.

At 1310 FO Force H ordered me to turn to 130° which was complied with at 1317.[1]

The arrival of the two Italian battleships prompted Holland's cruisers to fall back on *Renown* and *Ramillies*. At this point Admiral Campioni in *Vittorio Veneto* chose not to press home his advantage, probably because *Ark Royal*'s aircraft were dominating the skies over the Italian ships which were being subjected to numerous air strikes. Campioni therefore withdrew his forces – as did Somerville who correctly recognised that his primary object was to protect a convoy which had been left dangerously exposed during the action. Winston Churchill was most aggrieved with Somerville's decision not to pursue the enemy and safeguard the convoy, insisting that the matter be investigated by a Board of Enquiry as soon as possible after

Force H's return to Gibraltar. Much to the Prime Minister's chagrin, Somerville was acquitted.

After the action, Vice Admiral Holland observed that 'HM Ships *Manchester* and *Berwick* [hit on 'Y' Turret at 12.22 hours by a shell which put both guns out of action and caused heavy casualties amongst the Royal Marine gunners and hit again on the right aft, damaging officers' quarters at 12.35 hours] were favoured by the enemy as targets and HMS *Manchester* was under continuous fire from 12.21 hours until about 13.00 hours when it became spasmodic. The ship was straddled on a few occasions and a considerable number of salvoes corrected for range fell close on one side or the other. Had it not been for the small alterations of course, judiciously carried out by Captain Herbert Annesley Packer RN, the ship would have almost certainly been hit.'[2]

Holland also recorded that during the action, *Manchester*'s 6-inch ammunition expenditure was 'A' Turret 304, 'B' Turret 265, 'X' Turret 175, and 'Y' Turret 168. Thus more than half of the shells were expended by the forward turrets. The passengers were very useful in transporting ammunition from aft to forward at the end of the engagement.[3]

Not long after the fleet action the merchant ships and their defending warships came under air attacks which went on all afternoon. At 16.45 hours *Manchester* opened fire at five Italian bombers which had been attacking Force H.

Meanwhile, the convoy, under the orders of Commodore West Indies in the cruiser *Despatch*, proceeded via the Galita Channel. At 17.30 hours Holland again took charge of the convoy now escorted by *Manchester*, *Southampton*, *Coventry*, *Hotspur* and four Mediterranean Fleet destroyers. *Clan Forbes* and *Clan Fraser* streamed otters. By 18.25 hours the convoy was in position 37° 31'N 09° 45'E steaming 14.5 knots and proceeding through the Skerki Channel.

At 01.37 hours on 28 November, in position 36° 57'N 11° 37'E, an underwater explosion was felt aboard *Manchester*. The course had been altered to 180° four minutes earlier and the explosion may have been of a torpedo that missed. At 07.47 hours, *Gloucester*, *Glasgow* and *York* were sighted, followed by *Warspite*, *Valiant* and *Illustrious* at 08.30 hours. Soon afterwards the C-in-C Mediterranean Fleet, Admiral Cunningham, ordered a number of dispositions.

Decoy and *Hotspur* were to escort *Clan Forbes* and *Clan Fraser* to Malta. *Coventry*, *Hereward* and *Defender* were to escort *New Zealand Star* to Alexandria, routed south of Medina Bank and thence through 35° 10' N 20° E. *Manchester* and *Southampton* were ordered to provide cover for this convoy. Subsequently, at 13.45 hours on 29 November, *Manchester* and *Southampton* were ordered to join the body of the Mediterranean Fleet leaving *Coventry* in charge. At 17.15 hours *Manchester* and *Southampton* were detached from the Mediterranean Fleet and ordered to proceed direct to

Alexandria, arriving at 14.00 hours on 30 November. The ships berthed alongside and proceeded to disembark all passengers and mails.

Subsequently, *Manchester* was ordered by C-in-C Mediterranean to sail at 13.30 hours on 2 December for Suda Bay, to arrive at 09.00 hours next morning. Thereafter in company with *York* of the 3rd Cruiser Squadron, *Manchester* sailed from Suda Bay through the Antikithera Channel to be in a position fifteen miles SW of Cape Matapan on a north-westerly course at dusk on 3 December so as to give the impression, if sighted, that the two ships were about to raid the Strait of Otranto.

After dark, *York* returned to Suda Bay leaving *Manchester* to proceed at high speed to Malta where she arrived at 12.00 hours on 4 December having been slightly delayed by low visibility when making land. *Manchester* sailed from Malta at 17.00 hours so that it would be dark before course was set to the westward.

The Narrows and Skerki Channel were passed without any enemy being sighted and high speed was maintained until midday on 5 December. Since nothing had been sighted by this time, speed was reduced to twenty-four knots for the remainder of the passage to Gibraltar where *Manchester* arrived at 11.00 hours on 6 December. Two days later *Manchester* sailed from Gibraltar bound for Plymouth in company with the destroyer *Jersey* and arrived at Plymouth on 11 December. *Manchester* was back in Scapa Flow on 13 December.

Finally a Refit
The New Year found *Manchester* in the Home Fleet's storm-tossed northern base at one hours' notice for steam. On 4 January 1941 the cruiser received an Admiralty message, sent at 15.04 hours the previous day, noting that the shortage of Walrus amphibians would necessitate a temporary reduction to one of the number normally carried by HM Ships *Queen Elizabeth, Suffolk, London, Edinburgh, Manchester, Kenya* and *Nigeria*.[4]

At 00.02 hours on 6 January *Manchester* and *Edinburgh* raised steam for two hours' notice and four hours later the two cruisers sailed, heading towards 63°N 04'W at twenty knots. Later that day C-in-C Home Fleet signalled to Admiralty 'Intend to sail *Manchester* to arrive South Shields for refit on 11 January'. At 15.40 hours on 7 January *Manchester* and *Edinburgh* arrived back in Scapa from patrol and the following day Vice Admiral Holland transferred his flag to *Edinburgh*.

At 01.00 hours on 11 January *Manchester* left Scapa and made a fast fifteen-hour-long passage to the River Tyne to begin an urgently needed thirteen week refit at Palmer's Shipbuilding and Engineering Company's yard. While in dockyard hands, *Manchester*'s main machinery was thoroughly overhauled, her hull was stiffened amidships and Type 279 air warning radar fitted at the mastheads. *Manchester*'s close range AA armament was strengthened by the removal of the two utterly useless quadruple 0.5-inch machine-gun mountings and the installation of a single Bofors 40mm Mk.III gun on a platform on top of 'B' Turret. Five single 20mm Oerlikon guns were also fitted. The bulk of the refit was completed on 27 March 1941 and four days later the cruiser left Hebburn for post-refit sea trials followed by further rectification of defects. Whilst it had been in refit most of the ship's company had been drafted to other vessels and consequently when *Manchester* left the Tyne on the afternoon of 10 April she had been effectively re-commissioned with a new crew. A few hours later the cruiser arrived at Rosyth where she underwent a short docking and maintenance period.

On the afternoon of 17 April, *Manchester* left the Firth of Forth en route for Scapa Flow, arriving at 06.21 hours the next day to re-join the 18th Cruiser Squadron and spend the rest of the month working-up in the relative safety of Scapa Flow and its environs. However, danger was ever present and on 24 April, while at sea in the waters around the Orkney Islands, *Manchester* was attacked by a Ju 88 which was driven off by the cruiser's 4-inch and 2-pounder gunfire.

Her work-up complete, *Manchester* left Scapa Flow on 5 May in company with the rest of the 18th Cruiser Squadron (*Edinburgh*, flag Vice Admiral Holland, *Birmingham* and *Kenya*) to provide ocean escort to an operation by the 1st Minelaying Squadron. The minelayers *Agamemnon*, *Menestheus* and *Port Quebec* had left the Kyle of Lochalsh on the west coast of Scotland escorted by the ex-American destroyers *Brighton* and *St Marys* and Commander (D) 20th Destroyer Flotilla in *Intrepid* and *Impulsive* from the Home Fleet sailed from the Kyle of Lochalsh at 0700 on that day for Operation *SN9A*. This operation was designed to reinforce lines 'SN 68' and 'SN 69' in the centre of the Faeroes–Iceland minefield. The field consisted of 1,490 Mk.XX mines which were laid on 6 May at a depth of eleven feet along a line joining positions 63°20′N 11°36′W and 63°57′N 12°02′W. The three minelayers returned to their base at 13.00 hours on 8 May on completion of their uneventful operation.[5]

As soon as the minelayers had completed their work, *Edinburgh*, *Manchester* and *Birmingham* were met by the destroyers *Somali*, *Bedouin*, *Nestor* and *Eskimo*, which had just refuelled at Iceland's Skaalfjord, to begin Operation *E.B.* The combined force then sailed to capture or destroy enemy weather reporting trawlers reported to be operating in areas 067° to 070° 30′ N 0001° to 007° W. At 17.10 hours on 7 May the weather ship *München* was found and boarded by *Somali* and, although the trawler's crew attempted to scuttle their ship, the boarding party managed to capture vital parts of her *Enigma* machine. The force returned to Scapa Flow at the end of a highly successful operation which had garnered valuable intelligence.

Even as the force was inward bound from Icelandic waters, significant personnel changes occurred in the Home Fleet on 8 May when Vice

Admiral Holland was appointed Vice Admiral commanding battlecruisers in succession to Vice Admiral W.J. ('Jock') Whitworth who became Second Sea Lord. Whitworth's flag was struck in *Hood* that afternoon while Holland hoisted his flag in the battlecruiser on 12 May. Sadly, just twelve days later he was killed when his flagship was sunk in the Denmark Strait by the German battleship *Bismarck* on 24 May. Holland's place in command of the 18th Cruiser Squadron was taken temporarily by Captain C.M. Blackman DSO of *Edinburgh* who was appointed Commodore Second Class.

Sinking the *Bismarck*

Fears that the recently completed battleship *Bismarck* might attempt to break out into the Atlantic led the C-in-C Home Fleet to increase his cruiser patrols in the Greenland–Iceland–UK gaps. Consequently, on 18 May 1941 *Manchester* and *Birmingham* left Scapa to relieve *Nigeria* and *Kenya* on the Faeroes–Iceland patrol. The following day *Bismarck*, accompanied by the heavy cruiser *Prinz Eugen*, left the Baltic port of Gotenhafen at the start of a foray into the Atlantic aimed at disrupting the vital British convoy system.

At 13.00 hours on 20 May the force was sighted by the Swedish cruiser *Gotland* and reported to the Swedish naval staff, one of whom passed it on to the Norwegian military attaché in Stockholm. By 21.00 hours that night the information had been received by the Admiralty who advised C-in-C Home Fleet, Admiral Sir John Tovey, of the suspected break out by German heavy ships. The report coincided with information, contained in decrypts of the Luftwaffe *Enigma*, that Focke Wulf Fw 200 Condor long-range aircraft had been carrying out intensive reconnaissance of the ice edge between Jan Mayen Island and Greenland. These reports had already prompted Admiral Tovey to instruct patrolling cruisers in the Denmark Strait to be especially vigilant.

At 11.00 hours on 21 May *Bismarck* and *Prinz Eugen* were located at Bergen by a high altitude photo-reconnaissance Spitfire. At 18.28 hours, following development of the Spitfire's film, the Admiralty was able to warn all naval commands that a sortie against the trade routes by a German capital ship was imminent. Consequently, that day *Manchester* and her sister ship *Birmingham* were ordered to refuel at Skaalfjord in Iceland and then resume their watch between Iceland and the Faeroe Islands to intercept any possible breakout of *Bismarck* into the Atlantic.

On 23 May 1941, the cruiser *Arethusa* joined *Manchester* and *Birmingham* on the patrol line. The following day (and just five hours before the tragic loss of *Hood*), *Manchester*, *Birmingham* and *Arethusa* were ordered to patrol north of Langanes, the north-eastern point of Iceland, in case Admiral Lütjens decided to double back and attempt to return *Bismarck* to Germany via the Denmark Strait. As is well known, *Bismarck* was subsequently hunted down and destroyed by the battleships *King George V* and *Rodney* on 27 May after a torpedo hit had smashed *Bismarck*'s rudders. On completion of the *Bismarck* operation, *Manchester* returned to Scapa Flow on 3 June 1941 when Captain Harold Drew DSC assumed command.

Captain Drew

Captain Harold 'Peter' Drew was born in the Shropshire town of Oswestry on 15 March 1895. He was educated at Oswestry Grammar School and the training ship HMS *Conway* and served in the Merchant Navy. He joined the Royal Naval Reserve in 1913 and served as a midshipman aboard the AMC *Mantua* in 1914, attaining the rank of Acting Sub-Lieutenant in September 1915.

That month he joined the destroyer *Lance*, before transferring to the Royal Navy on 29 January 1916. Because of meritorious service in command of the coastal motor boat *CMB 9* off the French coast, for which he was awarded the Distinguished Service Cross on 12 May 1917, he was promoted to Acting Lieutenant on 15 November of that year. Drew then joined the battleship *Emperor of India* which was part of the Grand Fleet based in Scapa Flow. His Lieutenancy became substantive on 15 March 1918 and soon after the cessation of hostilities Drew was appointed to HMS *President*.

Drew decided to become a gunnery specialist by January 1920 and, after appropriate training, was appointed to the 6-inch gun-armed light cruiser *Dragon* on 1 January 1923 as her gunnery officer. His next appointment, on 29 November 1924, was to HMS *Pembroke*, the gunnery school in Chatham after which he transferred to HMS *Excellent*, the gunnery school at Portsmouth on 20 July 1925. While serving in HMS *Excellent* Drew worked in the Experimental Department and was involved in developing the Royal Navy's AA gunfire control systems and was promoted to Lieutenant Commander on 15 March 1926.

His appointment to the Portsmouth gunnery school ended in July 1927. He went on to serve as the gunnery officer aboard the then new 8-inch gun cruiser *Suffolk* on the China Station from 7 February 1928 until mid-1930. Subsequently, from September 1930 to January 1932, he served aboard the battleship *Royal Sovereign* as her gunnery officer and First Lieutenant-Commander in the Mediterranean, being promoted to Commander on 31 December 1931 at the age of thirty-six.

Having returned to the United Kingdom in 1932 Drew was appointed to the Training and Staff Duties of the Admiralty (HMS *President*) for two years after which, from September to November 1934, he underwent a tactical course in HM Dockyard Portsmouth (HMS *Victory*). In December 1934 he was appointed as the Executive Officer aboard the cruiser *Amphion* which was fitting out in Portsmouth Dockyard having been launched on 27 July and remained with her until February 1938.

By now it was obvious to all that the outbreak of war was but a matter of time and Harold Drew's next appointment in July of that year was for duty with the Admiral Commanding Reserves and particular gunnery duties with the RNVR. During this phase of his career he was promoted to Captain on 30 June 1939, at the age of forty-four, and a few months later he became Deputy Director of Personnel Services (Training Establishments) at the Admiralty. One of his first jobs was to commandeer all of Billy Butlin's holiday camps for use as naval establishments. He remained in this post until 31 May 1941 when he was appointed to command the cruiser *Manchester* joining her on 3 June at Scapa.

Captain Drew had just six days to get to know his new command before *Manchester* left Scapa Flow for the Denmark Strait via Iceland. On 11 June 1941, the cruiser left Iceland to relieve *Hermione* in the Denmark Strait, returning to Hvalfjord seven days later, in company with the destroyer *Achates*, having been relieved by *Suffolk*. Two days earlier, on 16 June, the C-in-C Home Fleet had ordered the number of cruisers on the Denmark Strait patrol to be reduced from two to one and to be accompanied by a destroyer because of reports of increased U-boat activity in the area. Consequently, the destroyer *Eclipse* accompanied *Manchester* when she left Hvalfjord on 23 June to relieve *Suffolk* on patrol in the stormy waters of the Denmark Strait. *Manchester* returned to Hvalfjord on 1 July and sailed the next day bound for Scapa Flow where she arrived on 3 July. Her next assignment would be to the warmer waters of the war-torn Mediterranean and her second Malta convoy.

Chapter 5

Operation Substance

Events in the eastern Mediterranean during the spring of 1941 had significant implications for the resupply of Malta. The sad catalogue of British decline had started on 26 March 1941 when the 8-inch gun cruiser *York* was hit by an Italian explosive motor boat while in Suda Bay becoming a constructive total loss which was finally abandoned on 22 May. Thereafter, the evacuation of British forces from Greece in April 1941 had put considerable strain on the Mediterranean Fleet while exposing it to the increasing power of the Luftwaffe which sank the destroyers *Diamond* and *Wryneck*. All told, 50,732 troops were embarked from nine beaches and taken to Crete during Operation *Demon* which began on 24 April and ended on 1 May.

Less than three weeks later the German invasion of Crete began with an attack by elite parachute forces operating under the umbrella of air supremacy. The British evacuation of the island was ordered on 26 May and the hard pressed Mediterranean Fleet managed to evacuate 16,500 out of 32,000 troops to Egypt. However, the cost was severe with British naval losses amounting to three cruisers (*Fiji*, *Gloucester* and *Calcutta*) and six destroyers (*Kashmir*, *Kelly*, *Juno*, *Greyhound*, *Hereward* and *Imperial*) sunk. Furthermore the battleship *Warspite*, the aircraft carrier *Formidable* and the cruisers *Orion* and *Dido* were so badly damaged that they required extensive repairs in dockyard facilities far greater than those available in Alexandria. Other ships damaged included the battleships *Valiant* and *Barham*, the cruisers *Carlisle*, *Naiad*, *Ajax* and *Perth* as well as seven destroyers. From 24 April to 2 June, forty-six Allied merchant ships totalling 137,934 tons were lost, while merchant ship losses in Greek waters during the period from March to June totalled 102 vessels.

On 2 June, with the Cretan debacle now over, Admiral Andrew Cunningham was able signal the Admiralty that, by 10 June, he hoped to have available a force of two battleships, five cruisers, two AA cruisers and fourteen destroyers patched up and ready for service. Cunningham went on to state that: 'The damage inflicted on the fleet during the evacuation of

Greece and Crete, together with the severe strain to which both ships and personnel had been exposed for so long, rendered the fleet temporarily unable to carry out any major operations. The absence of an aircraft carrier fit to operate, coupled with the enemy's possession of well-placed air bases restricted fleet movements to the eastern Mediterranean.'[1] Earlier that day, at 11.22 hours, in a signal to the First Sea Lord, Cunningham had discussed the problem of the resupply of Malta and observed that 'as we in the Eastern Mediterranean seemed to be absorbing the most of the attention of the Luftwaffe it would be a good idea if a convoy were run in to Malta from the west.'[2]

The successful German invasion of Crete led the British, who were unaware of the true extent of the enemy's casualties, to assume that this would soon be followed by a similar assault on Malta. Consequently, Lieutenant-General Dobbie, the Governor of Malta, was granted substantial reinforcement of his troops and equipment. However, with the Axis now firmly dominating the seas between Crete and Cyrenaica, any reinforcements would have to be run in from the Gibraltar. A plan was therefore made to escort six store-ships and one troop transport to Malta (Convoy GM 1), while, at the same time, bring out the fast auxiliary ship *Breconshire* and six empty merchantmen (Convoy MG 1) which had long been detained in the island. The reinforcements for Malta, approximately 5,000 troops and RAF personnel, were to be transported in Convoy GM 1 in an operation which was allocated the appropriate code-name *Substance*. In preparation for this operation, during 26 June to 1 July, Force H undertook a pair of 'Club Runs'[3] flying-in a total of fifty-six Hurricanes[4].

Operation *Substance* was a significant beneficiary of the German invasion of Russia which began on 22 June and involved the bulk of the Luftwaffe, including the crack anti-shipping unit Fliegerkorps X, being redeployed to the Polish border. However, this still left some 200 Italian aircraft, based on Sardinia and Sicily, which were available to contest Convoy GM 1's passage eastwards from Gibraltar.

If Admiral Cunningham can be credited with initiating Operation *Substance*, it was Vice-Admiral Somerville, the Flag Officer commanding Force H at Gibraltar, who was responsible for its implementation. Somerville's plan for the execution of Operation *Substance* was as follows:

> All forces and convoy to rendezvous east of Gibraltar am 21 July and form two groups, Group 4 comprising RENOWN, ARK ROYAL, HERMIONE, and six of the destroyers proceeding to Malta and Group 5 comprising NELSON, EDINBURGH, MANCHESTER, ARETHUSA, MANXMAN and the remaining destroyers escorting the *Substance* convoy, under the command of Rear Admiral commanding the 18th Cruiser Squadron. BROWN RANGER, escorted by BEVERLEY to be in company.

Group 4 to keep to the eastward of Group 5 during D.1 [21 July] and D.2 [22 July]. Destroyers of Group 5 to refuel from BROWN RANGER during D.2, the latter returning to Gibraltar on completion.

Group 4 to rendezvous with Group 5 early on D.3 [23 July] or late pm on D.2 if it appears that the enemy were aware of the operation.

In the event of enemy surface forces appearing in a position to intercept during D.3, Group 5, less MANXMAN, AVON VALE, FARNDALE, ERIDGE and the convoy, would be ordered to concentrate and form part of Group 5.

On arrival off Skerki Channel about 1700 on D.3 in position 'U' (37°45'N 10°00E), Force H comprising RENOWN, NELSON, ARK ROYAL and six destroyers turn west. Force 'X' consisting of the remaining warships and the convoy to proceed east with the object of arriving in position 'Y' (135° Pantelleria 50 miles) by 0600 on D.4 [24 July]. Fulmars to give protection to Force 'X' until relieved by Beaufighters from Malta or until about1830.

Convoy MG 1 to sail from Malta in company until reaching a position south of Pantelleria at dark on D.3 then to proceed independently in three groups. These groups should reach the following approximate positions by dawn on D.4: Group 1 315° Cani Rocks 17 miles, Group 2 070° Cani Rocks 10 miles and Group 3 120° Cani Rocks 30 miles. ENCOUNTER to remain with Group 2 until reaching position 'AA' (37° 18' N. 08° 30' E.), then to join Group 1.

EDINBURGH, MANCHESTER, ARETHUSA, AVON VALE, FARNDALE and ERIDGE to leave Convoy *Substance* at about 0700 on D.4, if no enemy surface units are in the vicinity, and proceed at best speed to Malta. COSSACK, MAORI, SIKH, NESTOR, FEARLESS, FOXHOUND and FIREDRAKE (last two using T.S.D.S.) to escort *Substance*. Subject to the submarine situation permitting, two destroyers at a time might be ordered by NOIC, Malta to proceed ahead of the convoy to discharge personnel and stores and refuel. Cruisers and Hunt class destroyers, followed by *Substance* final escort, to be routed on leaving Malta so as to reach position 'U' by approximately 0430B and 0530B on D.5 [25 July] respectively.

Subject to any interference by enemy air or surface forces, I intend to adjust the position of Force H during D.4 so as to achieve the following objects: (a) to divert attention from or cover the three groups of MG 1, (b) to disguise the subsequent intended westwards route of Force 'X'.

Subject to there being no enemy forces at sea, six Swordfish aircraft for Malta will be flown off early am on D.5 so as to arrive at Hal Far at 0530 D.5.

P.138 Force H and Force X to rendezvous to the westward of Skerki Channel shortly after daylight on D.5 and retire to westward covering MG 1.[5]

The plan also included a conspicuous diversionary sortie by the depleted Mediterranean Fleet on 23–24 July while two of Cunningham's submarines radioed manoeuvring signals from positions west of Crete to simulate the apparent westwards progress of the battleship *Queen Elizabeth* and her consorts as they returned to Alexandria under the cover of darkness. It remained to be seen how these well-laid plans would survive contact with the enemy.

Preliminary Moves – The Convoy Sails from the United Kingdom
Convoy WS 9C, which consisted of the Military Transports (MT) *City of Pretoria, Durham, Melbourne Star, Port Chalmers* and *Sydney Star* plus the troopship *Leinster*, escorted by *Nelson, Manchester, Manxman, Arethusa, Cossack, Maori, Sikh, Nestor, Jupiter, Lightning, Gurkha* and *Garland* left Clyde on 12 July for Gibraltar and Operation *Substance*. In order to avoid U-boats, the convoy and its escorts steamed well out into the Atlantic before turning south and this roundabout route meant that the passage to Gibraltar took eight days.

In early July the Admiralty informed Somerville that the five MT ships would pass through the Strait of Gibraltar during the night of 22/23 July with the battleship *Nelson*, which was to refuel at Gibraltar becoming the Senior Officer's ship for the operation. In his reply Somerville stated that it was undesirable that *Nelson* should refuel at Gibraltar but, provided the following arrangements were accepted, D.1 could remain 21 July:

D.-7 [14 July] Sail the destroyers of DF 8 to rendezvous with SUBSTANCE. D.-5 [16 July] Sail three Hunt class destroyers to rendezvous with SS PASTEUR. D.-4 [17 July] Destroyers of DF 8 to rendezvous with SUBSTANCE at 0700.

Group I comprising MANCHESTER, PASTEUR and three 'J' class destroyers plus Group II comprising ARETHUSA, SS LEINSTER and three Tribal class destroyers to break off from convoy and proceed direct to Gibraltar (Group I at best speed and Group II so as to berth at Gibraltar 0330 D.-1

D.-3 [18 July] Three Hunt class to rendezvous with Group I at 0700 and all to berth not later than 1800 D.-2. MANCHESTER before parting company with Group I before coming in sight of Cape Spartel and to join Group II. D.-1 [20 July] After transfer of stores and personnel, sail EDINBURGH, AURORA, three 'J' class and three Hunt class at 0250 to rendezvous with the SUBSTANCE convoy. DF8 to arrive at Gibraltar to refuel.

D.-1 SUBSTANCE convoy to pass Europa Point about 0143. Force H, MANCHESTER, ARETHUSA, three Tribal class destroyers and SS LEINSTER to sail so as to be clear to the eastward before dawn and rendezvous with SUBSTANCE at 0800.[6]

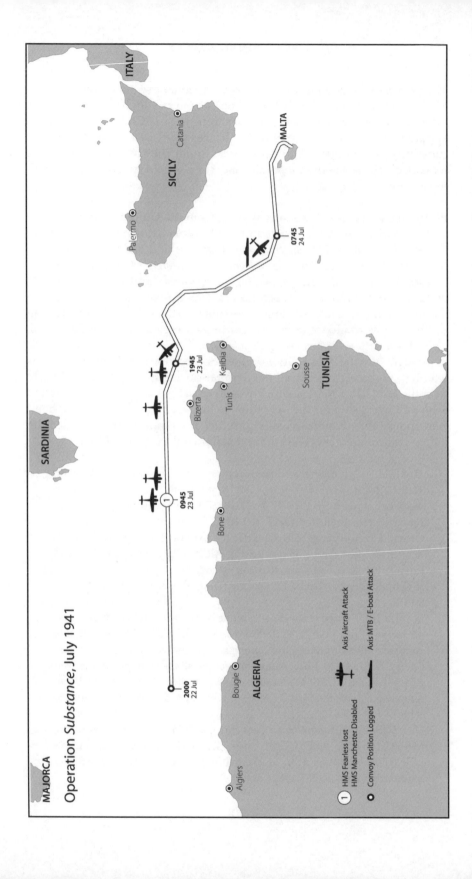

Rear Admiral E.N. Syfret (Flag Officer commanding CS18) arrived in Gibraltar aboard *Edinburgh* on 10 July and the cruiser then underwent a four day docking period. The same day Somerville signalled the Admiralty to pass the following instruction to SO of the escort in *Nelson*:

SS PASTEUR, carrying troops for Gibraltar and for transfer to Malta to fly the quarantine flag before arrival and until further orders.

No ships of SUBSTANCE escort or convoy to have any communication with the shore except by my permission.

No soldiers dressed as such to be visible in warships when in sight of merchant ships and, only a reasonable number of men to be on deck at any one time in any case. Not more than 1000 to be on deck in PASTEUR, and numbers visible in LEINSTER to be kept to the absolute minimum.

PASTEUR to be ready to disembark stores for EDINBURGH into lighters on arrival and to disembark personnel simultaneously by land to EDINBURGH and AURORA [actually her sister *Arethusa*] and by boat to JUPITER [withdrawn from the Operation on 15 July[7]], NESTOR, LIGHTNING and the Hunt class destroyers at 2159 on D-2 [19 July].

Personnel for Gibraltar to remain on board their ships until further orders.[8]

In preparation for *Substance,* on 11 July oiling-at-sea trials were undertaken by the destroyers *Foxhound* and *Eridge* with the oiler *Brown Ranger* using the trough method. *Foxhound* reported that these were not successful, and that further investigation and trials would be necessary before the convoy entered the Mediterranean.[9]

That day Somerville, who was clearly concerned about his obvious weakness in cruisers, signalled the Admiralty requesting that the recently modernised 8-inch gun cruiser *London* should be included in the reinforced Force H for *Substance*. However, their Lordships declined his request pointing out that this was impossible because of Home Fleet commitments which meant that *London* was required for patrol duties.[10]

Another concern was the passage of Convoy MG 1, consisting of seven empty merchant ships, from Malta to Gibraltar. Plans envisaged that they would leave Malta in company, escorted by the destroyer *Encounter*, to be in a position south of Pantelleria by dark on 23 July (D.3). Thereafter they would split into three groups and the hope was that the passage of MG 1 would not be detected by the Italians until the following day. Worries about the safety of MG 1 resulted in an exchange of signals between Somerville and the C-in-C Mediterranean Fleet which culminated in Somerville agreeing, on 13 July, to the proposal that *Encounter* should bombard Pantelleria harbour on 23 July if MG1 was sighted during its perilous passage eastwards on D.3.[11] However, Admiral Cunningham was still concerned that the MG 1 would remain wide open to surface attack on D.3

and, that by being at sea and moving westward, it might nullify the effect of any diversionary demonstration being made by the Mediterranean Fleet on D.3 and D.4 (23 – 24 July) by showing the real operation was the passage of the *Substance* convoy and the safe return of the escorting warships. Consequently, he signalled the Admiralty requesting that Convoy MG 1 should sail on D.4. The Admiralty disagreed and affirmed that the decision to sail MG 1 on D.3 must stand.[12]

At 05.00 hours on 16 July Somerville sailed the Hunt-class destroyers *Farndale, Avon Vale* and *Eridge* to rendezvous with *Manchester* and the troopship SS *Pasteur* in position 38°25′N 16°10′W at 07.00 hours on 18 July.[13] That day, intelligence reports concerning the disposition of the Italian fleet revealed that on 14 July there were two Littorio and two Cavour-class battleships (one of the latter in dock), three 6-inch cruisers and a few torpedo boats in Taranto. Furthermore, on 16 July there were four cruisers and five destroyers in Palermo and a further three cruisers and three destroyers in Messina.[14]

Meanwhile, the build up to the operation continued with SS *Pasteur*, escorted by *Lightning, Nestor, Avon Vale, Farndale* and *Eridge* entering Gibraltar harbour at 15.48 hours on 19 July and berthed at the detached mole. *Pasteur* was flying the quarantine flag and was ordered to have no communication with the shore. Personnel embarked for Gibraltar were ordered to be retained on board the troopship until after the forces engaged in *Substance* had sailed. The cruiser *Edinburgh* and the fast minelayer *Manxman*, which had arrived 04.00 hours that day, were also berthed on the detached mole and were similarly embargoed. Troops and their equipment were duly transferred to the warships and at 02.00 hours on 20 July Rear Admiral Syfret in *Edinburgh* left Gibraltar with *Manxman, Lightning, Nestor, Avon Vale, Farndale* and *Eridge* in company and sailed to the westward to meet Convoy WS 9C escorted by the battleship *Nelson* and destroyers at 12.00 hours on 21 July.[15]

Some two hours after Syfret had sailed the cruisers *Manchester* and *Arethusa* accompanied by the Tribal-class destroyers *Cossack, Maori* and *Sikh* plus the personnel ship SS *Leinster* arrived. The two cruisers occupied the berths vacated by *Edinburgh* and *Manxman* respectively in the hope that an inexpert observer might be deceived into thinking that *Edinburgh* and *Manxman* were still in Gibraltar. However, as Somerville observed acidly, the 'raspberry-ice colour of *Arethusa* did not assist the subterfuge.'[16]

Vice Admiral Somerville had clearly taken the issue of security seriously but he remained concerned about lapses that occurred in the United Kingdom before sailing. His worries were confirmed by the Commodore of Convoy WS9C and the Commanding Officer of HMS *Manxman* who reported that certain mail bags and stores were labelled with their ultimate destination, and, that in some cases, military personnel appeared to be aware of their port of disembarkation. Furthermore, the destination of ratings for HMS *Cormorant*[17] was written on their draft notices. Time did not permit a full enquiry before the operation but Somerville considered it desirable to inform the Admiralty at once in order that more stringent precautions might be taken [in future].[18] The following personnel and stores were embarked in the ships of the escort for *Substance*[19]:

EDINBURGH: 32 officers and 712 other ranks of the Lancashire Fusiliers, 50 tons of equipment, 20 tons of RAF small arms ammunition, 20 tons of Army ammunition.

MANCHESTER: 32 officers and 713 other ranks of the King's Own Regiment, 16 other ranks of the Royal Artillery, 50 tons of equipment, 25 tons ammunition, 7 tons of Bren guns and equipment, 2 Bofors guns and 15 tons of equipment and ammunition, 16 cases of dry batteries, 48 bags of confidential mail.

ARETHUSA: 25 officers and 436 other ranks of the Dorsetshire Regiment, RASC and Royal Artillery, 13 tons of baggage, 1 ton of Bren guns, mortars and ammunition, 2 tons of RAF ammunition and equipment, 63 bags of confidential mail.

MANXMAN: 25 officers and 433 other ranks of the Buffs, Lancashire Fusiliers and Royal Artillery, 10 tons of baggage, ammunition and weapons, 366 packages for the King's Own Regiment, 12 cases of films.

COSSACK: 4 officers and 51 other ranks, mostly of RAOC.

MAORI: 5 officers and 47 other ranks of the Royal Corps of Signals and RASC.

SIKH: 4 officers and 50 other ranks of the Dorsetshire Regiment.

NESTOR: 4 officers and 52 other ranks of the Royal Army Services Corps.

FOXHOUND: 4 officers and 46 other ranks of the Royal Army Pay Corps and Royal Artillery.

FIREDRAKE: 4 officers and 48 other ranks of the Hampshire Regiment.

FARNDALE: 1 officer and 11 other ranks of the Royal Ordnance Corps.

AVON VALE: 1 officer and 13 other ranks of the Royal Army Pay Corps.

ERIDGE: 1 officer and 3 other ranks.

Diversionary and Submarine Operations

Part of the plan for passing the fast convoy (Operation *Substance*) from Gibraltar to Malta consisted of attempts made in the Eastern Mediterranean to tempt Italian naval forces to come out, by creating the impression that the convoy for Malta was in fact going on to Alexandria. This had in fact happened as recently as the first two weeks of May 1941 when the *Tiger* convoy had made the passage from Gibraltar to Alexandria with the loss of just one ship. Operation *Tiger* had coincided with MW 7, a convoy from Alexandria to Malta covered by the Mediterranean Fleet, after which the returning warships escorted the four remaining *Tiger* ships safely to Alexandria.

Consequently, at 21.00 hours on 22 July the main body of the Mediterranean Fleet, consisting of the battleships *Queen Elizabeth* and *Valiant*, the cruisers *Naiad*, *Phoebe*, *Neptune* and *Hobart*, the fast minelayers *Abdiel*, and *Latona*, plus the destroyers *Jackal*, *Nizam*, *Kipling*, *Kimberley*, *Griffin*, *Hasty* and *Havock*, left Alexandria.[20] This force was joined at 04.00 hours on 23 July by the cruisers *Ajax* and *Leander* and the destroyers *Jervis*, *Jaguar*, *Kandahar* and *Kingston* which had left Haifa the previous afternoon.[21] The battlefleet was shadowed by enemy aircraft during 23 July but no attacks developed and, at dark, the ships turned back and steamed eastward at high speed. Having caught the enemy's attention, the Mediterranean Fleet quietly returned to Alexandria late on 24 July.[22] However, the fiction that the Mediterranean Fleet was still at sea and sailing westwards was maintained by the submarines *Perseus* and *Regent* which were employed sending dummy wireless messages indicating that the British Fleet was still at sea.

The Italian fleet based at Taranto, Messina and Palermo was capable of deploying overwhelming strength against the convoy as it started the final phase of its journey to the besieged island of Malta. Consequently, eight British submarines were sent to patrol off the Italian bases and on the probable sortie routes of their surface units as the convoy voyaged from Gibraltar to Malta. Two submarines were detailed to patrol south of Messina plus one off Palermo and one off Marittimo. The U-class boats *Upright*, *Unique*, *Urge* and *Upholder* were detailed to occupy these positions and left Malta as necessary so as to be in their designated patrol positions by 22 July. *P 32*, another U-class submarine, which was on passage to join the Malta submarine flotilla and had left Gibraltar on 17 July, was stationed off Cavoli Point, Sardinia from 21 to 26 July but sighted nothing and arrived at Malta without incident on 31 July. None of the submarines reported any incidents except for *Urge* which unsuccessfully attacked a small convoy on 22 July. Two days later *Upholder* proceeded to Cape St Vito to attack the Italian coastal route and to intercept any naval forces leaving Palermo. Later that day she attacked and damaged a large supply ship and then proceeded to the Marittimo area. On the evening of 28 July *Upholder* sighted a southbound force of two cruisers and their destroyer escort. The torpedo hit obtained during the resulting attack on the rear cruiser, *Giuseppe Garibaldi*, put her out of action for some months.[23]

Once More into the Mediterranean

At 22.00 hours on 20 July embarkation of another 536 officers and men of the King's Own Royal Lancaster Regiment began and was completed by 01.45 hours the next morning. As usual, to avoid early detection by Axis intelligence, the warships left Gibraltar incrementally, while the transports slipped through the Strait of Gibraltar on the night of 20–21 July 1941. A novel feature was the addition of the oiler *Brown Ranger*, escorted by the four-funnel destroyer *Beverley* (ex-USS *Branch*), from which Syfret's destroyers refuelled on 22 July to improve their endurance. *Manchester, Arethusa, Cossack* (Captain (D) 4th Destroyer Flotilla), *Maori, Sikh* and SS *Leinster*, were ordered to sail at 01.50 hours but because of fog and heavy Levanter squalls which commenced at 01.15 hours, sailing was delayed until 03.15 hours. Unfortunately, the troopship *Leinster* ran aground in the fog and had to be docked in Gibraltar. Consequently, about one fifth of the 5,000 troops intended for Malta had to be left behind including maintenance crews for Royal Air Force aircraft operating from the island. Soon afterwards, Force H, comprising *Renown* (Flag Officer commanding Force H), *Ark Royal, Hermione, Faulknor* (Captain (D) 8th Destroyer Flotilla) *Foresight, Fury, Forester, Fearless, Foxhound, Firedrake* and *Duncan*, also delayed by fog, sailed at 04.25 hours for Operation *Substance*. On joining the convoy, *Manchester* took station either astern of, or between, the two columns of the convoy as it began its journey to Malta. The various forces joined around 08.00 hours on 23 July and it was about that time that the Italians became aware of the true nature of the operation.

Italian aircraft had spotted the warships south of the Balearics on 22 July, but, on the assumption that Force H was conducting another flying-off operation, the Italian battle fleet remained in port. By the time that a second aircraft had discovered the convoy off Bone on 23 July it was too late to intervene with the three battleships at Taranto. However, the Italian air force soon made its presence felt.

At 07.45 hours on 23 July as the convoy approached the sector most easily reached by aircraft from Cagliari, Force H joined Force X and the convoy. Somerville's flagship, the modernised battlecruiser *Renown*, along with the Dido-class cruiser *Hermione*, protected *Ark Royal* forming an outer port column of the convoy which provided anti-aircraft protection while at the same time remaining free to manoeuvre for flying. *Nelson, Manchester, Edinburgh, Arethusa* and *Manxman* were stationed close to the convoy as it sailed eastward at thirteen and a half knots. A crescent-shaped screen of destroyers was spread ahead of the entire formation.

At 09.15 hours small formations of Italian aircraft were detected to the north-east by *Hermione*'s radar. Half an hour later eight high-level SM 79 bombers flew overhead from south to north and dropped their bombs on the convoy itself. While the gunners were distracted by the high-level bombers, six torpedo-armed SM 79s attacked from right ahead and then split into two groups of three and sheering off as the destroyers in the van put up an AA barrage. One aircraft from each group attacked the destroyer *Fearless* which was stationed on the starboard wing of the screen while the two remaining aircraft on the port side attacked the merchant ships, as did their compatriots on the starboard side of the convoy. The two aircraft which attacked *Fearless* released their torpedoes from a height of seventy feet and ranges of 1,500 and 800 yards respectively. One torpedo passed less than 1,000 yards ahead but the second hit *Fearless* causing very severe damage. Her sister *Forester* went alongside, took off survivors and then torpedoed and sank the burning wreck.

Manchester Torpedoed and Returns to Gibraltar

Captain Drew's 'Report of Proceedings', written on 27 July, provides a graphic account of *Manchester*'s part in Operation *Substance* and the effectiveness of the *Regia Aeronautica*:

> The ship made a rendezvous with Convoy WS9C as ordered by Flag Officer Force H at 0730 21 July. At 2130 on 22 July FURY was watered, 30 tons of boiler water being transferred. This was done at a speed of 8 knots. There were on board at this time some 700 officers and other ranks of the 8th Battalion of the King's Own Royal Regiment, some were employed as look-outs and on other suitable jobs. At 0515 on 23rd the ship's company went to Action Stations, and assumed second degree of readiness at 0550. The 1st degree was resumed at 0924 when it was apparent from HERMIONE's reports that an air attack on the convoy was developing.
>
> The attack commenced at 0943 when a high level formation of enemy aircraft was sighted to starboard crossing from starboard to port. Bombs were dropped which straddled EDINBURGH and CITY OF PRETORIA. This formation was in groups of seven and three. The leading ships of the convoy were then commencing a turn in succession to 060 degrees, a turn of 30° to port.
>
> 0944 FEARLESS on the starboard screen of the convoy was observed to be hit; a column of smoke rose to some hundreds of feet and flames were seen in the ship. The leading ships were altering back to 090 degrees.
>
> 0944.5 The torpedo bombers delivered their attack. Two torpedoes were fired from the port side in the general direction of the convoy, and a turn to port made to comb the tracks.
>
> 0945.5 Two torpedoes passed down the port side. Another torpedo passed astern to starboard.
>
> 0946 In order to avoid collision with PORT CHALMERS and resume station in the convoy, a turn to starboard was commenced. At this time one torpedo bomber (Savoia 79) flying low, fired a torpedo between SS DURHAM and PORT CHALMERS. The wheel was reversed in an attempt to avoid this, but the torpedo struck the port side aft.

0947 At this time the short range weapons were firing heavily on the port side at torpedo bombers, one of which passed between MANCHESTER and PORT CHALMERS. Hits were scored on these aircraft and in fact both were probably hit by several ships.

The immediate effects of the hit were that the ship listed 12 degrees to port and lost speed. She was still turning slowly to port. The steering was changed over to after steering, and the ship remained under reasonable control and endeavour was made to regain the course ordered (090°). This was done by 0955. The steering motors then failed and hand steering was used from 0958.

By this time reports were being received from the Damage Control Parties, and it was apparent that the After Engine Room was being abandoned and various compartments abaft that were flooding or had flooded.

At 09.49 hours, Drew reported to Flag Officer Force H, repeated Rear Admiral Syfret in *Edinburgh*, that *Manchester* had been hit by a torpedo and at 10.00 hours Vice Admiral Somerville, whose concern for the convoy was paramount, ordered *Manchester* to return to Gibraltar keeping along the French North African coast. At this time, ships in the convoy, which had been taking avoiding action and were pointing in different directions, were gradually reforming. As *Manchester* was already turning slowly to starboard, this turn was continued and course 230 degrees was set. Reports were received that only one engine, the starboard outer, was available. The Hunt-class destroyer *Avon Vale* was detailed to escort the crippled cruiser so as to provide additional AA support and, if the worst came to the worst, evacuate *Manchester*'s complement and the military personnel. *Manchester*'s speed was gradually increased until about twelve knots was attained.

Drew reported that for 'the next hour or two repair and rescue parties were busy between decks'. The explosion had travelled upwards through the decks including the wardroom anteroom, on the upper deck, driving enormous quantities of oil fuel upwards into all compartments affected. Water and oil fuel flooded the after engine room, 4-inch magazines, main W/T office, 'X' magazine and other compartments in these regions. The rescue parties were able to extricate about forty men before they were overcome by fumes of oil fuel and after treatment the majority recovered, and were able to go about their duties. Emergency leads to the steering motors were run and mechanical steering was restored by 1315. By this time it was apparent that a large number of compartments were flooded between 179 and 209 bulkheads, and it was decided not to try to trim by counter flooding. Trimming was effected by transferring fuel from port to starboard and by shifting military stores on the upper deck from port to starboard and by ordering all people not actually closed up to remain on the starboard side.

The shipwright repair party then constructed a coffer dam in 'X' Turret flat between 'X' Turret barbette and 198 bulkhead on the main deck, and shored up various bulkheads to guard against the risk of water flooding the compartment abaft 'X' Turret. Large parties, including military other ranks taking passage, then worked incessantly to try to reduce the very large quantities of oil fuel in the various compartments between decks. This was regarded as a matter of great urgency as further attacks were expected and the danger of fire had to be met. At 13.45, when North of Cape de Garde, an Italian Cant seaplane was observed shadowing. This continued at intervals until about 1700.'

At this point Captain Drew addressed the ship's company and whilst praising them for their splendid efforts, warned them that further demands would be made on them before they could consider that they were out of the wood. Soon after he finished addressing *Manchester*'s crew, three torpedo aircraft were sighted low down on the horizon on the starboard quarter at 17.31 hours and at a range of about 20,000 yards. At this time the French African coast in the region of Cape Bougaroni was abeam to port and the Italian aircraft, flying a few feet above the water in line ahead, followed the coastline close inshore without regard to territorial waters. They passed right ahead and disappeared over the horizon in the rays of the sun. Captain Drew then described what happened next:

> At 1805 the three aircraft reappeared low down on the starboard bow approaching the ship. HMS AVON VALE proceeded at high speed and subjected them to a heavy flank fire at the same time leaving the range open for MANCHESTER to fire also. Fire was opened with 6-inch guns – 'A' and 'B' turrets in barrage fire, and the starboard 4-inch battery also engaged them. They [the torpedo bombers] opened out with the apparent intention of attacking from different points. As the attack had been expected, I had decided beforehand that if simultaneous attacks were delivered , avoiding action, which would be slow, having regard to the state of the ship, would be taken in relation to the unfired at aircraft, relying on heavy gunfire to make the other attacks inaccurate.
>
> Actually one aircraft fired his torpedo near the destroyer [AVON VALE], the other two appeared to be so deterred by the volume of fire that they fired their torpedoes at long range. One of the torpedoes was just seen breaking the surface towards the end of its run in the rays of the setting sun, and course was altered in time to avoid it. This torpedo detonated shortly afterwards some distance astern.
>
> Course was then altered to round Cape Bougaroni nearer the coast in the hope of finding concealment in offshore mists, as the day had been hot so

there was some hope of this. The object of this, of course, was to counteract the menace of attack by surface craft during the night. There was no mist. Course was altered to 278° at 2130 in order to rendezvous with VIMY and VIDETTE in position 37° 20′ N. 3° 10′ E. at 0900 of the 24th.

That evening, the first of three burial services was held aboard *Manchester* as the bodies of ten members of her ship's company and twenty-three soldiers were committed to the sea. The following day while *Manchester* was being screened by *Avon Vale*, *Vimy* and *Vidette*, the port screen reported ASDIC contact with a submarine,and systematic attacks were carried out by *Vimy* and *Avon Vale*. The four ships were within range of air cover from Gibraltar by the late morning of 24 July and from 11.00 hours onwards a Sunderland flying boat provided anti-submarine escort. Later, at 19.15 hours that day, *Avon Vale* was secured to the starboard side of the cruiser and ninety tons of oil fuel was transferred to her. This was done whilst still moving at eleven knots to enable her to proceed in accordance with Flag Officer Force H's instructions to her to screen the damaged *Firedrake* and her escort *Eridge* which were also retiring to Gibraltar. On completion of fuelling *Avon Vale* then sailed to join the crippled *Firedrake* and help escort her to Gibraltar.

At 13.00 hours on 25 July the tugs *Rollicker* and *St Omar* escorted by MLs 173 and 169 were ordered out of Gibraltar to stand by *Manchester*, a corrupted signal having been received indicating a possible breakdown in her steering gear.

There were no further alarms and *Manchester* duly entered the North entrance of Gibraltar harbour at 00.55 hours on 26 July. The two tugs assisted the cruiser as she was secured alongside Gibraltar's detached mole. However, difficulty was experienced in berthing alongside because the port outer screw was resting on the bottom. The torpedo explosion had fractured the port outer 'A' bracket causing the shaft, propeller and barrel of the bracket to hang down below the keel. Consequently, the port outer shaft, which had broken away with most of its 'A' bracket, had to be lifted and secured to the after capstan before the stern of the ship could be brought alongside. Once alongside, the ship's divers inspected the damaged hull while the troops were disembarked and the injured transferred to a hospital ashore. By 19.30 hours that evening, *Manchester* had been taken into Gibraltar's No.2 Drydock for detailed examination of the torpedo damage and initial repairs.

Captain Drew's report finished with a brief note of the casualties caused by the torpedo's explosion. Thus, three naval officers and twenty ratings had been killed, three ratings were missing and one wounded. The military casualties amounted to five officers and seven men killed plus one officer and four men wounded.

Chapter 6

Back Home

While the crippled *Manchester* made her way back to the safety of Gibraltar, the convoy battled eastwards towards Malta in the face of enemy air attacks, but thanks chiefly to the *Ark Royal*'s fighters, which beat off many enemy attacks, the convoy and its escort reached the entrance to the Skerki Channel at 17.00 hours that day without having suffered further loss. At this point, Admiral Somerville hauled round to the westward with the heavy ships, while Admiral Syfret's cruisers and destroyers carried on to Malta with the convoy. At 17.13 hours on 23 July, *Hermione* was detached from Force H with orders to replace the damaged *Manchester* in Force X. Air attacks continued until dusk and another destroyer, *Firedrake*, was disabled and towed back to Gibraltar by *Eridge*.

Rear Admiral Syfret, the Flag Officer commanding the 18th Cruiser Squadron and Force X provided an account of the passage of the *Substance* convoy from the Skerki Channel to Grand Harbour in a report submitted on 27 July soon after his return to Gibraltar: [1]

> The damage to HMS FIREDRAKE during the air attack at 1945 was doubly unfortunate in that it deprived the port column of TSDS[2] protection. Nevertheless, the ill-luck was not so bad as it would have been had it occurred later; as it was, a decision to send FIREDRAKE back to Gibraltar under the escort of ERIDGE presented no difficulty. The loss of FEARLESS left only NESTOR as spare TSDS destroyer; but time had already been wasted and I did not want further delay while NESTOR streamed her sweep. Furthermore, the destroyer screen was already undesirably thin. Consequently, I decided to accept the increased risk of damage by mines, retain NESTOR for her original purpose and push on without further delay.

During the night of 23/24 July, Syfret in *Edinburgh* took the bold action of steering north eastwards for a time, directly towards Sicily. In the same way as had been done with Operation *Excess* the previous January he ordered two large changes of course under cover of darkness. These course changes kept the convoy and its escorts, in deep water, free of mines and away from Italian reconnaissance. It also avoided a submarine patrol line, though it was attacked near Pantelleria by Italian MAS boats. Syfret's report described what happened during that night:

> The long and tortuous route through the Sicilian Straits proved, contrary to my early fears, most excellently chosen. There is no doubt that the enemy expected the convoy to take the more or less direct route from the Skerki Channel to the Pantelleria Strait. In fact, they must have felt certain of this since they made no attempt to keep the convoy under air observation during the critical period before and just after sunset, and in consequence the alteration of course to 075° at 2000 on D.3 was unobserved and the anticipated attack at dusk, which I feared most of all, never materialised. The method of search employed by the enemy aircraft, viz. towing flares, was new to me, but I was unable to judge its effectiveness.
>
> The alterations of course without signal during the night D.3/D.4 were made without difficulty and the convoy never lost formation. Accuracy of navigation along the selected route, commencing as it did with a period of manoeuvring to avoid air attack, seemed to me a very difficult problem, and that Pantelleria was sighted on the appropriate bearing and at the correct time reflects, I think, much credit on my Squadron Navigating Officer Commander M.H. Brown, RN.

The period between 2250 on D.3 and 0013 on D.4 when the convoy entered the Italian convoy route, I had previously considered to be the most dangerous from the point of view of mines, and in view of the absence of the TSDS destroyer ahead of part of the column and of two Military Transport ships being without paravanes, I was very relieved when this period had passed without incident.

The meeting with E-boats off Pantelleria on D.4 might have had very different results had their attacks been carried out more resolutely. It seemed that they were not expecting us, and this surprise in our favour discounted their tactical advantage. The E-boats [actually the Italian MAS532 and MAS533] were difficult to see and always the presence of one was not disclosed until it went ahead on its engines at high speed. One felt that they would have achieved more had they kept quiet whilst and after they fired their torpedoes. I did not regret the decision not to use star-shell. As usual, the handicap of not having a flashless propellant was keenly felt.

By 0400 on D.4 the E-boat threat appeared to be over. Some ships were out of station but it was evident that all of these were doing their best to reform. It was too dark to be able to count the number of ships in company, but I was pleasantly surprised by the number that I could see. At 0345 I was able to see all but one MT ship and sent COSSACK around to look for lost sheep. While she was doing this a long message from NESTOR revealed that she was assisting the damaged ship.

It transpired that SS SYDNEY STAR, No.2 in starboard column, was hit by a torpedo and No.1 [hold] flooded at about 0250. She dropped astern and NESTOR then went alongside and embarked 600 (approximately) military personnel and stood by her until arrival at Malta, being joined by HERMIONE. SYDNEY STAR was able to steam at 12 – 14 knots, and she and her escort, proceeding by way of the route North of Malta, arrived off Grand Harbour at 1330. Great credit is due to the Commanding Officer of NESTOR, Commander AR Rosenthal RAN, for his initiative, able handling of the situation and display of seamanship in a position 4.5 miles off Pantelleria Island during the period of the E-boat attacks.

On D.3 the absence of protection on the evening of D.3 given by Beaufighters from Malta caused me some apprehension as to the effectiveness of air protection that would be afforded the following morning before the convoy reached Malta. At one time it appeared if all our efforts to get the convoy to Malta might be frustrated unless all the cruisers and destroyers remained with the convoy to the end. The comparative failure of direction of Beaufighters from Malta was no doubt largely due to not having worked with them before, but the number of frights given the convoy through the Beaufighters not identifying themselves by IFF or other means seemed quite unnecessary.

In accordance with your [i.e. Vice Admiral Somerville with Force H] instructions the cruisers and one remaining Hunt destroyer were due to part company and proceed to Malta at 0700 if I was satisfied with the situation as regards enemy surface forces. All enemy surface forces had been reported as in their respective harbours on the previous day, but 0700 no morning reconnaissance had been received from Vice Admiral Malta. I had never felt unduly worried about this but nevertheless I was not prepared to leave until I was happier about the NESTOR and SYDNEY STAR situation. Sounds of gunfire at 0630 and 0655 and a call for 'Help' showed NESTOR was in difficulties and consequently, at 0701 I detached HERMIONE, who could be spared since she had no equipment or troops to disembark to join her. At 0730 the situation appeared easier and as I realised that any further delay might jeopardise the arrangements planned for getting the convoy into Grand Harbour and for Force X re-joining Force H, I decided to take HM Ships EDINBURGH, ARETHUSA and MANXMAN on to Malta and leave HMS FARNDALE with her good AA armament, to augment the force at Captain (D) 4th Destroyer Flotilla's disposal for the defence of the convoy.

At 1000 SYDNEY STAR and NESTOR were attacked by 8 Ju 87 dive bombers and two high level bombers but fortunately neither were hit, nor in the two earlier attacks before the arrival of HERMIONE was any damage done. One of the dive bombers was shot down by HERMIONE. At 0705 the main convoy was attacked by three torpedo bombers at long range. Avoiding action was taken and no hits were scored.

At 0830 Vice Admiral Malta's reconnaissance report was received which removed what little fears yet remained as regards attack by surface forces and at 1130 EDINBURGH, ARETHUSA and MANXMAN arrived off Valletta. By 1200 all three cruisers had berthed and disembarkation followed three-quarters of an hour later and proceeded independently.

Force X received a great reception on entering Grand Harbour by the people of Malta and on leaving was given a most stirring and inspiring send off by the troops and crews of the Military Transport ships.

On arrival at Malta I visited the Vice Admiral to discuss with him the return route for Force X. At his suggestion it was decided to adopt the route south of Pantelleria Island and close inshore along the Tunisian coast, which had been used by MG 1.

The return passage was made without incident. Apart from a few fishing boats passed when steaming along the coast nothing was sighted and at 0750 (D.5) Force H was sighted ahead, Captain (D) 4th destroyer flotilla in COSSACK with MAORI, SIKH, NESTOR and FOXHOUND in company (FARNDALE had to stay in Malta owing to engine room defects), being then five miles astern of EDINBURGH.

The conduct of HM Ships and the initiative shown by their Commanding Officers throughout the operation were exemplary. The motto that you [i.e. Vice Admiral Somerville in a pre-convoy briefing in Gibraltar] had given us was inspiring and appealed to all, I am sure that from first to last there was never a doubt in Force X but that the CONVOY WOULD GO THROUGH.

The complete success of Operation *Substance* exceeded even the most sanguine hopes in view of the extremely hazardous nature of the enterprise. All the *Substance* ships arrived safely and their 65,000 tons of cargo included three months' supplies for the Maltese population, as well as 10,000 tons of ammunition and torpedoes for Malta's submarines. Obviously, losses were bound to be suffered but only one destroyer was sunk with one cruiser and another destroyer badly damaged while almost all the stores destined for Malta and all the reinforcements, except those left behind in *Leinster*, had been delivered. The transport *Sydney Star* had also been badly damaged but was able to reach Malta albeit in a sinking condition with twice her normal draft. Clearly, the skill of the veteran fighter pilots of the *Ark Royal* and the determination and experience of the cruisers and destroyers were vital to the success of the operation but, without, in Admiral Somerville's words, the 'steadfast and resolute behaviour of the merchant ships themselves success could not have been accomplished'.

Convoy MG 1, which had sailed from Malta early on 23 July with a single destroyer as escort was equally successful and, despite numerous air attacks, all of its vessels had reached Gibraltar by 28 July. Admiral Somerville, who had steered to the west after leaving the convoy on the evening of 23 July, altered course again the following afternoon and steered to the east to meet and escort Rear Admiral Syfret's returning cruisers and destroyers. Once again, *Ark Royal*'s fighters protected the fleet from high-level and torpedo-bombing attacks and, during the forenoon of 27 July all ships were back at Gibraltar.

The Italian Attack on Valletta During Night of 25/26 July 1941

Following the arrival of the *Substance* convoy in Valletta the Italians decided to mount an audacious attack, using the *X MAS* stealth unit of the Regia Marina, on the merchantmen before they could be unloaded. After dark of 25 July the fast sloop *Diana*[3], transporting ten Motoscafo Turismo (MT) boats[4] accompanied by MAS 451 and 452[5] sailed from Augusta to attack Valletta. Between them they were transporting ten MTs and a Motoscafo Turismo Lento (MTL)[6] carrying two Siluri a Lenta Corsas (SLC)[7]. SLCs were self-propelled human torpedoes and they were tasked with entering the series of creeks that make up the Grand Harbour to attack as many targets as possible including the submarines based at Lazaretto on Manoel Island. By midnight *Diana* and the two MAS boats were, as scheduled, fifteen miles offshore but the operation was delayed by about an hour because of a fouled propeller on one of the boats. All that then remained for them was to enter Valletta and create as much mayhem as possible.

The two mole extensions marking the entrance to the Grand Harbour were closed by booms. On the northern side, the mole was connected to the land at Fort St Elmo by a bridge and, as the gap beneath was known to be closed off by steel nets, one SLC was tasked with blasting a passage through for the nine explosive motor boats. The whole operation was to take place under the cover of air raids during the early hours of 26 July but, thanks to 'Ultra' decrypts, the British defences were fully aware of the enterprise. The state of alert was further heightened when *Diana* was detected on radar. The scene was set for what became known in Italian literature as the 'Glorious Failure'.

One of the SLCs turned out to be defective and consequently was not sent in. The second human torpedo headed for the boom but exploded without breaching the nets. Two of the explosive motor boats were then sent in but the first failed to explode after the pilot bailed-out. The second exploded with the pilot still on board but succeeded in bringing down the whole bridge span thereby blocking the planned route of ingress.[8]

At this point the operation became a fiasco as searchlights in Forts St Elmo and Ricasoli illuminated the whole flotilla whose every move had been tracked by radar. The luckless Italians' craft were hit by a storm of fire from the rapid-firing twin 6-pounder guns of the coastal defences and the unit's leaders were killed. Within two minutes the assault force all but ceased to exist. At dawn the MAS boats, the MT command boat and the MTL, which had stayed further offshore, were hunted down by RAF Hurricanes and all, except for MAS 452, destroyed. The latter was attacked by a Hurricane flown by Pilot Officer Winton of 185 Squadron about thirty miles north of Malta. Winton, who was shot down by a Macchi 200 sent to protect the surviving units on their return to Sicily, swam two miles to the drifting MAS 452 and, after boarding, he found eight dead Italians in the craft. Three hours later a rescue Swordfish floatplane from RAF Kalafrana arrived, took MAS 452 in tow and brought it into Valletta.[9]

Operation *Style* – The Completion of Operation *Substance*
On 28 July Vice Admiral Somerville received information from the Admiralty that the RAF personnel who had been left behind in Operation *Substance* because of the grounding of SS *Leinster*, were urgently required to maintain the air offensive against lines of communication in Tripoli. All told, because of the return of the damaged *Manchester* to Gibraltar there were some 1,800 troops and airmen to be carried to Malta. It was therefore desired that these, together with as many Army personnel as practicable, should be sent to Malta in *Hermione*, *Arethusa* and *Manxman* and Somerville was requested to plan an operation to cover the passage with Force H (Operation *Style*).[10]

Early on 31 July *Hermione*, *Arethusa*, *Manxman* and two destroyers sailed from Gibraltar with the last of the reinforcements. At 05.10 hours on 2 August, when nearing Malta and in position 36°21'N, 12°40'E, *Hermione* sighted a submarine in surface trim and apparently stopped fairly broad on the port bow at a distance of a third of a mile. The cruiser immediately increased to full speed and rammed the submarine at 28 knots as it was submerging with 'a lovely crunch'. The Italian submarine *Tembien* was sunk and *Hermione* suffered some flooded compartments forward and her ASDIC dome put out of action.[11] Later that day, the five warships arrived safely at Malta, left again the same afternoon and were back at Gibraltar on 4 August. Thus, within days, the Royal Navy had delivered the vital RAF personnel stranded with *Leinster* plus the *Manchester* contingent and sank an Italian submarine in the process.

The Damage Inflicted on *Manchester*
Because *Manchester* had been torpedoed in the Mediterranean on 23 July 1941 and was then sent to the USA for repairs, it was not possible for the damage to be inspected by a representative of the Director of Naval Construction in accordance with Confidential Admiralty Fleet Orders. Consequently, the damage report of the incident[12] was compiled and forwarded by Captain Drew through Rear Admiral Commanding 18th

Cruiser Squadron and Admiral Sir John Tovey (Commander-in-Chief, Home Fleet) to the Director of Naval Construction Stanley (later Sir Stanley) Goodall. The latter then reproduced Captain Drew's report (see Appendix II) for circulation on 27 February 1942. Captain Drew was commended for the quality of his report by the Rear Admiral commanding the 18th Cruiser Squadron, the C-in-C Home Fleet, the Engineer-in-Chief and the Director of Electrical Engineering.

Captain Drew reported that the torpedo struck at 09.46 hours on 23 July 1941 at 202 station in Y4 oil fuel tank, completely wrecking the port lower compartments between stations 179 and 209, driving the port side deck of 'X' flat to the upper deck and putting out all lighting in 'X' and gunroom flats. The limits of flooding were found to stretch from station 155 to 227. Unfortunately, the after section damage control headquarters was situated in 'X' flat. There were few survivors here, and they were unable to resume duty after rescue, thus there was some little delay before concerted action was taken. The majority of the after medical distributing section were also immediate casualties or else rendered unconscious soon after by fuel oil gas and explosion fumes. The number of casualties was increased by the fact that all fire and repair parties, magazine crews and medical parties were backed up by military other ranks that were embarked for the operation.

In 'X' flat most of the port side deck was blown up to the deckhead. All compartments beneath were missing with reflected sunlight showing up over a considerable area. However, the ship's side remained intact to well below the waterline. The gunroom flat, which was forward of 'X' flat, had water pouring over the coaming of the port after door and eventually became soaked with fuel oil to a depth of five feet on *Manchester*'s port side. The gunroom flat remained in darkness and the air would not support unaided breathing for long, while thick white smoke prevented the useful employment of torches. A considerable number of oil-covered casualties were collected in a heap at the foot of the ladder. Secondary and emergency lighting remained in operation in 'Y' flat but a mixture of fuel oil and seawater was entering through distorted communication doors. In due course the water/oil level in 'Y' flat reached about two feet on the port side. In the gunroom flat, the port after communication door was secured by one clip and then securely shored with leakage into the flat through a cracked bulkhead, being stopped with soft wood wedges. Similarly the manhole door to Midshipman's chest flat was shored up, and soft wood wedges employed to stop leakage of fuel oil.

The trunk to the 4-inch magazine was tested, the hatch opened and survivors were found clinging to the ladder with fuel oil being half way up the trunk. These survivors were rescued and the hatch closed and clipped. In 'X' flat, as free water was washing across from the port side, little could be done and any hope of rescue for 'X' magazine's crew was out of the question as the trunk proved to be full of water. The 'X' shell room crew had already left their shell room, closing the trunk upper hatch and evacuating casualties in the process. 'Y' magazine and shell room crews were similarly evacuated.

On the 24 July, the hatch to 'Y' pump space was re-opened and an emergency electricity supply was fed to the fifty ton pump. 'X' shell room trunk had been opened up some time before and was found to be flooding because of the distorted door of the warhead room in the trunk which allowed water to leak down the trunk. Unfortunately, the pump was unable to obtain suction on 'X' shell room which had to be clipped shut about one third full of water. The gyro room was also opened up and partially pumped out, but when the extent of the leak, through cable holes with no glands fitted, was ascertained this was abandoned, as it would have required the constant service of a portable pump which was more urgently required elsewhere. Instead the bulkhead was shored up across the slop room passage.

That day a collision mat was rigged to port of the dam in 'X' flat. This was made as neat a fit as possible and was installed to absorb the surge of free surface water and prevent damage to the wooden bulkhead should heavy seas be encountered. As the weather was deteriorating, the starboard forward door of 'X' flat, was replaced by a sound one and 'X' flat was isolated, work being continued by means of 'X' magazine upper deck embarkation hatch. Fortunately, the weather remained good. During the passage to Gibraltar bailing parties were employed in all three flats. The embarked military personnel supplied most of the manpower, as hands were closed up at action stations most of the time because further attacks were expected although only one of these materialised.

Prior to being torpedoed, *Manchester* was steaming at 124 revolutions, in units with two boilers connected in each unit. At about 09.46 hours the ship received a severe shaking from the explosion of a heavy bomb, but this was no worse than that which recently had been experienced as a result of a near miss. Indeed, in the interval before reports were received, it was thought that this had occurred, and that the list, which was being assumed, had been caused from the resulting minor damage and heeling the ship over under full wheel. The first report received was that the port telemotor lead had failed, causing one steering motor to stop, and that the ship was steaming by mechanical wheel in the after steering compartment. In the after compressor room, which was a centreline compartment, all lights went out and oil fuel gushed in from Y.4 oil fuel tank from a large hole in the port bulkhead. The hole was made by the projection of a piece of 'F' plummer block.

After the explosion the port outer shaft tended to speed up and was checked. In the after engine room all emergency lights and half the main lighting went out and all supply and exhaust fans stopped. The lower power air compressor stopped and smoke issued from the starter box. Both fire and bilge pumps stopped, and the after one was being splashed with oil fuel. The after plummer block on the port outer shaft had been torn off the inner bottom and the propeller shaft was bent. Oil fuel, followed by water, gushed into the engine room from port shaft bulkhead glands, which had been blown in. On loud bumping being heard, the port inner shaft was eased, but when it was discovered that the outer shaft was damaged, the inner shaft was re-started and 124 revolutions were obtained with approximately the same receiver pressure as before. It was assumed that the damaged plummer blocks and bulkhead glands were acting as brakes.

Within ten minutes however the flooding was already above the starting platform on the port side, and *Manchester* was listing 12.5 degrees to port. It was clear that the circulators and steam ejectors were not overcoming the flooding which increased rapidly and, with no ventilating fans running, the unpleasant fumes from the fuel oil made breathing very difficult. With the list on the ship and the oil covering the steering platform it was difficult to stand or move about, and with personnel affected by the fumes it was decided to abandon the after engine room. There was no damage to any machinery in 'B' boiler room, apart from contamination of the feed system and boilers.

After the aft engine room was abandoned, a call was received from the bridge for all possible speed, and the starboard outer engine was worked up steadily to 260 revolutions. At this, the L.P. relief lifted. Speed was decreased to 220 revolutions to ease the pressures and reduce vibration, which was excessive and especially violent in the after part of the ship. Eight sprayers at 100 lbs pressure indicated just under full power for this shaft and the speed attained was twelve and a half knots initially but this fell away to eleven and a half knots for no apparent reason after one hour.

Minor leakage into shaft passages, plummer block, and gland compartments took place through the shaft bulkhead glands. These glands had given trouble through overheating during the contractor's trials, and were the subject of correspondence. Consequently, they were only loosely packed in order to avoid overheating at high speeds, it being considered that they could be tightened up if required to produce watertightness. In the event, however, only those glands accessible in the forward engine room could be and were tightened up to stop the leakage from the shaft passages into the engine room. The shaft passages under the diesel rooms and lubricating oil store were kept pumped out down to the level of the plummer blocks.

The explosion also caused considerable disruption of electrical supply in the after part of the cruiser and, in particular, No.6 port ring main breaker had opened on overload thereby causing the numerous breakers to fail.

The sequence of events with regard to damage caused by the explosion to the armament and its control systems was as follows:

With regard to the 6-inch gun armament, communications between the Transmitting Station (TS) and 'X' and 'Y' turrets were mostly destroyed. In 'Y' Turret, all communications were dead while in 'X' Turret the multiphone to the TS was still functional and orders were relayed to 'Y' Turret by shouting. Primary and secondary lighting in both 'X' and 'Y' turrets failed. 'X' shell room was evacuated and 'X' magazine was flooded, so arrangements were made to supply 'X' from 'Y' using the troops on board. Power to the 6-inch transmitting station (TS) failed for a short period. 'X' gunhouse and cordite gallery were evacuated for a few minutes while thick smoke and fumes were cleared. Power supply to 'X' and 'Y' turrets failed, though their crews shortly reported 'Ready' with everything in hand. Furthermore, the after 6-inch DCT reported that although power training failed and the rangefinder was out of action, hand training was still possible. 'Y' magazine and its shell room were evacuated because of the danger from adjacent flooded compartments and panting of decks. Consequently, it was considered inadvisable to bring 'X' and 'Y' turrets into action because of the danger to adjacent structures already severely damaged by the explosion.

With regard to the 4-inch HA armament, the after HA.DCT was put of action because of shock to the instruments and its crew reported that they were ready to relieve the forward HA.DCTs as necessary.

Port and starboard HA gunnery control tables were affected adversely by shock but repairs were affected quickly. The 4-inch magazine was reported flooded, evacuated and closed down and consequently the 4-inch ammunition was reduced to that remaining in the ready use lockers.

In summary, the torpedo hit had reduced *Manchester*'s main armament to the six 6-inch guns in 'A' and 'B' turrets which remained under director control while, the 4-inch AA guns also remained under director control but had only a limited ammunition supply. The close-range AA weapons and torpedoes had been unaffected by the explosion.

With regard to assisting casualties the after medical distributing station was situated in the Warrant Officers' mess in the gunfire flat. This compartment is immediately forward of 'X' flat under which the torpedo struck and the Medical Officer and two Sick Berth Attendants were rendered unconscious inside a minute by carbon monoxide while two of the stretcher party outside the Warrant Officers' mess were killed and the remainder rendered immediate casualties. This was unfortunate as all casualties had to be brought to the forward distributing station situated in the Chief Petty Officers' mess. The first casualties arrived within in a few minutes of the explosion and quickly developed into a stream that threatened at first to become overwhelming. The rate of arrival made it possible to give only the roughest treatment at first, and distribution became an urgent question. This was solved by laying a line of stretchers along the alleyway. This line soon stretched far down the well deck. When the rush eased, sorting became feasible. Those already dead were carried away and covered, the wounded and unconscious being taken into the sick bay and the Chief Petty Officers' mess, both of which had been cleared of lighter cases. By this means it was possible to keep the more serious cases under supervision. Fortunately, most of the injured suffered from blast and carbon monoxide poisoning, and the weather allowed these to be taken to the well deck for artificial respiration. The number wounded was small and mostly not severely so, one case only urgently requiring operation. Shock and gas so affected survivors that their memories of the event were hazy and unreliable.

By the afternoon fifteen dead had been collected with twenty-one missing presumed trapped in flooded compartments. Those suffering from blast and carbon monoxide poisoning gradually recovered and were up and about by 22.00 hours, with the exception of eight who recovered the next morning. In all, seventy-four casualties received treatment. One of the ten wounded died. Three military officers, two military other ranks, and two ratings were landed for treatment on arrival.

The value of the prone position was well borne out in 'Y' flat where two ratings here, lying flat, were thrown bodily up to the deckhead which they actually hit without receiving damage. On the other hand four Army officers who died of head injuries were understood to have been sitting at the time of the explosion playing cards, in spite of the fact that they had been instructed previously to lay on the deck.

The damage caused by the torpedo on 23 July 1941 was summarised as follows:

> Generally between Stations 186 and 213 inclusive on port side.
>
> Port strakes – A, B, C, D, E, F of outer bottom together with transverse and longitudinal frames torn away and crumpled over a length of forty feet, and depth of twenty-five feet, platform and lower decks thrust up to upper deck. Upper deck buckled and holed above seat of damage.
>
> 'X' gundeck holed.
>
> Port transverse bulkheads buckled and split.
>
> Port longitudinal bulkheads buckled and split. The compressor room bulkhead abreast the point of contact perforated by a piece of plummer block projected from below.
>
> Internal armour abreast 'X' magazine and shell room slightly buckled with magazine port bulkhead set in towards centre line.
>
> Port outer shaft 'A' bracket both arms broken off one foot from plating.
>
> 198 bulkhead below platform deck shattered and two internal armour plates dislodged.
>
> 213 bulkhead torn in wake of bent inner shaft.

Port shafting – one tail section badly distorted, one bent. One intermediate section badly bent, two slightly bent.

Starboard shafting – plummer bearings out of alignment.

Port bearings – four plummer bearings and four bulkhead glands fractured, or missing in their entirety.

Plummer block compartments and contents destroyed.

Port propellers, both damaged.

Port outer stern gland casting fractured and stiffeners bent and torn away, shipbuilder's tube extensively damaged.

'X' Turret supporting structure slightly distorted.

4-inch magazine – fifty per cent bottle rack stowage buckled and beyond repair.

Installations in after engine room, after gyro compass room, main W/T office, after compressor room and No.5 breaker room submerged in oil fuel and water, also complete outfit of electrical spare gear submerged in oil fuel and water.

Repairs and Return to the Home Fleet

HMS *Manchester* entered Gibraltar's No.2 dry dock on 26 July 1941 for temporary repairs prior to being sailed to the USA for permanent repairs and a refit. As she was immobilised at Gibraltar, *Manchester* was reduced to a special complement, and fifteen officers and 157 ratings were sent back to the UK in SS *Pasteur* on 5 August.[13] On 5 August 1941 Commander Ian L. Fleming of Naval Intelligence Branch was at Government House, Gibraltar to discuss intelligence and 'Y' work with HM Excellency the Governor and Somerville and it is tempting to speculate that Captain Drew might have met the future author of the *Chitty Chitty Bang Bang* and the James Bond stories at this time. With temporary repairs complete during the second week of September 1941, *Manchester* was detached from the Home Fleet and sent to the USA for repair. She left Gibraltar on 15 September escorted by the destroyer *Firedrake* (repaired in Boston Navy Yard) and arrived at Philadelphia on 28 September.[14] During the five months spent under repair in Philadelphia's Navy yard, *Manchester*'s torpedo damage was made good while equipment changes included the removal of the already obsolete Type 286 radar. *Manchester* was made ready for the installation of more up-to-date radar including types 273, 279, 282, 284 and 285 as well as three single 20mm Oerlikon guns following the cruiser's return to United Kingdom. For those of *Manchester*'s complement who remained with the ship during her five-month-long stay in Philadelphia it must have been a welcome relief from wartime Britain with its air raids, rationing and Government controls.

However, there was little rest for Captain Drew, who after suffering the strain caused by skilfully nursing his crippled ship back to Gibraltar, was now responsible for getting his battered command into a condition fit to return to the fray. In addition to supervising the repairs, he was also responsible for the well-being of *Manchester*'s company. However, he was also the senior Royal Navy officer in Philadelphia and consequently, there was no-one more senior to look after his welfare.

Repairs were completed on 12 February 1942 and *Manchester* sailed for two days of trials after which she was dry-docked for a further six days. Eventually, on the last day of February, the cruiser left Philadelphia for seven days of post-refit trials and, each evening, anchored in Chesapeake Bay. On 8 March *Manchester* left United States waters for Bermuda from where, after refuelling and re-provisioning, she sailed for Portsmouth arriving on the 18th of the month. Subsequently, *Manchester* spent the next six weeks at Portsmouth where she was fitted with Type 284 surface gunnery radar, Type 285 anti-aircraft radar and Type 273 surface warning radar.

For her ship's company, conditions in Portsmouth at the time, while not as pleasant as those in Philadelphia, were better than in 1941 because there were no air raids on either the city or the dockyard during the cruiser's refit. *Manchester* left Portsmouth for the last time on 2 May 1942 escorted by the destroyer *Berkeley* and sailed through the Irish Sea for Scapa Flow arriving two days later. She had left the barren, wind-swept base in early July 1941 to participate in an operation expected to last no more than twenty-one days. However, thanks to the Italian Air Force she had been away for ten months.

Manchester spent most of the rest of May working up in and around Scapa Flow and, on completion, she left the anchorage on 29 May to join *Kenya* and the destroyer *Newark* for yet another patrol in the Iceland - Shetlands gap. During this patrol *Manchester* provided surface cover for Operation *SN 72* which started when the 1st Minelaying Squadron (*Southern Prince, Agamemnon, Port Quebec, Menestheus* and *Adventure* escorted by the destroyers *Newark, St Mary's* and *Saladin*) left the Kyle of Lochalsh on the night of 29 May. During Operation *SN 72*, 2,332 moored magnetic mines were laid in the Denmark Strait on 1 June and *Manchester* provided cover as far as longitude 20° west.[15] The cruiser returned to Scapa Flow three days later and 6 June was visited by HM King George VI, who was on an official visit to the Home Fleet in its northern wartime base.

Manchester remained in or around Scapa Flow during the first two weeks of June participating in day-running exercises with other ships of the Home Fleet, including on one occasion the heavy cruiser USS *Wichita*. On 18 June she escorted the newly completed battleship *Anson* from Scapa Flow to Rosyth before returning to the anchorage the next morning, where she hoisted the flag of Vice Admiral Stuart Bonham Carter, the Flag Officer commanding the 18th Cruiser Squadron. For the next two weeks *Manchester* remained in the Scapa area making just one short passage to Greenock where she loaded stores and equipment for Norwegian commandos. The latter were embarked at Scapa Flow before the cruiser left the anchorage on 27 June en route to Seydisfjord, Iceland where she refuelled before sailing for Spitsbergen on 30 June. Some weeks previously a small Norwegian force had been landed at Spitsbergen to run a radio and weather station on the island. *Manchester*, escorted by the destroyer *Eclipse*, was tasked with delivering stores and reinforcements of military personnel which were landed on 2 July.

After leaving Spitsbergen, *Manchester* joined the battleships HMS *Duke of York* and USS *Washington*, the aircraft carrier *Victorious* and the cruisers *Cumberland* and *Nigeria* and nine destroyers to provide distant cover for the ill-fated Convoy PQ17 during 3-4 July. After the dispersal of the convoy on 4 July *Manchester* sailed for Scapa Flow where Rear Admiral Bonham Carter left the ship. Thereafter, she was detailed to join the large naval force that was being assembled to provide the escort for what possibly was the most famous and most important single convoy operation of the Second World War – Operation *Pedestal*.

Chapter 7

Operation Pedestal

Between March and June 1942 Malta received only very small amounts of supplies in addition to fighters flown in from aircraft carriers. The long overdue deployment of Spitfires to Malta resulted in the climactic air battles over the island in early May. The subsequent period of relatively light Axis air attacks led the British to believe that the opportunity had come to attempt a major resupply of Malta by running simultaneous convoys to dissipate Axis air and naval power.

The June convoy from Gibraltar, code-named *Harpoon*, with fighter protection being provided by the old and slow aircraft carriers *Eagle* and *Argus*, was a modest success not least because these old ships carried only twenty-two fighters between them an could keep only ten of these aloft at any one time. This became a serious problem on 14 June when the convoy came within range of the Sardinian airfields and consequently was subjected to numerous air attacks during the first of which *Manchester*'s sister *Liverpool* was crippled by a torpedo. The damage was very severe and the cruiser had to be towed back to Gibraltar and was not returned to service until after the war in Europe had ended. The Dutch merchant ship *Tanimbar* was also sunk. Late that day, when the convoy reached the Sicilian Narrows, Beaufighters from Malta were able to offer a limited degree of protection.

At 06.20 hours on 15 June a Beaufighter reported that an Italian force of two cruisers and four (actually five) destroyers was fifteen miles to the north of the convoy. Admiral da Zara's ships opened fire at 06.40 hours and Captain Hardy (Senior Officer, in HMS *Cairo*) decided to divide his force so as to provide air cover for the merchant ships while at the same time stopping the Italian surface ships from getting amongst the convoy.

In the ensuing action both sides sustained damage but the Italians were unwilling to penetrate the smokescreens that were emitted and withdrew so as to intercept the convoy in a gap between an Italian minefield and Pantelleria. Meanwhile air attacks sank one freighter, *Chant*, and disabled another, *Burdwan*, as well as the tanker *Kentucky*. This forced the convoy to reduce speed to just six knots. Hardy decided to scuttle the two cripples and concentrate on getting the undamaged *Troilus* and *Orari* to Malta.

The Italian squadron reappeared at 13.55 hours and sank the disabled *Kentucky*. They further damaged the already crippled destroyer *Bedouin* which was finally sunk by an Italian air-dropped torpedo. The convoy ran into an Italian minefield off Malta losing the Polish destroyer *Kujawiak* and reached Valletta that night exhausted. Between them the transports *Troilus* and *Orari* delivered about 15,000 tons of urgently needed supplies. Strategically Operation *Harpoon* was a minor success for the British but, tactically it was a victory the Axis.

By contrast, the sister convoy, bearing the code-name Operation *Vigorous*, had been a disaster having been subjected to continuous air attacks since 14 June, suffering heavy casualties amongst both the escorts and transports. U-boats and E-boats added to the casualty list. On 15 June the presence of the Italian battlefleet twice forced the convoy to turn back towards Alexandria. The Italian force was subjected to regular air attacks from Malta and at 15.15 hours that day abandoned its pursuit of the convoy. However, the convoy was subjected to further air attacks which caused more damage and so depleted the AA ammunition of its escorts that it had become impossible to consider attempting to 'fight' the damaged remnants through to the Grand Harbour. The failure of Operation *Vigorous* showed that a convoy from Alexandria was simply not feasible under the conditions then existing in the eastern Mediterranean.

In comparison, *Harpoon* demonstrated that for a convoy from Gibraltar to be successful it would need several modern aircraft carriers with better fighter direction equipment and improved training in fighter direction. Furthermore, a heavy anti-aircraft barrage was essential to deter close range air attacks. Finally, it was apparent that the through-escort from the Sicilian Narrows to Malta had to be strong enough to deter attack by an Italian surface force consisting of cruisers and destroyers.

Malta as a Base for Offensive Operations in 1942
The distinguished historian Correlli Barnett described the situation of Malta in 1942 as the 'Verdun of the Maritime War'. He went on to observe that for much of 1942 the besieged island of Malta was more of a hostage to the enemy than a British strategic asset because Axis air superiority had forced the remaining surface warships to be withdrawn in April. The submarines followed shortly afterwards because the ferocity of the bombing was such that they had to remain submerged during daylight. The submarines did not return until August and in the interim period Axis shipping losses dropped to less than one per cent.

In effect, Malta was incapable of supporting offensive operations and had, indeed, become the Verdun of the maritime war. In the words again of Correlli Barnett 'for just like Verdun and the French leadership in 1916 – or for that matter Stalingrad and Hitler in 1942-1943–Malta became for the British leadership a matter of prestige and pride, a symbol of heroic resistance. Like Verdun it triggered tremendous emotions that it must be held at all costs.'[1]

Furthermore, it can be argued that because of previous disasters, the very survival of Winston Churchill's premiership was dependent upon the survival of Malta. Thus, although Churchill's fighting spirit had kept Britain in the war since June 1940, he was also responsible for several major debacles since becoming Prime Minister. These included the Greek fiasco of March and April 1941, the sinking of *Prince of Wales* and *Repulse* off Kuantan on 10 December 1941 and the humiliating surrender of Singapore on 15 February 1942. The loss of Tobruk and the headlong flight of the 8th Army in June 1942 resulted in a further loss of Churchill's prestige at home and a concomitant increase in the number of those prepared to question his leadership. The capture of Malta, or even worse the island's abject surrender because of a lack of food, would undoubtedly have had significant political consequences both at home and abroad.

Any objective analysis will reveal that the damage done to Axis communications by the minor submarine and air forces able to operate from the island during June-October 1942 did not justify the severe losses inflicted on the Royal Navy and the Merchant Navy to keep the island supplied with the bare essential of food, fuel and ammunition. A major study undertaken by Martin van Crefeld revealed that 'at no time, except for perhaps November-December 1941, did the aero-naval struggle in the central Mediterranean play a decisive part in events in North Africa, and even Rommel's difficulties were due as much to his impossibly long – and vulnerable – line of communications inside Africa as to losses at sea ... and the Axis decision not to occupy Malta was of far less moment to the outcome of the struggle in North Africa than the fact that the port of Tobruk was so small and hopelessly exposed to the attacks of the RAF operating from Egypt.'[2] It can be argued, therefore, that the survival of Malta had become a matter of honour driven partly by a fear of the political consequences of its capture.

Operation *Pedestal*

By early July, Malta faced starvation and a target date was set for surrender if no supplies could be got through. Consequently plans for Operation *Pedestal*, a major resupply convoy, were drawn up and completed by 27 July.

Operation *Pedestal*, under the command of Acting Vice Admiral Sir Edward Syfret, KCBN, Flag Officer Commanding Force F (SO (F)), had as its object the safe passage of thirteen fast modern freighters (*Almeria Lykes, Brisbane Star, Clan Ferguson, Deucalion, Dorset, Empire Hope, Glenorchy, Melbourne Star, Port Chalmers, Rochester Castle, Santa Elisa, Wairangi* and

Waimarama) and a tanker (*Ohio*) through the Western Mediterranean to Malta. For this purpose, Force F was sub-divided into Force Z and Force X, the former under the direct orders of SO Force F and the latter under the command of Rear Admiral H.M. Burrough CB, DSO, Rear Admiral Commanding Tenth Cruiser Squadron (CS10). It was the intention to cover the convoy with Force Z as far as the entrance to the Skerki Channel leaving Force X as escort for the convoy to Malta. Force Z was then to turn back and operate in the vicinity of Sardinia until safe passage of the convoy and return of the escort had been assured.

Force Z consisted of the battleships *Nelson* (Flag SO (F)) and *Rodney*, the aircraft carriers *Victorious* (Rear Admiral Arthur Lyster), *Indomitable* (Rear Admiral Denis Boyd), and *Eagle*, the cruisers *Charybdis, Phoebe* and *Sirius* and the destroyers *Laforey, Lightning, Lookout, Quentin, Somali, Eskimo, Tartar, Ithuriel, Antelope, Wishart, Vansittart, Westcott, Wrestler, Zetland* and *Wilton*. Between them, the carriers *Victorious, Indomitable* and *Eagle* embarked seventy-two fighters and twenty-eight strike aircraft. A fourth aircraft carrier *Furious*, escorted by the destroyers *Keppel, Malcolm, Amazon, Venomous, Wolverine* and *Vidette*, was to fly off thirty-seven Spitfires for Malta in a subsidiary operation code-named *Bellows*. A fifth carrier, *Argus*, was also at Gibraltar.

Force X, the through-escort, consisted of the modern cruisers *Nigeria* (Flag CS 10), *Kenya* and *Manchester*, the AA cruiser *Cairo*, and the destroyers *Ashanti, Intrepid, Icarus, Foresight, Fury, Pathfinder, Penn, Derwent, Bramham, Bicester* and *Ledbury*. A replenishment group, Force Y, consisting of the fleet oilers *Abbeydale, Brown Ranger* and *Dingledale* escorted by the destroyers *Matchless* and *Badsworth*, was provided to top-up the fuel tanks of the escorting destroyers during the first two days of the operation.

This concentration of naval strength was only possible because the Russian convoys had been suspended in July after the disastrous Convoy PQ17. Consequently, the Admiralty was able to draw heavily upon the units of the Home Fleet. Furthermore, the Japanese defeat at Midway allowed a reduction of British naval forces in the Indian Ocean.

The convoy and its through-escort were to proceed to a position south of Zembra and Zembretta islands, through position 000° Cape Bon one and a half miles off the Tunisian coast to a position 'R' which was approximately ten miles to the South West of Kelibia Light. A minefield (Q.B.B.255) was reported between Sicily and the Tunisian coast, but a clear passage was known to exist within two miles of the coast between Cape Bon and Kelibia. Arrangements were made with Vice Admiral Malta for fighter protection to be provided for Force X and the convoy from 19.30 hours to dark on 12 August 1942, and from daylight on 13 August until the arrival of the convoy at Malta. HM Ships were warned against opening fire on the grounded wreck of the destroyer *Havock* which was situated in the vicinity of Kelibia Light.

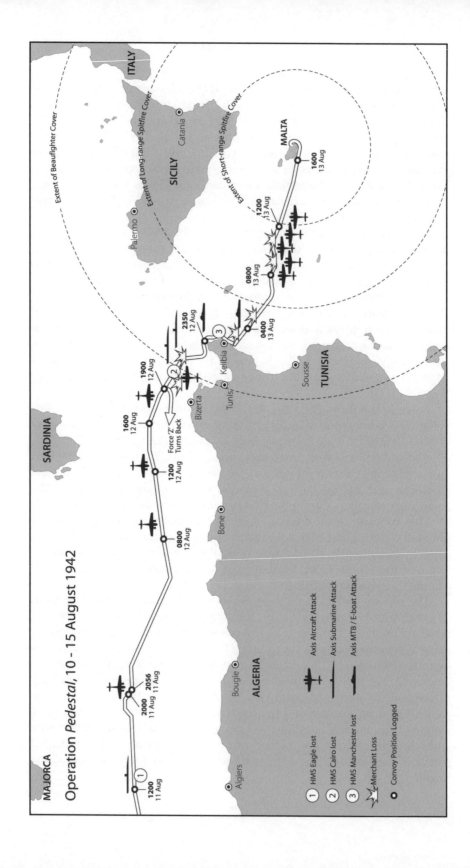

Operation *Pedestal*, 10 - 15 August 1942

MAJORCA

SARDINIA

ITALY

SICILY

Palermo

Catania

MALTA

TUNISIA

Bizerta

Kelibia

Tunis

Sousse

Bone

Bougie

Algiers

ALGERIA

Extent of Beaufighter Cover

Extent of Long-range Spitfire Cover

Extent of Short-range Spitfire Cover

1200
11 Aug

2000   2056
11 Aug 11 Aug

0800
12 Aug

1200
12 Aug

1600
12 Aug

1900
12 Aug

Force 'Z'
Turns Back

2350
12 Aug

0400
13 Aug

0800
13 Aug

1200
13 Aug

1600
13 Aug

① HMS Eagle lost

② HMS Cairo lost

③ HMS Manchester lost

Merchant Loss

Convoy Position Logged

Axis Aircraft Attack

Axis Submarine Attack

Axis MTB / E-boat Attack

Most of the convoy forces assembled at Scapa Flow on 27 July sailed south on 2 August and passed through the Strait of Gibraltar on 10 August. Other ships joined from Freetown and Gibraltar.

On 30 July *Manchester* was at Greenock awaiting orders to sail to Gibraltar. The main body of the convoy and escorts left the following day, but *Manchester*'s departure was delayed because the carrier *Furious* grounded while loading Spitfires in Glasgow's King George V Dock. The carrier also had difficulty in stowing these RAF fighters which lacked the folding wings of their Fleet Air Arm contemporaries. Eventually, at 23.50 hours on 4 August, *Manchester*, *Furious* and the Polish destroyer *Blyskawica* sailed from Greenock to join the convoy and its escorts.

After sailing at high speed for two and a half days the three ships met the convoy off the west coast of Portugal, but as *Manchester* was running low on fuel she was detached with certain other ships to refuel at Gibraltar. She re-joined the convoy on 9 August but was still some 600 tons short of furnace fuel oil because the oiling programme had not been successful and consequently the cruiser was again detached to Gibraltar to refuel the same day. *Manchester* re-joined the convoy at 11.30 hours on 10 August in the Mediterranean.

As soon as the convoy was reported by their spies in the Strait of Gibraltar and by a Vichy French airliner, the Axis powers started to position their submarines in the western Mediterranean while at the same time increasing their fighter and bomber forces. These amounted to some 650 Italian and 255 German aircraft, in Sardinia, Sicily and Pantelleria. Furthermore, Rear Admiral Angelo Parona's force of four cruisers and eight destroyers was assembled to intercept the convoy and its through-escort near Pantelleria. Finally, Italian MAS-boats and German S-boats were positioned in the central Mediterranean between Cape Bon and Pantelleria.

At 13.16 hours on 11 August 1942, the aircraft carrier *Eagle* was hit by four torpedoes fired by *U-73* and sank in just eight minutes with the loss of 173 officers and men and all but four of her complement of twenty Sea Hurricanes. At the time *Furious* was flying off Spitfires for their long flight to Malta, and as soon as this had been completed was ordered to return to Gibraltar. The Fleet streamed paravanes on the same day and there was a heavy but unsuccessful air attack on the Fleet at dusk. By this time the oilers had successfully refuelled three cruisers and twenty-six destroyers.

On 12 August there were few moments when neither air attack, submarines, torpedoes nor Asdic contacts were being reported. One merchant ship, *Deucalion*, was damaged by a near miss at 13.50 hours and the Hunt-class destroyer *Bramham* was ordered to escort her to Malta. Her sister ship *Wilton* of Force Z replaced *Bramham* in Force X. At 16.16 hours that day, as the force was approaching Galite Island just north of the border between Algeria and Tunisia, the destroyers *Pathfinder* and *Zetland* depth-charged the Italian submarine *Cobalto* which was forced to the surface and rammed and sunk by *Ithuriel*. The latter rescued forty-one Italian sailors but suffered serious damage to her bows as a result of this seemingly rash and unnecessary action.

At about 18.30 hours when the convoy was approaching the Skerki Bank, a large force of German Ju 87s, Italian SM 79 torpedo bombers and scores of fighters was intercepted by Sea Hurricanes from *Victorious*. The scale of the attack was such that *Foresight*, which was one of the four TSDS Destroyers of Force X, was torpedoed by an Italian SM 79. Her back was broken and her propellers were wrecked and, later, when it proved impossible to tow her back to Gibraltar she was torpedoed and sunk by the Tribal class destroyer *Tartar*. The flight deck of the aircraft carrier *Indomitable* was hit by three bombs from a Ju 87 and rendered useless as an operational carrier.

The damage to *Indomitable* caused Vice Admiral Syfret to turn Force Z to the west at 18.55 hours, twenty minutes earlier than intended. Force X and the convoy were ordered to keep close to the Tunisian coast from Cape Bon to Ras-el-Mustafa before sailing almost due east to Malta.

The departure of Force Z left the four cruisers and twelve destroyers of Force X to guard the convoy at a time when Italian submarines were taking up station in the northern approaches to the Sicilian Channel. Flotillas of torpedo boats were also positioned between Tunisia and Pantelleria, and Rear Admiral Parona's cruisers and destroyers were gathering north of Sicily.

The operation had proceeded reasonably well until Force Z turned back but then the situation deteriorated very quickly as a result of Axis air and submarine attack.

In his report compiled on 15 August, Acting Captain Onslow (Captain D6 Destroyer Flotilla) described the misfortunes which overtook the unlucky Force X about an hour after the departure of Force Z:

> At 1915 12 August Cruising Disposition No.25 was formed with ASHANTI in position 'J'. At this time I ordered destroyers of the close A/S screen to drop single depth charges in succession every 10 minutes, hauling out to five cables to do so. As this signal had not cleared by 1945 ASHANTI hauled out at that time and dropped one charge. At 1956 ASHANTI was about to repeat this preventative measure when HM Ships NIGERIA and CAIRO and No.32 [OHIO] in convoy were torpedoed. Destroyers on the port screen (ASHANTI, PENN and DERWENT) increased speed and steered outwards dropping depth charges. No contact was obtained or periscope sighted. NIGERIA took a heavy list to port and was steaming in a clockwise circle at about 12 knots. CAIRO was stopped and settling by the stern. I ordered BRAMHAM to stand by

CAIRO while ASHANTI went alongside NIGERIA, the remaining destroyers with the exception of the TSDS destroyers provided A/S protection.[3]

Nigeria had been hit by a torpedo abreast the bridge and at once assumed a list to port of thirteen degrees and circled to starboard. By 20.10 hours the ship was under control and at 20.15 hours was stopped to transfer Rear Admiral Commanding CS10 and his staff to *Ashanti*. Very prompt damage control had by this time reduced the list to five degrees and by 20.30 hours the ship was able to proceed to Gibraltar at fourteen knots despite being eleven feet down by the head with *Bicester* and *Wilton* as escort. The destroyer *Derwent* later joined the group protecting the crippled cruiser as she made for Gibraltar.[4]

Cairo, whose stern was blown off and engines disabled, was sunk by the destroyers *Pathfinder* and *Derwent*. *Pathfinder* had to fire four torpedoes to sink *Cairo* because the first three missed; the fourth hit the starboard side under her bridge but did not immediately sink the cruiser. *Pathfinder* reported that two torpedoes had faulty runs. Even a pattern of depth charges under *Cairo's* stern failed to send her to the bottom and consequently *Pathfinder* left *Derwent* to finish the job and sailed off the rejoin the convoy.[5]

The torpedo that struck *Ohio* exploded amidships aft of the bridge blowing a hole measuring twenty-four feet by twenty-seven feet in her hull. The tanker caught fire and came to a stop. When she was eventually able to resume her voyage *Ohio* could only manoeuvre slowly in circles.

The torpedoing of *Nigeria, Cairo* and *Ohio* took place at a time when the convoy and escorts were disorganised for various reasons and the Italian submarine *Axum* had fired her four torpedoes from outside of the screen such as it was at this time. This salvo of torpedoes must rank amongst the most effective ever fired, because in addition to causing chaos and confusion, the torpedoing of *Nigeria* and *Cairo* eliminated both of Force X's fighter direction-equipped ships at a stroke.[6] At 20.20 hours S.O. (F) detached *Charybdis, Eskimo* and *Somali* from Force Z to reinforce Force X. Meanwhile Rear Admiral Burrough commanding CS 10 in *Ashanti* proceeded to close and direct the convoy.

At 20.38 hours, some twenty-five minutes after sunset, a heavy attack by dive-bombers and torpedo bombers developed and lasted until 21.00 hours. *Empire Hope* was hit by a torpedo and two bombs and her burning wreck had to be torpedoed and sunk by the destroyer *Penn*. *Brisbane Star* was torpedoed by an He 111 and left the convoy heading south to hug the Tunisian coast as she proceeded independently to Malta. *Clan Ferguson* was also hit by an aerial torpedo and blew up as 2,000 tons of aviation spirit countermined 1,500 tons of ammunition. At 21.12 hours *Kenya* was hit on the forefoot by a torpedo from the Italian submarine *Alagi* which was seen by the cruiser. One other torpedo passed under her and two more narrowly missed her stern.

At 21.21 hours the Commanding Officer of *Kenya* reported by emergency signal that he was in command of Force X, an incorrect statement that did not help to improve an already confused situation. At 21.30 hours *Deucalion*, which had been proceeding independently with *Bramham*, sank after being torpedoed by a torpedo-bomber near the Cani Rocks. *Bramham* proceeded to join Force X.

The effect of this series of disasters was to cause the convoy to become scattered although the ships generally continued on their course for Cape Bon. The disorganisation following the dusk attack and the lack of destroyers made it virtually impossible to round up the convoy during the night and it was therefore a relatively easy prey to E-boats. There was a mass of burning oil on the water, and some ships had altered to a northerly or north-westerly direction and were rounded up by the Hunt-class destroyer *Ledbury*. Captain Onslow in *Ashanti* recorded that:

> At about 2020 I embarked RA Commanding CS 10 and his staff & he hoisted his Flag in ASHANTI. ASHANTI then proceeded to the rear of the convoy which had become scattered to investigate the situation. While there, a heavy dive-bombing attack was delivered on the convoy and several ships were hit – at least two burning fiercely. A torpedo-bomber attack developed shortly afterwards and HM Ships ASHANTI and PENN laid mixed Black & White smoke clouds between the convoy and the western horizon. One torpedo was observed approaching the starboard bow and was avoided by only a few feet.
>
> On completion of the torpedo attack ASHANTI closed BRISBANE STAR and OHIO who were lying stopped for the Admiral to pass them instructions. ASHANTI subsequently proceeded to the van of the convoy. At this time there were only three merchant ships in company with KENYA and MANCHESTER and the three TSDS destroyers but when PATHFINDER rejoined later she reported eight ships in company although badly strung out.
>
> Single line was formed astern of the TSDS destroyers at about 2100 in the order of HM Ships MANCHESTER, KENYA and ASHANTI followed by two merchant ships which were then the only ones in visual touch. Cape Bon was passed at 2354.[7]

At this time, and while coming down the Tunisian coast, the state of Force X and the convoy was as follows. The convoy was led by the destroyers *Intrepid, Icarus* and *Fury* with their TSDS sweeps streamed. Following were the cruiser *Manchester, Ashanti* (Flag SO Force X), the damaged cruiser

Kenya, the merchant ships *Almeria Lykes, Glenorchy, Wairangi* and *Santa Elisa*, the destroyer *Pathfinder* and the freighters *Melbourne Star, Waimarama* and *Rochester Castle* in that order. *Ledbury* was escorting the damaged *Ohio* and rounded Kelibia approximately an hour after the leaders. The destroyers *Penn* and *Bramham* together escorted *Port Chalmers* and rounded Cape Bon at 02.30 hours about two and a half hours after the leaders. The 4.5-inch gun-armed cruiser *Charybdis* and the Tribal-class destroyers *Eskimo* and *Somali*, which had been detached from Force Z to reinforce Force ' were coming up astern and rounded Cape Bon at about 00.10 hours. Of the fourteen merchant ships that set out on Operation *Pedestal*, three had been sunk and at least two were damaged by this time – but the situation was about to get a lot worse.

Manchester Torpedoed
The weather was calm and very dark, with good visibility. Then, shortly after midnight, a mine exploded ahead of *Manchester*'s port bow as she was passing Zembra island. Although no damage was caused, Captain Drew decided to change the ship's company's action stations by moving the shell room and magazine crews and other exposed personnel up one deck to the lobbies. When *Manchester* had been torpedoed in July 1941, several men had been killed unnecessarily and Drew hoped that by moving men up a deck he would minimise casualties while at the same time not reducing the fighting efficiency of his ship. At about 00.40 hours on 13 August there was an engagement with the German *Schnellboote* (torpedo-armed fast attack boats, also referred to as E-boats) *S 58* and *S 59* on the port side of the van. Searchlights were used to illuminate the targets which were engaged by several ships of Force X including *Manchester*, which opened fire with all guns that could bear. *S 58* was damaged and both boats broke off the attack.

Captain Onslow's report of the action noted that, 'at 0038 13 August two E-boats were detected by 286 radar [on *Ashanti*] on the port bow and were engaged simultaneously by all ships with all available weapons. A running fight developed with these and a further two on the starboard side until Kelibia Light was passed. The E-boats used smoke to avoid punishment and it is possible that one was blown up [both survived].'[8]

A lull then followed until 01.02 hours when the leading units of the unlucky Force X were sighted off Ras Mustafà by the Italian *motosiluranti MS 16* (Capitano di Corvetta Giorgio Manuti) and *MS 22* (Tenente di Vascello Franco Mezzadra). The Italian historian Francesco Mattesini described what happened next:

> The light of a searchlight, which suddenly lit up on one of the ships, identified by Comandante Manuti as an Arethusa class cruiser [actually the much larger *Manchester*], and which illuminated other shapes ahead, allowed the two motosiluranti to select targets. The MS 16 headed slowly

at the cruiser and at 0104, from a range of 800 metres, fired her starboard torpedo at it. Deviating from its course, probably due to poor functioning of the control mechanism, the weapon missed the target and passed ahead of the MS 22, which at that moment found herself 200 metres ahead of the MS 16 and was aiming at the central unit of the enemy line, identified as a Tribal class destroyer [*Ashanti*].

Declining to fire the second torpedo against a receding target, MS 16 turned to aim at one of the following ships and, unexpectedly, found herself in a favourable position to attack another cruiser [*Kenya*] that was astern of the unit attacked earlier. The same target [actually *Manchester* and not *Kenya*[9]] was also picked out by MS 22 which, at the last moment, gave up the attack on the destroyer to aim at the cruiser. In that way, at 0107, the two motosiluranti, which had lost sight of each other during the turn, attacked the same ship. MS 16 fired her second torpedo from a range of 800 metres and after twenty-seven seconds saw the after part of the cruiser [*Manchester*] rise up and illuminate itself with a red-orange flash. MS 22, which in relation to *MS 16* was further ahead, attacked from a range of 600 metres launching two torpedoes. The first of these passed ahead of the target because of an angling error, while the second was seen to explode after thirty seconds by the after funnel. [10]

Contrary to this report, *Manchester* was only hit by one torpedo on 13 August and it is more likely that it was fired from *MS 16*. Immediately afterwards the two *motosiluranti* disengaged, passing along the convoy under an intense fire. Turning to zig-zag, to interfere with the correction of the fire, they headed inshore at high speed ending up aground in shallow water. *MS 16* after having turned around the wreck of the destroyer *Havock*, which she had mistaken for a unit of the convoy, beached herself in the vicinity of Ras el Mihr with *MS 22* beaching in the lee of Ras Mustafà. After several attempts both succeeded in refloating themselves with the assistance of tugs *and MS 16* returned to Trapani on 15 August and *MS 22* to Pantelleria on 20 August.

Prior to this attack, Captain Drew had been looking for the wreck of the destroyer *Havock* when at about 01.10 hours, and in a position some two miles east of Kelibia Light, he observed an E-boat on the starboard bow. The armament and searchlights were ordered onto the target and the rudder was put hard-a-starboard and the port engines full ahead. Seconds later as *Manchester* began to swing to starboard, he and others heard the sound of torpedoes being discharged, after which there was the noise of petrol engines being started as two Italian MAS boats *MS 16* and *MS 22* disengaged from the convoy under intense fire which caused some damage to *MS 22*.

The tracks of two torpedoes were seen approaching from the starboard side, one torpedo passed close ahead but the second torpedo struck *Manchester* aft on the starboard side abreast her after engine room. Power to the steering motors having failed as a result of the explosion, the rudder remained hard-a-starboard until centred by hand pump shortly afterwards. An officer and eight ratings were killed instantly by the explosion. The cruiser heeled to starboard and lost speed, her after boiler room, 4-inch ammunition magazine and fuel tanks all flooding fast. After circling to starboard and losing way, the cruiser came to rest heading 160 degrees between two and three miles to the eastward of Kelibia Light.

Captain Drew's avoiding action slewed *Manchester* to starboard across the bows of *Almeria Lykes* and *Waimarama* which had to take evasive action to avoid collision with the already listing cruiser which gradually came to a stop.

At 01.15 hours the Tribal-class destroyer *Eskimo* passed the damaged *Manchester* and a destroyer (possibly *Ashanti*) off Kelibia. *Manchester* seemed to be moving slowly; her loud hailer said, 'What ship is that? How are you Eskimo?'[11]

At about 01.40 hours *Pathfinder* (Commander E.A. Gibbs) came upon *Manchester* which was stationary and listing. Gibbs informed Drew of his emergency orders from Rear Admiral commanding CS 10 and, after embarking about 150 of *Manchester*'s 'spare' crew, sped off to join CS 10 to ward off an anticipated attack by further Italian surface forces.[12]

For now we will leave the crippled *Manchester* and briefly follow the progress of the convoy and its escorts to Malta.

Operation *Pedestal*, 13-15 August 1942

The E-boats continued to pick off the ships of the convoy as they made their way along the Tunisian coast that night. The first to go was *Glenorchy* which was torpedoed in the engine room by *MS 31* at 02.00 hours. Her crew left in boats but her master, Captain George Leslie, went down with his ship. Rear Admiral Burrough in *Ashanti* can have had little real knowledge of the situation unfolding around him as the night progressed, although he must have been heartened to learn that *Charybdis*, *Eskimo* and *Somali* had joined Force X at 02.46 hours. The damaged *Kenya* was some miles ahead and still in contact with *Wairangi* and *Santa Elisa* which were preceded by the minesweeping destroyers. The latter, which occasionally fired starshell to illuminate any torpedo boats lying in ambush, were gradually losing their effectiveness as minesweepers as they lost their TSDS sweeps.

At 03.00 hours a second wave of MAS/S-boats attacked, hitting *Wairangi* at 03.10 hours forward on the port side abreast No.3 hold and quickly reducing her to a hulk. She remained afloat for some hours and was attacked again at 06.00 hours by torpedo-carrying He 111s whose torpedoes missed. The water-logged transport disappeared beneath the waves about three hours later. At about 03.30 hours, *S 30* and *S 36* made a determined attack on *Almeria Lykes* hitting her forward in No.1 hold at the same time that *Wairangi* was hit. Her American crew abandoned ship even though she was in no danger of sinking. When the destroyer *Pathfinder* arrived her commanding officer thought that *Almeria Lykes'* crew should return to their ship and refused to pick them up. At 09.30 hours she was still afloat when *Somali* picked up the American seaman and took them to Gibraltar. *Santa Elisa* was torpedoed on the starboard side forward and petrol in Nos. 1 and 2 holds ignited. Her crew abandoned the blazing ship and were picked up by the destroyer *Penn*. The burnt-out hulk was attacked by a Ju 88 at 07.15 hours and five minutes later *Santa Elisa* had gone. At 03.30 hours *Rochester Castle* was torpedoed on the starboard side abreast No.3 Hold but was not in immediate danger of sinking and was able to maintain a speed of thirteen knots.

Having passed through the lines of S- and MAS-boats the surviving ships gradually reassembled with the expectation of air cover as they approached Malta. The ships of Operation *Pedestal* were now on their final leg to the east-south-east heading for the entrance to the swept channel into Grand Harbour about 100 miles away. Along their route lay Kesselring's He 111s and Junkers dive bombers as well as the torpedo bombers of the Regia Aeronautica. Unfortunately, because of the loss of *Cairo* and the withdrawal of *Nigeria*, the convoy and its escorts were unable to benefit fully from what air cover was available. The Luftwaffe resumed its attacks in the early hours of 13 August and found *Rochester Castle*, leading *Waimarama* and *Melbourne Star*, some thirty miles southeast of Pantelleria at 08.10 hours. One of the three Ju 88s that attacked *Waimarama* scored four hits on her and the ship's deck cargo of high octane fuel and ammunition exploded. The ship disintegrated leaving the sea covered in burning fuel and a huge column of black smoke which darkened the sky. *Charybdis* reported seeing two aircraft diving into *Waimarama* but only one coming out of the dive, the other being presumed destroyed in the explosion.

The concentration of Kesselring's pilots on the derelicts *Santa Elisa*, *Almeria Lykes* and *Wairangi* was an elementary error because it gave Force X the chance to regroup and gather up the remainder of the convoy. Thus, at dawn on 13 August Rear Admiral Burrough commanding CS 10 in *Ashanti* had in company with him, HMS *Kenya*, *Charybdis*, *Intrepid*, *Icarus*, *Fury*, *Eskimo*, *Somali* and the transports *Melbourne Star*, and *Rochester Castle*. *Ledbury* with *Ohio* was five miles astern, *Pathfinder* and *Bramham* with *Port Chalmers* were ten miles to the northwest while *Penn* was observed beyond *Port Chalmers* which was near the burning remains of *Waimarama*. *Dorset* was sighted later to the northward and ordered to join the convoy. The following day it was learned that *Brisbane Star* spent the night of 12/13 August and part of the 13th in the Gulf of Hammamet. Whilst in Vichy territorial waters she was boarded by the French authorities, who after protest behaved well and took a seriously injured man ashore to Sousse. *Brisbane Star* eventually reached Malta at 14.30 hours on 14 August.

At 07.12 hours Rear Admiral Burrough sent *Somali* and *Eskimo* to search for *Manchester*'s survivors, during which operation they rescued survivors from *Wairangi* and *Almeria Lykes*. However, the two freighters were left afloat in the hope that either they could be towed to Malta or act as targets for aircraft that might otherwise attack other more viable ships of the convoy. Finally at 10.40 hours *Eskimo* and *Somali* rescued 150 of *Manchester*'s men from Carley floats inshore. Not half a mile away on shore they saw several hundred of apparently *Manchester*'s ship's company being marched away. Having recovered all survivors, the two destroyers sailed for Gibraltar.

Further attacks by Stuka dive bombers accompanied by Italian aircraft laying parachute mines ahead and on the flanks of the convoy occurred at 09.25 hours. The dive-bombers targeted *Ohio* which sustained several near misses. One Ju 87 which was shot down by the combined efforts of *Ashanti* and *Ohio* crashed into *Ohio*'s side.

The Malta Beaufighters and long-range Spitfires were now in sight of Force X and were seen to take down four enemy aircraft in the distance. Rear Admiral Burrough, observing that they had no fighter direction aid from Force X, reported that the fighters performed a magnificent job of work throughout the day. At 09.41 hours *Kenya* was near-missed by dive bombers and at 10.17 hours and 10.50 hours similar dive-bombing and minelaying attacks occurred. During these raids *Dorset*, which was re-joining the convoy, and *Ohio*, were both near-missed and stopped. *Penn*, *Ledbury* and *Bramham* stood by *Ohio* and *Dorset*. The latter was eventually sunk at 20.14 hours after being set on fire by more air attacks. At 11.20 hours, Italian torpedo bombers carried out an attack combined with the dropping of parachute mines or circling torpedoes. The torpedoes were dropped at long-range and, except for one which became entangled in *Port Chalmers*' paravane and was subsequently cleared safely, none appeared to endanger the convoy and its escorts. Fortunately, by 12.30 hours Force X was within range of Malta's short-range Spitfires and was unmolested thereafter.

At 14.30 hours the Malta Escort Force under the Senior Officer, Minesweepers, in *Speedy*, reinforced the escort and at 16.00 hours Force X less *Bramham*, *Penn* and *Ledbury*, which continued to stand by *Ohio*, and *Dorset*, retired to the west. *Port Chalmers*, *Melbourne Star* and *Rochester Castle* were turned over to the local escort and eventually entered harbour at Malta safely at 18.25 hours. The severely damaged tanker *Ohio* entered Grand Harbour at 07.55 hours on 15 August after an epic struggle by her gallant master and crew and her escorts *Bramham*, *Penn* and *Ledbury*.

Force X's withdrawal was uneventful in the initial stages but when off Cape Bon at 01.30 hours on 14 August it was attacked by E-boats which were engaged and driven off. At 04.50 hours, when off Fratelli Rock, a submarine attacked the Force just missing *Ashanti*. *Kenya* sighted the submarine and attempted to ram but the latter was inside her turning circle. By daylight Force X was south-southeast of Galite Island and shortly afterwards the first enemy reconnaissance aircraft appeared.

At 09.12 hours the first of a long series of air attacks commenced with a number of Ju 88s. *Kenya* was near-missed at 09.42 hours and had a small fire in her forward boiler room which necessitated a short reduction in speed. From 10.00 hours to 13.00 hours attacks were almost incessant and included dive bombers, high level bombers and torpedo bombers and the dropping of mines or circling torpedoes by low flying aircraft. Fortunately Force X came through untouched and at 18.00 hours joined Force Z in position 37° 29'N, 03° 25'E.

Operation *Pedestal*, which was a major naval operation rather than a convoy, demonstrated that the lessons of Operation *Harpoon* had been well and truly learned with the August convoy being allocated four aircraft carriers with effective fighter direction. Furthermore, the sheer volume of fire put up by the *Pedestal* escorts so disconcerted the Axis airman that hardly any damage was done by air attack in the initial stages. Finally the through-escort was more substantial and effectively deterred intervention by Italian surface forces apart from E-boats.

As anticipated by Winston Churchill, the Axis powers proclaimed the aero-naval battle of mid-August a great victory, claiming to have destroyed the convoy. They had indeed sunk nine of the fourteen merchant ships as well as an aircraft carrier, two cruisers and a destroyer in addition to damaging another aircraft carrier and two cruisers. However, the Italian moment of triumph was short-lived, for although the siege was not yet lifted, Malta had received enough supplies to last several months while Italian fortunes had long passed their apogee. Furthermore, their German allies would never again be able to make such a large number of aircraft available to attack Malta and its supply convoys. The siege of Malta was lifted on 20 November 1942 with the arrival of four ships, carrying 32,000 tons of supplies, from Alexandria (Operation *Stoneage*).

Chapter 8

Torpedo Strike

At about 01.10 hours[1] *Manchester* was attacked by the Italian torpedo boats *MS 16* and *MS 22* which fired their 533.4 mm (21-inch) torpedoes at the cruiser. These torpedoes had a warhead containing 270kg of TNT, and Italian accounts of the attack suggest very strongly that both *MS 16* and *MS 22* used the high-speed (fifty knot) setting on these weapons[2].

The attack was witnessed by Yeoman of Signals Thomas Cardiff who recalled that:

'I was on the compass platform at the time of the explosion. I saw an E-boat on the port side [NB *Manchester* was hit by a torpedo on the starboard side] in the gloam of a searchlight. I saw two [torpedo] tracks. One passed very close on the bow and the other hit what I imagined was the centre of the ship. As soon as the report 'Torpedo approaching starboard bow' the Captain gave the order 'Hard-a-starboard'. The ship gave a shudder there was a flash and [*Manchester*] started to heel over to starboard. Immediately after the explosion the Captain gave the order 'Hands to Emergency Stations'. This involved all people not actually on watch going to abandon ship stations. The Captain also gave a pipe for the Commander [Hammersley-Johnston] and Engineer Commander [Robb] to come up to the bridge. Also piped around the ship 'Clear the Carley floats ready for lowering in the water' – about 15 minutes after the explosion.'[3]

Able Seaman Walter Pearce, whose action station was in the Starboard Torpedo Control Position, said:

'As the night was dark I spotted a dark object in the water which I presumed was an E-boat which attacked us. I reported a dark object low in the water and I took my eye away from the object for a moment to turn towards the Captain to shout to him and, when I looked back at it, it showed a light [a torch presumably]. When I reported that it had shown a light I looked forward to the Captain. During this time he [i.e. the MAS boat] had fired his torpedoes. I saw their wakes. One struck the ship. The other I presume went 8–14 feet clear of the bows forward.'[4]

Colour Sergeant Joseph Mullins RM observed the E-boats and the torpedo that struck *Manchester* and recorded:

'My action station was closed up round the forward torpedo platform with a Bren gun. We had been closed up near enough 48 hours. Immediately before the explosion we were steaming along and we got a damage bearing 'Red 150°'. The ship that was immediately behind us [*Ashanti*] put on a searchlight and I saw some E-boats between four and six hundred yards away. Just before the explosion I remember speaking about the light ship [actually a lighthouse] which was on Cape Bon, she seemed to have an extra brilliant light, she seemed to flash long beams and then turn and flash three dots on shore. When the torpedo hit, the blast came right up through the after control like a big red flame; the ship started to list, the ship went to about 16°. I then left my position and went down to the flight deck to help clear away Carley floats should the order 'abandon ship' be given. I left my action station about 10 minutes after the explosion. I could not make out any ship on the starboard side [which could have fired the torpedo] but I saw the torpedo when it was about three yards off the ship.'[5]

Able Seaman Leonard Excell was on the bridge when the torpedo struck and stated that the Captain ordered 'Emergency Stations' as *Manchester* heeled over. He had heard reports that the port [outer] propeller was turning and the starboard [inner and outer] was not and they could not stop the port. Asked how long after the explosion the ship was able to make some headway, he replied 'about half an hour, she went round in a large circle.' He could not remember feeling any large vibration or unusual noise from the engines.[6]

For some time after the explosion, the majority of officers on the bridge, including the Gunnery and Torpedo Officers, were occupied in passing orders by loud hailer to ships in the vicinity in order to avoid collision.

The State of HMS *Manchester* Prior to the Attack[7]

The ship's company, including the damage control parties, was at action stations, except that shell room and magazine crews had been ordered up to the lobbies above because of the explosion of a mine ahead. All boilers were in use and all four dynamos were running, with the ring main split in four sections. Approximately seventy-nine per cent of fuel oil remained. The armament was in efficient order and ready for action. The training motor on number one searchlight (starboard) was out of action. The ASDIC equipment was out of action as a result of a near-miss earlier in the operation. The radar equipment was in efficient running order with the surface warning Type 273 transmitting while the air-warning Type 279, the main armament gunnery, Type 284 and the 4-inch HA gun Type 285, were ready for instant transmission. The Main W/T and Remote Control Offices were manned but the secondary and auxiliary W/T were not manned though the equipment was available for use.

The Effect of the Explosion on the Ship

Manchester's hull was penetrated on the starboard side in the neighbourhood of 175 station adjacent to the after end of the after engine room. The platform deck immediately abaft the after engine room split in two places. Compartments which were open to the sea flooded rapidly, including the after engine room, the 4-inch magazine, the starboard shaft passage, the starboard watertight compartment abreast the after engine room, the starboard plummer block compartment, the starboard gland compartment and the starboard cable passage abreast the after engine room as well as X.5, X.7 and Y.1 oil fuel tanks. Some compartments including the main W/T Office flooded slowly and this had not been controlled by the time the ship was scuttled. The effect of this flooding was that the ship quickly listed from ten and a half to eleven degrees to starboard. Counter flooding measures were promptly taken which ultimately reduced the list to about four and a half degrees starboard by about 02.45 hours.

The after engine room was flooded thereby putting out of action the port and starboard inner shafts. The starboard inner shaft was probably damaged but the port inner was running for a short time. The after boiler room was suffering from controllable leaks and the boiler fires had been put out because of sea water in the furnace fuel oil. With regard to the forward engine room, the starboard outer shaft was damaged and useless. There were also minor defects and leaks which were very soon rectified. Crucially, the port outer turbine and shaft were in working order, but port circulator had tripped. A full head of steam of 340lb was at all times maintained in both boilers of the forward boiler room until *Manchester* was abandoned.

No.4 steam dynamo situated in the after engine room was put out of action by flooding. The remaining three dynamos were not affected. Power failed on after sections of the ring main to port and starboard. The steering gear and motors were mechanically sound, but power failed to the steering motors.

The 6-inch gun armament was undamaged mechanically except that power was not available to train 'X' and 'Y' turrets. The structure to 'X' Turret was possibly affected by the explosion. There was a temporary failure of electric power to 'A' and 'B' turrets. The 4-inch gun armament was mechanically undamaged but the ammunition supply was limited to the 350 rounds outside the 4-inch magazine. The short range weapons were unaffected.

The DCT on the bridge was fully functional, unlike the after DCT which lacked electric power and had been damaged by the explosion. All three High Angle Directors were mechanically sound but the starboard and after HA.DCTs reported difficulty in training. In all probability fire control communications in the fore part of the ship remained intact but the after circuits must have been damaged. Internal and external communication systems were largely undamaged and the damage control headquarters remained in communication with the bridge. All gunnery radar sets remained serviceable except for the Type 284 in which a fuse had blown, but this was immediately replaced. The Type 279 was probably put out of action owing to destruction of generators. The Type 273 remained in action.

All-in-all the damage inflicted by the explosion of a 21-inch torpedo with a 270kg warhead was remarkably similar to that suffered on 23 July 1941 when *Manchester* had been hit on the port side abreast the after end of the After Engine Room by a 17.7-inch (450 mm) aerial torpedo with a 170kg warhead. All that remained was to get the ship underway and to a friendly port – if possible in view of the cruiser's dangerous area location. Clearly a successful outcome would be dependent upon a large slice of luck as well as some friendly support.

The After Engine Room Floods

As a result of the torpedo hit, one officer and eight or nine ratings were killed in the after engine room which flooded very quickly. Leading Seaman Albert Slater was standing on some plates about twenty feet above the engine room floor when the explosion plunged everything into darkness. He was blown off the plates and only the water rushing into the compartment saved him from injury that would have made it impossible for him to get clear. The water carried him up and there appeared to be nothing to stop his being drowned like a rat in a trap when the water reached the top of the compartment. Suddenly it ceased to rise, and Slater pulled himself on to a turbine where he sat in pitch darkness, half stifled by heat and steam. A slight glimmer of light through some pipes gave him fresh hope, but he could not climb over the pipes without being badly burned, so he plunged into the water and came up at a point where the air was a little better. Groping along the deckhead, he cut his hand on a broken lamp; but the lamp told him where he was. He went on until he found himself beneath an open hatch. He was pulled clear a few minutes before it became necessary to clamp down the hatch against the advancing water[8].

Another lucky survivor was Stoker Robert Holding who was in the after engine room at the time of the explosion:

'I seemed to be dropping a long way; you could not see anything it was that black, all the lights went out. The first thing that I did was to blow my life belt out and then I was floating in the water with oil on top of the water. I tried to find the hatch to get up, it was so black I could not see a thing. I tried to get round the turbine but could not see anything then. The water came up sharp and then it stopped about 3 feet off the top of the after engine room. Then it came in very slowly after that. One of the lads took me on deck and someone else picked me up and took me to a destroyer [*Pathfinder*] alongside. They took me to the Sick Bay.'[9]

Stoker Petty Officer Alcwyn Williams was outside the Warrant Officers' Mess when the torpedo struck. 'The first thing that I knew about it was there was a great rush, it sounded like water running in. We had a lot of stores outside the Warrant Officers' Mess and they all came on top of me. I know nothing after that, I was knocked out.' When he came to he said:

'The water was running in from 'X' flat through No.19B bulkhead. I put the clip on the watertight door. No more water came in. I could not get through the door to the Wardroom so I went through the transit door on the bulkhead. I got in the Pay Office Float which was full of steam and oil fuel on the deck. I had a look round to see what I could find as I could hear all this water running in[to] the After Engine Room. The hatch was blown off, I pulled several clips on one side. The next thing I did, as the steam was getting stronger, I made my way up to the upper deck to get assistance. Two ratings came in through the Officers' Heads and then we pulled all the people clear of the oil and took them on the upper deck. By this time the after engine room was flooded right up. We had to be careful going across the flat because a big flap on top of the engine room was blown right off. I had to go on the upper deck because I was getting overcome with fumes. When I came to I was on the upper deck on the port side.'[10]

The Forward Engine Room and the Port Outer Engine
Warrant Engineer Oliver George was in the forward engine room during and after the attack and recalled that:

'At about 0110 on 13 August 1942 there was a sudden 'Emergency full speed' order – an explosion followed at 0115 and the ship took a list if 11° to starboard immediately. Amongst other things, the Port Main Circulator had tripped–this was rectified in about 2 minutes. The gauges in the Forward Engine Room showed that there was between 340–350 lbs of pressure in both boilers in the Forward Boiler Room. The port outer shaft was still running. I subsequently received, about 10 minutes after being hit, an order from the bridge by word of mouth to stop the port outer shaft. This was done by shutting off the steam and this was made known by way of the reply gong. A turbo-generator in the Forward Engine Room was running and I knew the diesel generators were going as I could hear them. No orders were received on the Engine Room telegraph. There was no communication with the After Engine Room and I noticed that there was no pressure showing on the gauges from the After Engine room. At this point the time was about 0135 and about 10 minutes later the ship got back to a starboard 7° list.'[11]

One of the key issues in the sorry saga of the loss of HMS *Manchester* concerns the port outer engine and whether it had been running after the torpedo exploded. Fortunately, there were many witnesses who were able to confirm that at least one engine was functional after the torpedo's warhead detonated. These included Sergeant Charles Coleborn RM who said he could feel an engine running after the explosion and stated that 'You could see the propeller [i.e. port outer] turning on the port side, there was one on the port side. It seemed as though we had eased down that is all. The screw seemed to be out of the water a bit, a thrashing noise as they were nearer the surface than usual.' This was obviously due to the starboard list.[12]

Petty Officer Albert Miller, Captain of 'Y' Turret, also confirmed that 'there was one shaft still just ticking over, I think that it was the port after [outer]. The screw was just a little bit out of the usual and it was just going over slowly. It did not make any undue noise.'[13]

Marine George Pritchard who had been stationed in 'X' Magazine said that, 'I went up to the quarterdeck and we stood there awaiting orders and the port [outer] screw was still running for about 10 minutes [i.e. 10 minutes after he arrived topside]'. He did not hear any knocking or grinding.[14]

Chief Stoker John Penn was stationed in Damage Control HQ at the time of the explosion and reported that 'we were still underway [after the explosion] so obviously there must have been one [engine running]. There was a lot of vibration, more aft than forward.'[15]

Mechanician George Williams was told by Engineer Commander Robb's messenger that the engine [port outer] was turning after the crash but it became necessary to stop that shaft to put the steering engines right. They fixed the steering engine but she would not go. Full boiler pressure was put on it but it made no difference.[16]

The starboard outer shaft was damaged by the explosion and was stopped because it was bumping badly. The port circulator tripped and steam was temporarily shut off to the port outer engine until the circulator was restarted. As soon as it was restarted the order was received by messenger from the bridge, at about 01.30 hours, to stop all shafts. The engine was subsequently tried under steam and was correct. Both main feed pumps tripped but were quickly restarted. The forward boiler room maintained a full head of steam at a pressure of 340lb pressure in both boilers until ship was abandoned.

No real progress was made in restoring power to the after sections of the ring main. Emergency leads were run along the upper deck to the steering motors and were connected up by about 02.20 hours, but were never tested. Steps were taken to restore electric power to the fore end of the ship.[17]

Armament and Magazines
The force of the explosion was felt by those in the 6-inch guns turrets. For example, Sub-Lieutenant Frank Munro RNVR remembered that:

> 'The turrets just suddenly seemed to be lifted. It seemed as if the whole structure of the turret lifted and all the lighting failed. There was a lot of water thrown over the turret ['X' Turret] and down through a manhole over the Officers' seat. All lights were extinguished aft and the power was cut off. The ship took a list to starboard immediately. After a moment or two, as no orders were received and the ship listing increasingly, I ordered 'X' Turret to be cleared. When all hands had left the gunhouse I followed. I ordered the men on the quarter deck to prepare the Carley floats. I went aft myself to make sure that the primers had been removed from the depth charges.'[18]

Ordinary Seaman Roland Hindmarsh's action station was on the centre gun of 'A' Turret, and he recalled that 'as I bent down for the next cartridge case, the turret floor suddenly thrust upwards, rocking me violently. An enormous and deep explosion resonated from within the ship. Then the floor, whipping from side to side, settled down again.'[19]

Petty Officer Albert Miller, who was Captain of 'Y' Turret, 'felt a terrific shaking at the time of the explosion. There were no orders given what to do, the lights went out. The majority of the gun's crew climbed out without an order being given.'[20] This was just one among many incidents where personnel simply walked away from their posts and wandered off to find things to do such as prepare Carley floats for launching.

'B' Turret reported by voice to the bridge that power to the turret had failed. If this was true, it was only temporary. At about the same time, the forward 6-inch DCT reported to the bridge that they were in communication with the TS, but that their onward communication to the turrets had failed. Gunnery Lieutenant Commander Duff, on his own initiative, then gave the order for the TS to be abandoned and the crew to remain on the mess deck. This order had a deleterious effect on internal communications while at the same reducing the 6-inch guns to local control. Duff also received reports that the starboard and after HA.DCTs were jammed in training. This was incorrect as regards the starboard HA.DCT. Unfortunately, this DCT was abandoned by the order of Lieutenant Daniels RNVR, who was the HA Control Officer and almost at once the HACP and remaining DCTs were abandoned by their crews. Very little action appears to have been taken to restore the fighting efficiency of the ship.[21]

Marine George Pritchard who was stationed in 'X' Magazine recorded that 'after the explosion the lights went out and smoke came down the ladder from the 4-inch gun deck into the wardroom flat'.[22]

Royal Marine Sergeant Charles Coleborn was also stationed in 'X' Magazine and was closed up in the cordite gallery when the torpedo exploded. He reported that 'all I felt was the ship shuddered and then all the lights went out. I got out of the turret up through the top manhole. I sought out the Captain of Marines and asked him about the confidential books. He said "they will have to be got up" so I took four marines and went down to get them up. I had them all [i.e. the cases of the Confidential Books] put on the upper deck and when the order was given to abandon ship I had them thrown over the side and we watched them sink. There were no officers there. The list at the time of abandoning ship was smaller than when it first started.'[23]

Leading Steward Harry Ironmonger, whose action station was in 'Y' Magazine, made his way to the quarter deck where he observed that 'oil was pouring out into the water, big patches of oil, coming from abreast 'X' Turret'.[24]

Steering

There is no doubt that the order 'Amidships' was given shortly after the explosion. The fact that the rudder was no longer being controlled by the wheel was observed by the Officer of the Watch and Chief Quartermaster in the lower steering position. Shortly afterwards, the latter seems to have received an order by voice-pipe from the bridge to 'come-up' and as a result the Chief Quartermaster and the Telegraphmen left the lower steering position leaving the port telegraph at 'full speed ahead' and the starboard telegraph at 'half ahead'. It is likely that Captain Drew gave the order to stop engines shortly afterwards but this was not received in the now-evacuated lower steering position. By about 01.20 hours the rudder had been centred by hand pump. Drew, realising that his ship was still going ahead, was endeavouring to pass orders to the engine room to stop engines. This order finally reached the engine room by messenger by about 01.30 hours.[25]

Shipwright 4th Class Leonard Blackman's action station was in the key board flat and Admiral's flat right aft. He recorded that 'there was a violent explosion and I was lying on the deck with head [facing] inboard. I saw no flash or smoke. The first thing I did was to put on the emergency lighting. I went forward and was advised not to go any further forward [than the foremost end of 'Y' flat] as it was flooded with oil fuel.' Asked if he could hear the sound of any water entering the ship or see any flooding he replied, 'only right aft, the tap in the Admiral's bathroom had gone'. He continued, 'I went aft to try to make my way forward from the Admirals' hatch aft on the quarterdeck. I was stopped by a Sergeant of Marines and told that nobody was allowed on the upper deck. I hung around for a bit and then we had orders to have a look at the after steering position. I did not go below but attempted to bring the wheel over and after about 10 minutes we got it amidships.'

Blackman reported that the quartermaster and 'a seaman' had gone below to have a look at the rudder and were satisfied that it was now amidships. He added 'as far as I know they relayed it [i.e. the rudder position] to the bridge'. Asked if he saw any emergency leads being run he replied that 'there was one being run down to the steering position'. He saw no water in the steering position and had been given no information about the damage caused by the torpedo. However, he observed that 'shortly after we relayed the message [rudder amidships] forward an engine or something stopped. I was told that the only engine that was going was stopped.'[26]

Engine Room Artificer 5th Class Albert Laverty was standing on the port side of the ship in the key board flat when the torpedo exploded and remembered that 'there was a loud bang, the lights went out and the ship shuddered and took a list to starboard. When the ship had settled I went forward into the next compartment aft, the Admiral's flat where there were several fellows trying to get the steering gear to work.' He said that it took about twenty minutes to get the rudder centred, during which time there was an engine running, but 'it stopped moving before we got the rudder amidships'.[27]

Temporary Warrant Electrician Percy Williams RN recalled that 'after the explosion a seaman told me that No.4 dynamo had come off power and No.5 Ring main breaker had opened leaving the whole after section dead. I immediately ordered a cable party to fit the steering motor from No.2 dynamo connection box. I made sure that they had found two drums of cables that I had just recently placed amidships and from there I went back again down to the workshop flat and made sure that the Electrical Artificer had gone to No.2 dynamo to make the necessary connections fitting to the upper deck. From there I went to the quarter deck. I waited until the connections were made to the steering motors. I remained on the quarter deck until the job was finished. When they were completed I then proceeded to the bridge and reported to the Navigator (Commander Gill] that I had supplied power to the steering motors. I asked the Navigator if I could have permission to try [the steering motors]. The Navigator told me to wait and not to apply the juice because he was waiting for a reply from the engine room. Someone said the "port engine fails to respond". The Navigator said to me then he would not require the steering motors. The list on the ship was very slight at the time of abandonment – perhaps 3-4 degrees.'[28]

'Emergency Stations'
At about 01.40 hours the order 'Emergency Stations' was given by Captain Drew. This order, coupled with an earlier order to evacuate certain

positions, resulted in the breakdown of internal communications. Concurrently with the order 'Emergency Stations', the order was given for all secret and confidential books and publications to be destroyed. This destruction now started, some books being burned and some being thrown overboard. Another disruptive effect of the order 'Emergency Stations' was that it caused a considerable number of officers and men to occupy themselves in preparing Carley floats for launching.[29]

Sub-Lieutenant Robert Williams was amongst those detailed to dispose of the confidential books and he recorded that 'my action station was in the after conning position-searchlight platform and the explosion was just about below where I was standing. Quite a lot of smoke came up from the Oerlikon gun deck which was just aft of the searchlight platform. There was only one bang. About five minutes after the explosion I received instructions from the Paymaster Lieutenant Commander to help dispose of the confidential books. I did not see any E-boats after the explosion.'[30]

Paymaster Lieutenant Cyril Kirk RNVR, who was in the gunroom flat at the time of the explosion, was another officer involved in the disposal of secret material and described his efforts to access the W/T office: 'When the torpedo hit the lights went out and I was knocked over and I lost my spectacles at the time. Immediately there were fumes and I had difficulty breathing. I made my way up one deck. Later I went down to the gunroom flat again to the entrance of the hatch into the W/T office where I encountered the Paymaster Midshipman who was in the cypher office at the time of the explosion and also Lieutenant Wake RN. Wake had on a smoke helmet and was endeavouring to get down to the cypher office but owing to the length of the tube he could not make it so he came back. I tried to get down myself. I got to the bottom of the steps but the fumes sent me back again.'[31]

HMS *Pathfinder* Comes Alongside

Hearing of *Manchester*'s plight Rear Admiral Burrough, who was still astern in *Ashanti*, ordered *Pathfinder* to stand by *Manchester*. At 01.40 hours *Pathfinder* came upon *Manchester* which was stopped and listing to starboard. The destroyer came alongside the crippled cruiser's starboard quarter at 01.54 hours. Commander Gibbs in *Pathfinder* stressed the greater necessity of escorting the merchant transports to which Drew readily agreed. However, Captain Drew took the opportunity to transfer the wounded and some members of the crew, who were serving no useful purpose, to *Pathfinder*.

After some consultation with Commander Hammersley-Johnston, the order was passed 'Port Watch to muster on the quarterdeck, stand fast high angle guns crew and short range weapons crews'. As a consequence 172 officers and men left *Manchester* and embarked in *Pathfinder*. The transfer to the destroyer was controlled by Commander Hammersley-Johnston and

Master at Arms Terry. A number of Carley floats were also transferred to the destroyer. *Pathfinder*, having embarked as many officers and men as she thought she could fit, cast off by the orders of Captain Drew and proceeded to re-join CS 10. Before HMS *Pathfinder* left, she was ordered by Captain Drew to report the situation to CS 10 together with a request that an aircraft or destroyer might be sent to see how matters stood.[32]

Yeoman of Signals Thomas Cardiff recalled that *Pathfinder* came alongside about twenty minutes after the explosion and remained alongside for a further fifteen minutes. Asked if he had heard any information as to which men were to go in HMS *Pathfinder* he replied, 'The Captain had piped "Port Watch to muster on the quarterdeck." After that had been done I read a signal from the *Pathfinder* saying that she had emergency orders to join up with the convoy fifteen miles from position "R". The Chief Yeoman took the signal off me and went up to the compass platform to give it to the Captain, after which the Captain hailed *Pathfinder* to push off and rejoin the convoy and also told him prior to pushing off that if he could take any more [men] he should do so.'[33]

The stories from the crew related thus far indicate how difficult and confusing the situation was on board the crippled cruiser. What, though, would happen next? The fate of the warship and its remaining crew hung in the balance.

Chapter 9

Scuttled

Engineer Commander William John Robb, who served aboard HMS *Manchester* from 30 November 1939 to 13 August 1942, described his experiences on that fateful night in a statement written for the court martial held in February 1943. His report, addresses the key engineering issue in detail and consequently is reproduced in full below:[1]

At about midnight on 12 August 1942, I was on the Flight Deck with the Senior Engineer Lt Sutton. There had been a lull. About this time I heard a near explosion. This brought everybody to the alert and I proceeded below. Gunfire from our own ship followed later. The order to 'Stand to' and 'Stand Down' was passed by loudspeaker. When at the 'Stand Down' during a few lulls I was either in the Workshop Flat or the E.A.s' [Engineer Artificers] Workshop above the forward engine room. Between midnight and 0100 there were some 'alarm[s]' with gunfire from our own ship. Manoeuvring of engines took place with 'Full Ahead' on one side or the other, from which I concluded that torpedoes were being avoided. I decided at about 0045 to remain below in the Forward Engine Room. Position below was as follows:

'Full Ahead' Port. I felt an explosion with severe shaking or bouncing of the ship and knew that ship had been hit. I looked at the after unit gauge board, which appeared normal. I heard a loud knocking on the starboard outer shaft. I gave orders on my own responsibility to stop the starboard outer shaft. I saw by the repeat revolution indicator from the after Engine Room that the Starboard Inner Shaft had stopped. Ship immediately assumed a list to starboard settling at about 10°. I then crossed to the port side of the Forward Engine Room to check the Port Telegraph which was showing 'Full Ahead'.

I gave orders to connect hose, and to flood the Port Wing Watertight compartment, i.e. counter-flooding. This was done to conform to Engine Room Department Action Orders as regards Damage Control, and in conformity with Damage Control Handbook, namely counter flooding was carried out immediately the list exceeded 10°, by flooding wing Watertight compartments adjacent to machinery spaces.

At the same time I noticed a cloud of steam on the Port side of the Forward Engine Room. I heard someone report to Mr George [Warrant Engineer] that they could not get the hose connection because of the blow of steam. Mr George said that he would have a go at it, and in spite of the escape of steam near the hose connection, got the hose connected to the wing compartment.

I asked Mr George and the C.E.R.A. [Chief Engine Room Artificer] if they could account for the escape of steam. It was suggested that there might be a crack or a steam joint blown out.

I then noticed from the gauges that the Port Main Circulator had stopped and deduced that the escape of steam was due to the Condenser or Turbine Relief Valve lifting. In such circumstances, i.e. loss of circulating water, with main engine developing high power, the lifting of this relief valve is not abnormal.

The Port Main Feed Pump had also tripped, and was restarted. I called the attention of C.E.R.A. James, and E.R.A. [Engine Room Artificer] Bacon on Port Throttle to the fact that the Main Circulator had stopped and ordered the C.E.R.A. to re-start it. I assumed that it had tripped either because of the shock or when increased to full speed. I gave orders to shut steam off the Port Outer shaft temporarily while the Main Circulator was being re-started. At about the same time I received a message from the Captain by C.E.R.A. Atkinson to stop all shafts. I repeated the order to Mr George and E.R.A. on Port Throttle and Mr George said that he would inform the After Engine Room.

Telegraphs still showing 'Full Ahead', Port.

I received a report that water was entering the Forward Engine Room by the Starboard Bulkhead Gland. This was stopped by tightening up the gland. Mr George then had the brake put on the Starboard Outer Shaft to stop it trailing, should the ship go ahead.

All the above took place within a few minutes, and no information had yet been received as to the state of the After Engine Room. The Port Inner Shaft was still revolving as shown on the indicator in the Forward Engine Room.

I received a verbal message by Marine Orderly to report to the Captain on the Bridge. I tried direct telephone to the After Engine Room without result and was told by a stoker that it was dead. I spoke to Mr George as to what I should tell the Captain and we agreed that I would report the Port Outer engine would be available but the Port Inner doubtful.

As I was leaving the Engine Room, C.E.R.A. James asked me if it would be all right to put steam on the Port Outer Engine after re-starting the main circulator. I replied 'Yes'. Notices had been posted at each Throttle position showing safe receiver pressures to use when steaming with reduced number of shafts as a result of trials recently carried out at Scapa Flow.

On the way to the bridge I called at the Damage Control H.Q. in the Workshop Flat. I told Lt Malin, the Damage Control Officer, the situation in the Forward Engine Room.

The situation as to damage was not yet clear. He informed me that the Office Flat above the After Engine Room was full of smoke and wreckage, there was a black-out aft, and that counter flooding and transfer of oil fuel was underway. I sent Senior Engineer Lt (E) Sutton to check the position re Steering Gear, in case Lt (E) Rambaut, the After Sectional Officer, had become [a] casualty.

The Standing Instructions to the Watch-Keepers, copy of which was posted in the After Steering Compartments, were to change over to Hand Steering Pump immediately on failure of the motors, without waiting for orders. Commander and Navigating Officer had copies of these orders, and I had shown them to the Captain after revision in May [1942], subsequent to fitting of the Duplex Telemotor System.

I told Lt (E) [Engineer Lieutenant] Malim to get a message to the After Engine Room to stop the Port Inner Shaft. I knew the After Engine Room was flooding by the leak through the shaft bulkhead gland into the Forward Engine Room, but not to what extent.

When I left the Forward Engine Room, Mr George was exhausted. I sent C.E.R.A. Pedder to relieve Mr George for a spell and to back up C.E.R.A. James, who was on watch. I told Lt Malim to inform the Senior Engineer, who had left to check up on the Steering Gear, what the situation was in the Forward Engine Room. I went to the Bridge via the Flight Deck, which was crowded with men.

I estimate that the events related above took approximately 10 mins so that I reached the Forebridge between 0125 and 0130. I then had a conversation with the Captain. Lt Russell, Lt Daniel, Lt Cdr Duff and Cdr (N) [the Navigator, Commander Gill] were present for all or part of the time.

Conversation with Captain: So far as I can remember, Captain first asked me if I could do something about stopping the shafts, as we were going round in circles, and he was afraid that we should run onto a minefield. I replied that I had stopped the Port Outer temporarily just as his order came, owing to the stoppage of main circulator but it would be available. Port Inner was still revolving but I had sent a message to have it stopped. I have not had time to complete picture but this is the situation as far as I know it. It looks the same as last time. Both starboard shafts are out of action. I am uncertain about the After Engine Room. There must be some flooding there as we had a leak from the shaft passage into the Forward Engine Room which we stopped by tightening the shaft bulkhead gland. But at least we have one engine available, and could do

12 – 13 knots, with hand steering connected, and leads would be run to the steering motors. Heel and Trim is in hand by counter flooding wing compartments, and by transferring oil fuel.

At this point a telephone call came from the Damage Control Officer, Lt (E) Malim, I asked the Captain to tell Lt Malim to make sure that the Port Inner Shaft was stopped.

Captain then asked, 'Is the engine which you had to stop ready to use now?'

I replied, 'It has not been reported to me as I had to leave the Engine Room, but if the trouble is what I feel sure it is, it is only a matter of re-starting the circulator.'

Captain, 'And if it is not what you think it is how long will it take to put right?'

I replied, 'I can't say without investigating.'

Captain, 'Will it take 2 or 3 hours?'

I replied 'I cannot say but I am confident that it will be alright and can quickly check up on it. If it is no good we will have to take our chance on the Port Inner, it was still revolving when I left.'

The Captain explained the Tactical situation of the ships in words to this effect: 'Well Robb, I will explain the position to you as I see it. I have to make the decision whether to try and save this valuable ship, against the risk of further heavy loss of valuable lives. We are on the edge of a minefield with E-boats all around us. I am afraid we may be put in a position where we could not move the ship and be captured by the enemy. I could not bear to think of this fine ship being captured.'

I replied, 'We have a chance, Sir, and are in the same condition as last year as regards machinery.'

At this point there was a shout from the destroyer alongside, 'All aboard who are coming?'

Captain went to the loud hailer and said, '*Pathfinder* shove off when ready, and thank you very much.'

Pathfinder asked whether they could do anything else. – 'we can take a few more if they are quick.' The Captain replied, 'No thanks very much. We will look after ourselves now. Please send something back to see what has happened to us even if it is only a 'plane.'

Pathfinder replied, 'Goodbye and Good Luck, sorry we can't do more for you.'

My conversation with the Captain continued along the following lines:

'I think we should go on, Sir.'

Captain, 'When you say go on, what do you mean? If we go on and try and reach Malta, we shall be attacked all the way, and we shall be sunk for lack of manoeuvrability or because we cannot manoeuvre.'

I replied, 'We can go back, Sir.'

Captain, 'To Gibraltar?'

I replied, 'Yes, Sir.'

Captain, 'If we turn round to go back, we will either run on a minefield or be caught by an E-boat. They are all around us. Listen, you can hear them.'

I could hear nothing because the Captain continued, 'We are no further use to the convoy, and it would be unfair to detach an escort for us.'

I suggested that we might get some help from Force 'Z'. Captain replied that they were miles away and could not possibly help us.

Captain, 'We cannot steer.'

I replied, 'We have the Hand Steering Pump, Sir.'

Captain, 'That is not of much use.'

I replied, 'Leads must be ready to connect up to the steering motors very shortly.'

I asked generally, 'Has anyone heard anything about the Steering Gear.' Someone said, 'We are on hand steering.'

Captain also said words to the effect that he was expecting another torpedo at any moment, and that if we tried to go back we were bound to be dive-bombed at dawn.

I replied, 'We can certainly stand another hit, Sir.'

Captain said words to the effect that he could not feel it would be right or justified to lose the lives of a further large number of gallant men. Here we are close to the shore, and if we act quickly we can get the Ship's Company ashore as a body, and they be of further service to the country.

Captain then said to me: 'If we decide to sink the ship, what do we have to do about it?'

I replied, 'We can sink the ship if we have to do it, but I hope we shall carry on.'

Captain repeated, 'What shall we have to do?'

I replied, 'Open up all Sea Cocks and Magazine Floods, remove Condenser Doors and get Torpedo party to place scuttling charges.'

Captain turned to the Torpedo Officer Lt Russell and said, 'Have we got any?'

Torpedo Officer, 'We will have to make them up, Sir.'

Captain, 'How long will it take?'

Torpedo Officer, 'About half an hour, Sir'

Captain then said to both of us: 'Well make your preparations, and let me know when you are ready.'

I said, 'We can make preparations as a precaution in case we get further damage.'

Captain, 'Yes make your preparations'.

I said, 'Well, can I check up on the Second Engine before you decide, Sir?'

Captain, 'Yes, but we must be quick, as I must decide quickly, so that we can all get away before daylight.'

I turned to leave the Bridge, hoping this question was still open and not finally decided. As I went away, I heard Commander [Hammerlsey-]Johnston calling out Commander (E) [Commander Robb]. I met Commander at the top of the ladder. The Commander said, 'Has the Captain told you what he wants?'

I replied, 'Yes, he told me to make preparations to sink the ship.'

The Commander said, 'Right' and moved towards the Captain who was calling [for him].

I would have spoken further to the Commander but I heard the Captain call out, 'Is that the Commander, is that you Johnnie?'

The Commander, 'Yes, Sir.'

Captain, 'Are you all ready?'

Commander, 'They are all falling in now, Sir. I've got them coming up now.'

The Captain said he would come along.

I left the Bridge and proceeded to Damage Control H.Q. via the Marines' Mess Deck. I took Lt Malim aside to the E.A's Workshop and told him the Captain wanted us to make preparations to sink the ship and I arranged with him to ensure the E.R.A.s were standing by the necessary valves.

I went below to the Forward Engine Room, and C.E.R.A. James reported that the Port Outer engine had been tried and was correct. I returned to the Damage Control H.Q. Lt Malim reminded me regarding getting the magazine and shell room hatches, and all scuttles open before opening the flooding valves. I agreed regarding the hatches, but not the scuttles, as that would undarken the ship. He had no further news regarding the After Engine Room, but he thought it was finished.

The ship still had 3 dynamos, namely one Turbo-Generator and 2 Diesel Generators. Damage Control Parties could still work at transferring fuel, investigating damage, shoring hatches and bulkheads, transferring weights, and rigging emergency leads to the Steering Gear.

I was not satisfied re lack of information concerning the After Engine Room and told Lt Malim I would take a party to investigate, and then go to the captain again and ask him to proceed on one shaft if the After Engine Room was out of action. I ordered the Central Repair Party with C.E.R.A. Atkinson to come with me. Stoker Petty Officer Lyford attached himself to this party. Bearing in mind Lt Malim's remarks about wreckage in the Office Flat I took them over the Flight Deck and sent them down the ventilator supply trunk to the After Engine Room where I previously caused a jumping ladder to be rigged. I went via the 4-inch Gun Deck and Officers' Heads to reach the Engine Room by a different route. The Flight Deck and Gun Deck were very crowded with men and it was difficult for me to get through. I met Lt Rambaut in the heads passage. I asked him what was the state of affairs. Lt Rambaut said the fumes were bad below, and that everybody seemed to have gone from the flats below. I continued on down the ladder to the lower deck and turned aft to the door leading to the Gunroom Flat. I saw Pay. Lt Kirk with a torch, and enquired where the damage was. He said, 'I don't know, everyone has gone away from here' I then turned forward through the Office Flat, and made my way to the trunk to the After Engine Room. I found one man covered in oil fuel astride the coffer dam of the Engine Room door, exhausted and calling for air. Fumes were fairly thick, but bearable and more like vapour. I put the man onto the fan chamber for air. I shone a torch into the Engine Room, which was flooded up to the crown. There was one man with his head above the oil fuel and grasping the top rung of the ladder, and another man was calling for help. I saw two casualties on deck near the hatch.

S.P.O. Lyford and the rescue party began to arrive down the fan trunk; Lt Rambaut also arrived having followed me down. I turned the situation over to them and left for the Bridge to report to the Captain.

I decided, as I was aft, to check position re Steering Gear, for myself. Made my way through crowds on Quarter Deck, and satisfied myself that the emergency leads and fire main hose were provided, and had been rigged in position. I shouted down the hatch 'Is anyone working on these leads?' A reply came, 'The electricians are working down below.'

I saw the stern of a destroyer alongside and Carley floats being passed to the destroyer. I asked some hands what they were doing with the Carley floats and was told that it was the Commander's order to pass them to the destroyer.

I proceeded forward and met two stokers carrying a leather oil fuel hose, who had lost their way in the well deck in the darkness. They said they had been told to rig it to Y.2 oil fuel tank. I led them back to the quarterdeck and directed them down the Gunroom Flat. I saw Midshipman Parker who said he was getting up the C.B.s.

On arrival at the Bridge, I called for the Captain, received no response and saw nobody there. I heard a cheer, and started down the ladder. I then met the Captain at the bottom of the ladder, returning to the Bridge accompanied by the Torpedo Officer.

I reported that the After Engine Room was flooded, rescue party working there, but that one engine was definitely correct, and the leads were ready for connecting to the Steering Motor and asked if there was a chance of going on.

Captain replied, 'We don't stand a hope, old Boy.'

I then asked him if he would order all magazine and shell room hatches to be opened, if he still decided to flood. He asked the torpedo officer to see to that. I then reported to the Captain, that flooding parties were posted and awaiting orders. Captain asked, 'Where will you be?' I replied, 'Damage Control H.Q. in the Workshop Flat.'

Captain: 'You had better be on the Flight Deck so that I can get to you.'

I made way towards the Office Flats, via the Flight Deck and 4-inch Gun Deck, but met a casualty being brought up via the Officers' Heads. I got extra hands from the 4-inch Gun Deck to assist.

I returned to Damage Control H.Q. and told Lt Malim to stand by for flooding and to have nuts on Condenser doors slackened.

Chief Stoker Gibson, the double-bottom Chief Stoker (Heel & Trim party) arrived from the damaged area by the Starboard passage and was exhausted. I made him sit down and explained the situation to him. I told him to cancel all heel and trim operations.

I returned to the Flight Deck and met the Commander and asked him what were the arrangements for abandoning ship. He said that he was trying to reserve whalers for the Captain and flooding parties. Carley floats were being manned and told to carry on for the shore. I went down to the Workshop Flat again, and told Lt. Malim to get everybody not required for flooding up from the Engine Room and Boiler Rooms.

While we were waiting for final orders, Lt Rambaut told me there would be no chance of flooding parties or watch getting into the whalers as they were crowded and that we should probably have to swim. After a pause I went over the Flight Deck again to the After Engine Room hatch to make quite sure that nobody was there, and that the casualties had been evacuated. I returned to the Flight Deck, via Cabin Flat to get a blue suit, and arriving on the Flight Deck saw the Commander who said that he thought it was time to carry on flooding. I saw the Captain standing on the Pom-Pom deck, I called up to him 'Commander says he is ready to carry on flooding, Sir.' Captain replied 'Carry on' and he came down to the Flight Deck.

I waited for the last raft to go out, then went down to the Damage Control H.Q. and gave orders to the Forward and After Sections to carry on flooding. After receiving reports from Lt Fletcher (fwd) and Lt Malim (aft) I ordered Mr Budden to open floods and abandon both Boiler Rooms. On receiving his report I ordered Forward Engine Room to flood and place scuttling charges. Mr George [Warrant Engineer] and Mr Casey [Torpedo Gunner] went down to the Forward Engine Room. Mr George asked me about the Engine Room Registers, and I said that we could not manage them if we had to swim, and we could not take them to internment.

List on ship was 4.5° and had been for a long time. This was checked by the indicator in the Forward Engine Room, when I called down. I checked that Diesel Watchkeepers were up, and ordered all Officers and men with no further duties to abandon ship. I enquired re Chief Stoker Gibson, who was flooding miscellaneous spaces. Lt Malim said that he would search for him, and later reported that he had been found and was on deck. All the Engineer Officers were reluctant to leave the Workshop Flat and I had to tell each one personally and definitely to go. Lt Rambaut returned to wait until we had finished in the Engine Room, and again I told him to leave the ship. Mr George's party with C.E.R.A. Pedder, removed condenser doors, came up and reported. I told them to abandon ship. I ordered Mr Casey to fix his charges.

Mr Casey was the last man to leave the Engine Room. I told him to abandon ship, and followed him up the ladder and went to the starboard waist. I found a crowd round the starboard whaler which was in the water and full. The Captain was in the Whaler. Suggested to the Commander that we should go aft to the quarterdeck until the scuttling charges had gone off. He agreed, and we began to make our way aft. Lt Sutton and myself got aft to the Quarter deck. In the darkness we could not find anything floatable. I missed the Commander and Lt Malim. I went forward to look for them I met the Commander who said, 'If you want to catch the Whaler, hop in now.'

I got back to the starboard Whaler and found Lt Cdr Duff and Mr Casey working with some ropes. I got down to the Whaler's falls. Lt Cdr Duff and Mr Casey got some kind of raft which was towed by the Whaler with them and two hands hanging on. The Commander and Lt Malim got a plank and were then picked up by the Whaler and taken on board. Lt Sutton was picked up by the 2nd Whaler off the Quarter deck.

Estimated it was 0500 when the Whaler left the ship.

As dawn was breaking, an Italian plane arrived and aimed a torpedo at the ship. It ran close to the Whaler, but missed ahead of the ship. Captain remarked: 'That proves it. That proves we did right.' After some time, the Captain said, 'I hope she will go all right Robb.' I replied, 'It will take a little time, but I think she will go all right.' The Captain later remarked, 'That was a very hard decision to take.'

On the way ashore planes circled the boats several times. It was said that one was a Beaufighter.

The ship listed over to starboard. We heard shell cases from the Pom-Pom deck rattling as they rolled down. The Diesels were still running. Stern of the ship went under and bow lifted up. Estimate ship sank after 0530 approx.

There was a large explosion from a merchant ship, with a huge cloud of smoke some distance away to port. We saw an E-boat examining our boats and rafts. Landed at Kelibia and were put in a compound about 0900. Heard Pom-Pom firing about half an hour later and saw two Tribal destroyers in the Bay.[2]

The Decision to Abandon Ship

At about 01.25 hours Commander Hammersley-Johnston made a brief report to Captain Drew on the bridge outlining the extent of damage based

98

on the tour which he had just made round the ship. He stated that the after engine room was flooded, that there was no fire, that men were being brought up from the flats immediately above the after engine room, and that the damage was confined between the forward bulkhead of the after engine room and the after bulkhead of the 4-inch magazine. He added that damage control HQ had not yet got out a complete statement. At about the same time, Lieutenant Malim, the damage control officer, reported by telephone to the Captain in person on the bridge that the after engine room was flooded, that the two inner shafts and the starboard outer shaft were out of action and that counter flooding measures were being taken. Lieutenant Malim also reported that the port outer shaft was either workable or that it remained intact and Captain Drew gave orders for it to be stopped.

At about the same time orders were given for the information to be passed to the bridge that steering by hand pump was available, but there is no direct evidence that this information ever reached Captain Drew or Commander Gill. Furthermore, it appears that no steps were taken to ascertain whether steering by this method was available, or to establish communication between the bridge and the hand pump.

A little later the gunnery officer reported to the Captain that the gun armament was virtually out of action, except for the close range weapons and that the 4-inch guns were in local control with a limited amount of ammunition. Furthermore, prior to 01.54 hours the Torpedo Officer reported that the search lights were no longer working and asked for permission to jettison the starboard torpedoes to reduce the list. This was approved. He had already reported that No.4 dynamo was not working, and that No.2 was unsatisfactory.

Commander Robb arrived on the bridge at about 02.10 hours in response to an order from the Captain. Robb undoubtedly had a fairly accurate appreciation of the extent of the damage and also knew that the forward boiler room and forward engine room were intact, and could be used. He also knew that the ship could be steered by the hand pump, and that the port outer engine had had to be temporarily stopped. He did not anticipate that this stoppage was due to any major defect but was not in a position to define the cause nor say with certainty how long it would before this engine could be used again. He also knew that power was being supplied to the steering motors and therefore that power steering would soon be available.

Captain Drew had by this time also received a fairly accurate report as to the extent of the damage to his ship but did not know that the rudder had been centred by hand pump, or when power would be available for the steering motors. He had received a very gloomy report on the state of the gun armament from which he gathered that the 4-inch and short range weapons alone remained usable at the time. He knew that the 4-inch ammunition was limited to the amount in the ready use lockers and that the searchlights had been reported out of action. He had already taken the decision to transfer a portion of the ship's Company to the destroyer *Pathfinder*, and this operation was in progress. He knew this reduced the offensive or defensive power of his ship. The secret and confidential books of all types were in the process of destruction. He knew of the presence of E-boats in the vicinity, and the general situation must have appeared thoroughly bad.

Evidence presented in Chapter 12 suggests that assuming that his ship could again be got underway, there is no doubt that by this time Captain Drew had decided to take *Manchester* back along his course in order to reach deep water off Zembra Island by daylight, which he estimated would take him just under three hours. Consequently, he felt that the ship must proceed by 02.45 hours at the latest. This critical conversation was interrupted from time to time by the Captain dealing with reports verbally and by telephone, as well as having to decide when to despatch *Pathfinder* while at the same time worrying about nearby E-boats.

Sadly the conversation turned out to be inconclusive and unsatisfactory with Robb certain that the port outer engine could be got working again without being able to say when. Drew on the other hand dominated the conversation and outlined the ship's dire tactical situation at length explaining that he could not delay a final decision for much longer. It was unfortunate that as a result of asking a leading question Drew gained the impression that he would not have steam for three hours. Nevertheless, by 02.20 hours, temporary leads had been run to the steering motors and the fact that this had been done was reported to Captain Drew on the bridge at about 02.25 hours.

There can be no doubt that scuttling as an alternative to getting under way must already have been present in the Drew's mind as he discussed it during the interview in question with Commander Robb, and by 02.30 hours had told Lieutenant Russell, the Torpedo Officer, to consider what preparations would be necessary. Lieutenant Russell suggested to the Captain that he should see what the ship could do before making up his mind to scuttle.

Robb left the bridge after this interview at about 02.40 hours with this knowledge, and must have felt his chances of getting *Manchester* underway again were slim. Robb's fears proved to be only too well founded because, at about the same time, Captain Drew instructed Commander Hammersley-Johnston to assemble the hands on the flight deck so that he could inform them that he had reluctantly come to the conclusion that he must scuttle the ship in her present position. At about 02.55 hours, soon after the Captain had finished his speech, Robb returned to the bridge with the news that the port outer engine was ready and that power steering was available.

Unfortunately the decision to scuttle had been taken already and as the orders had been given accordingly it would have been very difficult to reverse the decision at that point because the whole ship had become disorganized by the preparations for abandoning ship.[3]

Mechanician George Williams whose action station was in the Staff Repair Party in the Workshop said: 'I proceeded to take the portable pump to the main W/T office to attempt to pump out there as ordered by the Chief Stoker. We ran into the Chief Torpedo Gunner's Mate and he said "What's up? Aren't you going to leave the ship?" I said, "Why, what's up?" He said, "Hands to abandon ship." I said, "that's the first I have heard about that." He said, "I am just putting charges around so you had better get up top." So I dismissed my party and went up top. I was down below when the Captain spoke and I only heard the three cheers.'[4]

Colour Sergeant Joseph Mullins went on to the flight deck while Captain Drew was addressing the ship's company and heard that they were going to abandon ship as the ship was not under control and, 'that we would be a sitting target if we were attacked again'. He recalled that, 'we were told that if we went into action again we should lose at least 75% of the men who were aboard and that they [i.e. the speaker, Captain Drew] considered it advisable to abandon ship and that we were required to pull towards the lighthouse on Cape Bon where we would be interned; that we would have plenty of time to go down below for any personal articles we would require. These were to be packed in a small bag if possible.'[5]

Asked if he heard a suggestion that it might be possible to get the ship underway again he replied, 'not from the person speaking. I was told it had been said that it might be possible to get the ship under way at about 12 knots in the morning.'[6]

Manchester Abandoned and Scuttled

On conclusion of the Captain's speech, the Executive Officer, Commander Hammersley-Johnston, addressed the ship's company and told them they could go to their lockers and pack any of their personnel gear in a small case. He told them to wear warm clothes, and return to their boat stations within ten minutes in order to prepare to abandon ship. He also told them that if they were made prisoners of war they were only to give their name, rank and official number and no other information. The ship's company commenced abandoning ship at about 03.45 hours and continued to do so until about 05.10 hours, when the last members including the Captain and scuttling parties left the ship. Meanwhile, preparations were being made for scuttling of the ship and the various parts of the ship were ordered to open all watertight openings in the ship except the scuttles and deadlights which would allow light outward. Sea cocks were opened and flooding valves eased off, shores already placed were knocked away and charges were placed under the main inlets in the Forward Engine Room. Preparations were made for removing the condenser doors in the Forward Engine Room.

Shortly before the order to scuttle was given, an attempt was made to get into communication by wireless with CS 10, using the emergency transmitter in the Remote Control Office. Soon after dawn an enemy aircraft appeared and dropped two torpedoes at *Manchester* but both missed ahead of the ship. At about 06.47 hours (Commander Robb's report has the sinking at 05.30 hours) *Manchester* sank stern first in a position approximately seventy degrees, two to three miles from Kelibia Light.[7]

Chief Petty Officer Cook Charles Williams remembered that 'the Captain spoke at, I should say, about two thirty and I actually got into the water at about three thirty'.[8]

Colour Sergeant Mullins recalled that after the Captain's speech, he 'left the flight deck and went along to the 4-inch HA to see that all the marines were clear from there. I then went to the Commander's flat to go to the cordite handling room of 'X' Turret. When I got into the Commander's flat I saw that the stanchions were bent and all the occupants were in a state of confusion from the explosion. I did not go to the cordite handling room but went towards 'X' Turret. I was informed that all marines were clear of the turret and that one Sergeant and some marines were getting up confidential books. I then proceeded back to the flight deck and consulted Sergeant Liversage about our raft and asked him if it was clear and ready for shipping. He informed me that it was, so we went for gear to abandon ship.'

He said that the order to abandon ship was given about an hour after the Captain's speech and Mullins remembered that, 'all of the rafts were got away without difficulty at all. Some sank to the bottom because they had been damaged by shrapnel. The boats were hoisted out by crane. We pulled towards a dinghy which was already in the water and we tied up to her stern. We found that the dinghy had no oars so we passed them over one of our paddlers. Three or more Carley floats came up and got astern of us but we found it too much for us so we cast off from the dinghy and made our own way towards the lighthouse [about five or six miles away]. It was becoming twilight.'

With regard to *Manchester*'s final moments, Mullins recalled that he had left the ship about an hour earlier and was about 'two or three hundred yards away' when the cruiser sank. He thought there were three detonations in the ship before she went down:

> She went down by the stern and her bow went up at an angle. After the ship sank we pulled for the lighthouse. We saw two E-boats, one we thought was close inshore. The other came out and was circling around the rafts. He did not actually come to my raft but I learned from other survivors that this E-boat circled their rafts and covered them with rifles and asked for the Captain of HMS *Manchester* – 'is he in your raft?'
>
> While this E-boat was circling the rafts an aeroplane was flying overhead. She appeared to flash to the E-boat who made off. We then saw

two destroyers [*Eskimo* and *Somali*] appearing over the horizon but thought they were Italian. As they approached we could see that they were of the Tribal class. They lay off the three-mile limit for approximately ten minutes before they decided to come and pick us up. We were then about three-quarters of a mile from the shore. She came in and told us to stay on the rafts and that she would not pick us up if we dived off, in case they were attacked they would tow the raft. We went alongside and were taken inboard. We were one of the first rafts off but were held up by currents. The destroyers picked up survivors from about five rafts.

A French fishing smack put out and was picking up off the rafts nearest the shore. She [Mullins didn't specify *Eskimo* or *Somali*] then put off to a raft that was going west. She had a boat in tow which appeared to me to be the pinnace belonging to HMS *Manchester*.

To the best of my knowledge she did three trips with survivors and was making her way inshore when the destroyers appeared. As the destroyers came in they opened fire on the aircraft which was overhead. We saw people on the beach being marshalled and marched towards a fort under armed guard.[9]

The Ship's Company after Abandoning Ship

One rating was drowned on the way ashore. The majority of the ship's company, with the exception of 172 officers and men embarked in *Pathfinder*, landed on the Tunisian Coast and were interned during the afternoon of 13 August 1942. A number of officers and men, estimated at sixty to ninety, who had embarked on rafts, were picked up by *Somali* and *Eskimo* at about 10.30 hours when making for the shore. These two destroyers had been detached by CS 10 at 07.13 hours on Thursday, 13 August to return and stand by *Manchester* and give her every possible assistance. CS 10 did this in response to a visual signal received from *Pathfinder* as it re-joined him, to the effect that the Captain of *Manchester* would be glad if a destroyer could be sent when one could be spared. Two officers were forcibly taken from a Carley float by an Italian E-boat. They were subsequently released through the intervention of a French officer and re-joined the other survivors ashore.[10]

Thereafter the survivors were taken to the infamous Laghouat internment camp in Algeria. This was used as a prisoner of war camp for British Empire and Commonwealth prisoners, including RN personnel captured after the destroyer *Havock* ran aground off Kelibia in April 1942. Laghouat Camp is best described as a Beau Geste style fort adjacent to a Saharan oasis. Escape was virtually impossible, given the expanse of desert that surrounded Laghouat. All officers and ratings from *Manchester*, with the exception of a few who had died, were released from internment after North Africa had been occupied by Allied forces in November 1942.

Chapter 10

Board of Enquiry

On 20 August 1942, Acting Vice Admiral Neville Syfret, who had commanded Force F during Operation *Pedestal*, sent a signal to the Admiralty saying:

> From reports from survivors from HMS MANCHESTER which I have seen so far seem to indicate that an enquiry into the loss of this ship is desirable.
>
> Enquires into the loss of HMS EAGLE and HMS CAIRO are not considered necessary.
>
> Enquiry into the loss of HMS FORESIGHT has been held but my recommendations must await report from her captain who was sent home in HMS VICTORIOUS and was not available for the enquiry.[1]

Two days later, the Admiralty received a message from Washington in which it was stated that on 17 August the US Consul in Tunis had talked to the Captain of *Manchester* who said that his ship was sunk by a torpedo from an Italian E-boat. The Captain said that this boat and one other were sunk. *Manchester* had sunk in twenty fathoms about four miles off Kelibia. All documents burnt, nothing compromised, RDF gear destroyed.[2]

On 24 August C-in-C Home Fleet was ordered to hold an enquiry into the loss of HMS *Manchester*. Three days later, the C-in-C Portsmouth signalled the Admiralty saying:[3]

> In his report Sergeant Mullins R.M. states that, 'The Captain said that it might be possible to get the ship underway by the morning at about 12 knots but that he considered that he would lose about 75% of the ship's company if the ship were engaged by the enemy and therefore he considered it best to abandon the ship and then scuttle her.'
>
> Mr Williams, Warrant Electrician, in his report states, 'The Captain addressed the ship's company and told them it was impossible to move the ship and had decided to get everyone away and then scuttle the ship.'

Mechanician GE Williams states, 'Steering gear was damaged and consequently the ship was unable to manoeuvre. It was estimated that the ship could have steered at 12 knots if the steering gear was in working order.'

Constructor Commander HE Skinner in his technical report to Flag Officer Commanding Force F states that, 'It is probable that the ship was abandoned due to tactical considerations.'[4]

C-in-C Portsmouth contacted the Admiralty again on 27 August observing that the forthcoming enquiry needed to address three questions namely, (a) the decision to abandon ship, (b) whether or not the ship was capable of steaming after being torpedoed and after counter flooding action had been undertaken or whether she could have in time been got underway and (c) the general question of damage control. C-in-C Portsmouth felt that question (a) could only be weighed by Acting Vice Admiral Syfret who had been Flag Officer commanding Force F and consequently requested Their Lordships direction on this point.

The Admiralty replied that questions (a), (b) and (c), were equally valid. However, in view of the lack of evidence from *Manchester*'s senior officers who were interned in Algeria, it was not anticipated that the Board of Enquiry would be expected to adjudicate on whether the cruiser's Commanding Officer was right or wrong.[5]

The Board of Enquiry
The Court of Enquiry had been undertaken by Captain E.M. Evans-Lombe (HMS *Glasgow*, President), Captain J.P. Gornall (RNAS Worthy Down), Commander (E) R.C.W. Bett (RN Barracks Portsmouth) and W.R. Andrews (Constructor, DNC Department Bath) who were appointed on 10 September with proceedings commencing on 16 September 1942[6]. The Board was tasked with reporting into the 'circumstances attending the loss of HMS MANCHESTER and the internment of the bulk of the ship's company, in so far as this is possible from examination of the witnesses available'.[7]

The Board heard evidence from twenty-four witnesses, three of whom were officers – Lieutenant (Special Branch) Harold McCormack RCNVR, Lieutenant Cyril Kirk RNVR and Sub-Lieutenant James Munro. The witnesses, all of whom had escaped capture and internment by the Vichy French, recounted their experiences aboard the cruiser from the time that *Manchester* was torpedoed until the time she scuttled.

The Board was particularly concerned with the order 'Emergency Stations' and asked Sub-Lieutenant Munro what he knew of this arrangement. He replied that he did not hear the order 'Emergency Stations'.

The organisation of this affected everyone on board, he stated: 'All watertight doors which were open in action for any reason were immediately clipped fully. Such compartments that had men in them had a sentry on the watertight door whose duty was to ensure that the door remained closed. Any hands who were not required for the HA armament were sent to their abandon ship stations. The HA armament remained closed up. Any preparations necessary for abandoning ship were made by hands at abandon ship stations'. Munro added that, 'if we were in two watches the watch below went to their abandon ship station while the watch on deck manned the HA armament'.

Asked how long HMS *Manchester* had had this organisation, he replied, 'In the whole time I was in the ship – I think it sprang from when she was torpedoed before in the Mediterranean'.[8]

Petty Officer Albert Miller was asked to describe the organisation known as 'Emergency Stations' and replied, 'Emergency Stations were the HA people closed up at action stations and the remainder after closing all doors, to go to their abandon ship stations'.[9] When asked about 'Emergency Stations' Colour Sergeant Joseph Mullins said, 'our emergency station was to close up to our abandon ship stations unless we were detailed for any other stations'.[10]

Able Seaman Alfred Shepherd was present when Captain Drew addressed the ship's company before the ship was abandoned and reported that he said, 'he had done the best for the men on the ship. We could beat the Italians, we could get to Vichy France to being taken prisoner of war … nobody said that it was possible to get the ship under way.'[11]

The Court of Enquiry report dated 17 September 1942 established the following facts:

(a) Ship's Company including damage control parties were at Action Stations when the cruiser was hit by the torpedo fired by an E-boat.

(b) Damage control at first degree readiness and as far as can be ascertained all gear provided and doors closed.

(c) No evidence that oil fuel tanks in any way abnormal at time of strike.

(d) The ship was altering course to starboard when struck.

(e) Ship hit by a single E-boat torpedo between stations 155 and 198 and probably included Y.3 oil fuel tank. Compartments known to be affected were the after engine-room, Y.1 oil fuel tank, 4-inch HA magazine, clothing issue room and associated stores and the main W/T office. It appears that the watertight compartments and oil fuel tanks on the starboard side of the after engine room were open to the sea.

(f) The after engine room flooded quickly to water level putting port and starboard inner shafts out of action. The starboard outer shafts out of action probably due to direct damage.

(g) No.4 dynamo was put out of action and no electrical power was available abaft 155 station thus putting the steering gear out of action.

(h) Steam was maintained for a considerable period before shutting down–doubt exists whether secondary flooding occurred into the after boiler room.

(i) A split occurred on the lower deck in the Gunroom Flat.

(j) The forward hatch to the after engine room was blown open.

(k) Oil fuel was present on the lower deck in 'X' flat, the gunroom and bathroom flats.

(l) There was some structural damage in the Ward Room Flat.

(m) The ship listed about sixteen degrees to starboard.

(n) The following machinery remained in action immediately after the explosion:

(i) Port outer shaft which continued to steam until stopped to prevent the ship circling.

(ii) Both boiler rooms

(iii) No.1 steam, Nos. 2 & 3 diesel dynamos & all electrical power before 155 station.

(o) The following remedial action was taken:

(i) Counter flooding of ship reduced list to six degrees.

(ii) The Fire Main was re-established aft.

(iii) The rudder was centred by hand.

(iv) Power was supplied by emergency leads to the steering motors.

(v) Attempts to re-start the port outer engine failed once it had been stopped. The cause of the failure cannot be determined. The Commanding Officer's decision to abandon ship followed closely in point of time to the report of this failure.

(vi) The Commanding Officer ordered 'Emergency Stations' immediately the ship was damaged.

(vii) The decision to transfer a proportion of the ship's Company to HMS PATHFINDER was taken before the final state of the port outer engine was known (ten officers and 163 ratings transferred to PATHFINDER).

(viii) At the time of the decision of the Commanding Officer to abandon and sink the ship, the ship was not in danger of sinking but was incapable of steaming. There is some evidence to show that the Commanding Officer believed at the time that there was a chance the ship could be repaired sufficiently to steam at slow speed. The position of the ship at the time and the consequent tactical considerations appear to have decided the Commanding Officer not to attempt this chance.

(p) The ship was sunk by three scuttling charges in a position approximately five miles from Cape Bon in between twenty and thirty fathoms.

(q) Ship's Company advised to proceed to neutral Vichy territory. The weather conditions were such that there was no immediate imperative to get ashore but had the effect that only a small proportion of the ship's company were rescued by SOMALI and ESKIMO which subsequently appeared on the scene.

(r) The damage control organisation appeared to work well.

(s) The evidence shows that a premature opinion was created in the ship that she would have to be abandoned as evidenced by:

(i) Emergency Stations were almost immediately ordered after the damage occurred.

(ii) HMS PATHFINDER was ordered to embark a considerable proportion of the ship's company before it was certain that the ship could not steam (even if the latter was actually true).

(t) The organisation adopted for 'Emergency Stations' was dangerous. It entailed all seamen and marines, other than HA personnel, leaving their stations and preparing to abandon ship. This must inevitably react upon the determination of the remainder of the ship's company–as in fact it did.

(u) The decision to abandon ship was taken after it was known that the outer engine could not be moved under steam. The Court felt unable to express an opinion as to whether this decision was premature. However, it appears possible that the whole of the ship's company could have been rescued by British destroyers if this decision had been delayed to daylight. Furthermore, there is no evidence to show what was the reason for the seizure of the port shaft or that it could not have been rectified within this extra time.

(v) The Court was unable to form an opinion whether the ship's company should have been ordered to remain together until daylight or whether they should to steer northward. We are of the opinion that the advice that they should immediately pull for shore was premature under the conditions prevailing.[12]

The Assistant Chief of Naval Staff (F)'s minute on outcomes of Court of Enquiry, dated 2 October 1942, stated that:

I generally agree with the findings of the Court of Enquiry but there is no one who can speak with authority as to what reports were made to the Captain.

It cannot be stated positively:

(a) Whether or not the ship could have been got under way in the morning.

(b) Whether the Captain knew that other destroyers were coming later who could have taken off the remainder of the Ship's Company and so save them from internment.

The position in which the ship was sunk is not precise and therefore the possibility of recovery by divers of books, *etc.* (even though thrown overboard in chests) cannot be precluded. There does not appear to have

Top: HMS *Manchester* entering Portsmouth in August 1938. Note the HF/DF aerial, fitted to facilitate raider hunting, at her foremast head. (Wright & Logan)

Above: Another view of HMS *Manchester* entering Portsmouth in August 1938. (Wright & Logan)

Right: Troops and equipment being unloaded from HMS *Manchester* at Åndalsnes, Norway, on 25 April 1940. (Geirr Haarr)

Above: HMS *Manchester* (right) and her sister HMS *Southampton* (left) seen from HMS *Sheffield* during the Battle of Cape Spartivento on 27 November 1940. (Author's Collection)

Below: HMS *Manchester's* flight deck in July 1941 soon after the cruiser had been torpedoed during Operation *Substance*. (US Navy)

Officers on HMS *Manchester*'s compass platform during the early stages of Operation *Substance* in July 1941. (US Navy)

A view of HMS *Manchester*'s 'B' Turret during Operation *Substance* and after the cruiser had been torpedoed. Note the single 40mm Bofors gun on the turret top. (US Navy)

Personnel on the quarterdeck, abreast 'Y' Turret, after HMS *Manchester* had been torpedoed during Operation *Substance*. Note that the cruiser is listing to port. (US Navy)

Left: An exhausted, oil-soaked Lieutenant Commander R.L. Matheson emerges from a lower compartment after HMS *Manchester* had been torpedoed during Operation *Substance*. (Author's Collection)

Below: A diagram showing the lower deck flooding on HMS *Manchester* caused by an Italian aerial torpedo in July 1941. It has been annotated from someone in the Director of Naval Constructor's department to show the likely positions of the torpedo strike on the cruiser's port side.

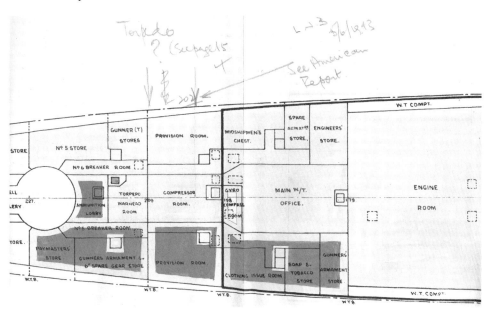

Above: An aerial view of the pillar that used to be part of the swing bridge between Sliema and the breakwater at the entrance to Sliema Creek after the failed Italian raid in the early hours of 26 July 1941. (Author's Collection)

Below: HMS *Liverpool* after being hit on her starboard side abreast her after engine room, by an Italian 17.7-inch aerial torpedo on 16 June 1942 during the *Harpoon* convoy to Malta. (Author's Collection)

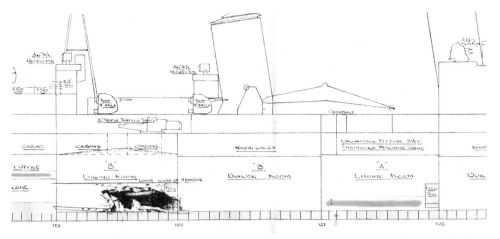

Above: A diagram showing the damage caused to HMS *Liverpool* when hit by an Italian aerial torpedo on 16 June 1942. Commander Robb believed that the torpedo that struck *Manchester* on 13 August hit abaft of the engine room on the starboard side.

Below: The AA cruiser HMS *Cairo* passing a burning merchant ship in the Mediterranean in 1942. Her loss on 12 August 1942 deprived the *Pedestal* convoy of one of its two fighter direction ships. (Author's Collection)

Below: HMS *Edinburgh* on 22 May 1942 showing her torpedo-damaged stern. The crippled cruiser was fought to the death in the freezing waters of the Arctic unlike her half-sister HMS *Manchester* which was scuttled prematurely in the much warmer Mediterranean. (World Ship Society)

HMS *Liverpool* in drydock showing the damaged caused by a torpedo hit abreast the starboard side of her after engine room on 16 June 1942. The damage caused to HMS *Manchester* on 13 August would have been similar but further aft.

Above: The Tribal-class destroyer HMS *Eskimo* pictured in 1942 wearing Western Approaches camouflage. She and her sister HMS *Somali* managed to pick up some of HMS *Manchester*'s survivors before they landed in Tunisia. (Author's Collection)

Below: HMS *Manchester* on 16 June 1942. Note single 40mm Bofors gun on 'B' Turret, type 284 gunnery radar on the LA. DCT on the bridge and type 273 surface warning radar in the lantern aft of LA.DCT. (Author's Collection)

Bottom: HMS *Manchester* in her final configuration. Note that there is a Walrus amphibian on her flight deck. (Author's Collection)

Above: The destroyer HMS *Pathfinder* on 22 May 1942. She came alongside the crippled HMS *Manchester* in the early hours of 13 August. The destroyer's certified engine room log was vital in the construction of the timeline showing the sequence of events after HMS *Manchester* had been torpedoed. (US Navy)

Below: A Walrus amphibian being catapulted from HMS *Manchester*. The cruiser used her amphibians to provide anti-submarine cover during the early stages of Operation *Substance*. (Author's Collection)

Top: HMS *Kenya* in drydock in Gibraltar on 18 August 1942 showing her torpedo damaged bow. Despite this damage she could still make 25 knots if required. (Author)

Above: Force 'X' under heavy air attack on 14 August 1942 while returning from Malta. HMS *Kenya*, seen from HMS *Charybdis*, is near missed by a salvo of bombs astern. (US Navy)

Above: The freighter *Dorset* on 13 August 1942 seen under air attack was lost later that day. It is possible to argue that the freighter might have reached Malta if the damaged HMS *Manchester* had been handled more resolutely. (Author's Collection)

Below: HMS *Nigeria* pictured after being torpedoed on 12 August 1942. The badly damaged cruiser was forced return to Gibraltar thereby depriving Force 'X' of its second fighter direction ship. (US Navy)

Divers swimming over the wreck of HMS *Manchester* – more specifically the 'A' Turret –
on 9 July 2009. (Chris Simons)

Above: Another view of HMS *Manchester*'s 'A' Turret taken by divers on 9 July 2009. (Chris Simons)

Below: Port side of HMS *Manchester*'s bridge showing LA.DCT on bridge and port HA.DCT. (Chris Simons)

Above: Divers examine the 6-inch guns of HMS *Manchester*'s 'B' Turret. Note the platform on which a single 40mm gun was fitted. (Chris Simons)

Below: Another view of the port side of HMS *Manchester*'s bridge taken by divers on 9 July 2009. (Chris Simons)

Above: Close up of the front of HMS *Manchester*'s bridge showing its rounded shape which was also found in her sisters HMS *Gloucester* and HMS *Liverpool*. (Chris Simons)

Below: Divers swimming over HMS *Manchester*'s 'B' Turret, 9 July 2009. Note the platform on which a single 40mm gun was fitted. (Chris Simons)

been any panic or disorganisation and the Captain appears to have made his decision deliberately and calmly and uninfluenced by immediate enemy action or danger of sinking.

Two courses appear to have been open to him.

(a) To sink her as he did because he believed the chances of getting under way were zero.

(b) To have taken the chance that she could steam slowly later in the morning. In this case he should have put his wounded and unnecessary personnel into *Pathfinder* and fought his ship through.

It is difficult not to feel after reading the evidence that the Captain's decision was wrong, unbalanced and showed a lack of determination. No further evidence or inquiry seems desirable at present but further enquiry into the whole circumstance should be made as and when other survivors return to the Country.[13]

The First Sea Lord's comment on the outcome of the Court of Enquiry on 7 October 1942 was predictable and damning:

As long as a ship remains afloat and has even one gun in action she may cause damage to the enemy. In spite of the sketchy nature of the evidence, I do not consider that there can be any doubt that MANCHESTER was sunk prematurely and that this shows a lack of determination on the part of the Captain which renders him unfit to command one of HM Ships. I am of the opinion that a notation should be made in the Captain Drew's record to the following effect:

All the available evidence pointing to the fact that HMS MANCHESTER *was scuttled prematurely. Captain Drew is not again to be employed in Command of one of HM Ships unless a further Board of Inquiry at which Captain Drew produces evidence which necessitates a reversal of the above decision.*[14]

The First Lord, A.V. Alexander, approved Pound's comments two days later and on 10 October the Naval Secretary recorded that the necessary notation had been made in Captain Drew's record.[15]

Chapter 11

Court Martial

On 25 November 1942, the Head of Naval Law reported that all interned survivors had returned to the UK. He observed that the Commanding Officer of HMS *Manchester* had not yet forwarded a report on the loss of his ship and should be ordered to do so. He also suggested that a court martial should be convened under section 92 of the Naval Discipline Act. Such an approach would be more rapid than convening a second Board of Enquiry followed by a court martial.[1]

Subsequently, on 30 November, Captain Harold Drew wrote to the Admiralty from his home in Oswestry acknowledging receipt of their letter of 30 November and stating that, as requested, he was preparing a report which would be forwarded as soon as possible. He went on to say that:

> It was not possible to prepare this during the period of internment at Laghouat after the loss of the ship, as I would have liked to do, as the French authorities were at that time pro-Axis in sympathy and seized any written matter. Otherwise, I would have had such a report ready for submission on landing in this country. In conjunction with some of my officers, I was however, able to draw up notes on the passage home, and it is from these that I am now preparing my report.[2]

Captain Drew forwarded his report to the Admiralty on 7 December 1942, and in his covering letter amplified his earlier remarks:

> I have had to prepare the report from notes which were made three months after the event, and it is probable that the times quoted are not accurate. The explanation of this is that I and other survivors were interned at Laghouat in Algeria, after the sinking. At this time the French authorities were not friendly towards us and had or appeared to have pro-Axis sympathies. All written material was removed from internees and occasionally searches were made of officer's quarters, and so I considered it inadvisable to write a report at this time. In order to prepare for the time

when a report could be written I discussed this with my navigator in the hope of keeping the facts as fresh in our memories as was possible.

As soon as we were out of the internment camp and on board the troopship homeward bound, I asked my navigator to write an independent appreciation of the situation after we were torpedoed which I have attached to my own. I also borrowed a chart from the captain of the troopship and with this we tried to reconstruct the time and track from the time that we parted company with the covering force until we were torpedoed.[3]

On 14 December 1942 it was announced that a court martial under section 92 of the Naval Discipline Act would be convened for the trial of HMS *Manchester*. Captain A.W.S. Agar VC, DSO, RN was appointed as Prosecutor.

Augustus Agar had won the Victoria Cross in 1919 for sinking the Bolshevik cruiser *Oleg* in Kronstadt harbour. He was appointed captain of the cruiser *Dorsetshire* in August 1941 and was on board her when she was sunk by Japanese carrier aircraft south of Ceylon on 5 April 1942. Agar was wounded in the leg by shrapnel and, when *Dorsetshire* sank, he was dragged down deep suffering the bends on the way up which caused permanent lung damage. He also swallowed furnace fuel oil on surfacing. The damage caused by the bends and the swallowed oil effectively ended his naval career and in 1943 he became President and Captain of Greenwich naval college. However, prior to taking up the appointment at Greenwich he had one last job as the Prosecutor at one of the longest courts martial in the history of the Royal Navy.

Captain Agar was particularly keen that Vice Admiral Sir Harold Burrough, who as a Rear Admiral, had commanded CS 10 and Commander E.A. Gibbs, the commanding officer of HMS *Pathfinder*, would be able to attend. However, wartime exigencies meant that neither could be made available and consequently Captain Agar had to make do with signed statements. Commander Gibbs also provided certified true copies of *Pathfinder*'s Deck Log and her Engine Room Rough Register.

Captain Agar was anxious to have the service of a Navigating Officer, an Engineering Officer and a Constructor to assist him in preparing his case and expressed this requirement to the C-in-C Portsmouth.[4] The latter made arrangements with HMS *Dryad* for the navigating officer but no Engineer Officer with sufficient modern experience was available locally. Consequently C-in-C Portsmouth approached the Admiralty inviting them to suggest a suitable Engineer Officer while at the same time asking if a Constructor Officer could be appointed.[5] The Admiralty replied on 28 December 1942 saying that Commander (E) F.B.C. Smith, was involved in the construction of the cruiser *Ceylon*, could be utilised as necessary, while the DNC wrote on 30 December that Mr Andrew RCNC will assist.[6]

During December, C-in-C Portsmouth announced that the court martial on the loss of HMS *Manchester* would be convened at Admiralty House, Portsmouth on 2 February 1943.[7] Prior to that on 22 January, C-in-C Portsmouth informed the Admiralty which officers were required to attend the Court Martial.

The Court Martial Convenes

The Court assembled on 2 February 1943, and was dissolved on 20 February. The Board consisted of Rear Admiral Clement Moody RN (President), Commodore 2nd Class Edward Chicheley Thornton DSC, RN, Captain Thomas Charles Armstrong DSC, RN, Captain Guy Hamilton RN, Captain Henry Gerard Laurence Oliphant, Captain Geoffrey Frederick Burghead and Captain Archibald Frederick Cooper OBE, RN, Deputy Judge Advocate of the Fleet.[8]

Before proceedings got underway Captain Drew asked to address the Court saying, 'I was very surprised when I arrived in Southsea last night, meeting several of my officers, to find that during the period I was at home, knowing nothing about what was occurring down here, the Prosecutor had been sending for them, that is the officers and men, and taking statements from them on the loss of HMS *Manchester*.[9]

Drew explained that he was not raising an objection but was concerned that they may both be contradicted and incriminating themselves as well as incriminating Drew himself. He expressed concern that any of his officers or himself might be confronted suddenly with a statement which because of lack of prior knowledge and therefore time to prepare a defence, could prove to be difficult to refute at the time. He went on say that 'my violent reaction to learning from my officers that they had been sent for, as far as I can make out, over a period of weeks and called upon to make and sign statements was that I sensed in it a considerable danger and possibility of complications'.[10]

The Deputy Judge Advocate pointed out that the Prosecutor had followed correct procedure. Captain Agar explained that he had no personal interest in the loss of HMS *Manchester* and that under King's Regulations and Admiralty Instructions (KR & AI) he had no option but to continue his duty and send for every officer and man on the ship, obtain a written statement of their evidence to be used, if necessary, as a summary of their evidence and to be placed in the Court.[11] The Deputy Judge Advocate then explained the procedure pointing out that there was no question of doing anything behind anybody's back. He explained that in this trial a witness will be called, and, if the Court thinks fit, will read from his written statement which was allowed in this particular section (KR & AI article 461) of the Act. He will then be examined by the Prosecutor verbally and then he will be subject to cross-examination by any person concerned. The Deputy Judge Advocate explained that any discrepancy in that statement can be dealt with in the cross-examination.[12]

Captain Drew replied 'that we have had plenty of warning of the questions to be answered but we do not know what anyone else has stated'. The President of the Court intervened saying, 'I think the Court will fully appreciate that view'.[13]

Proceedings then got underway with the presentation, to the Court, of certified true documents, including charts and the Deck Log of the destroyer *Pathfinder* that summarised the *Pedestal* operation. A statement, made by the Rear Admiral Commanding CS 10, was also read into evidence. A signed, written statement from Commander E.A. Gibbs was also read into evidence. In his testimony the commanding officer of HMS *Pathfinder* wrote: 'At 0140 I came upon *Manchester* stopped and listing to starboard in a position 095 degrees Kelibia Light 2.2 miles. This was my first knowledge of *Manchester* being in trouble.'

The destroyer's Deck Log for Thursday, 13 August 1942 read:

> 0142 Sighted MANCHESTER.
> 0154 Went alongside MANCHESTER which was stopped in positon 095° Kelibia Light, embarked 172 officers and Ratings.
> 0220 Cast off from MANCHESTER and proceeded at 30 knots.
> 0327 Sighted and engaged enemy E-boat.
> 0332 Sighted ALMERIA LYKES torpedoed and stopped. Persuaded crew to rejoin and endeavour to steam her to Malta. Signed EA Gibbs, Commander in Command.[14]

Captain Drew's Written Statement to the Court Martial

The next stage in the proceedings was that Captain Drew's statement was read into the evidence:[15]

> At 0120, whilst looking for the wreck of HMS HAVOCK in the vicinity of Point Kelibia, I sighted a suspicious object on the starboard bow, under the land. I suspected that it might be an E-boat. It was stationary. I ordered hard a starboard, full speed ahead port, and just as the ship commenced to swing to starboard, I heard the discharge of two torpedoes. The E-boat then started up its engines and went off at high speed towards the shore.
>
> The tracks of the two torpedoes could be seen approaching and the first one passed ahead of the ship. The second one struck the ship abreast the after engine room.
>
> The ship continued under rudder which remained hard over for a while, engines were stopped. She took a list of about 12 degrees to starboard. The position was 070 degrees -2 miles from Point Kelibia. After circling right round and then continuing to plane round until losing way, the ship came to rest heading 160 degrees.

113

We were about two miles from the shore in about 20 fathoms, on the edge of a minefield which was close to seaward on the port side. The ship was at that time unable to steam, stopped and listing to starboard. The night was very dark and there was no wind.

We were 38 miles from Pantelleria, and about 16 miles from Cape Bon.

While waiting for reports of damage I considered the situation, and what I might be able to do if later we were able to steam. The track towards Malta would pass within 22 miles of Pantelleria, the Italian E-boat and torpedo bomber base, i.e. four hours steaming at 10 knots.

The track towards the west at 10 knots was one and half hours from Cape Bon, two and three quarters from Zembra Island and six from Cani Rock. This route would have committed the ship to navigating the narrow channel one and half miles from the coast inside the minefield, until clear of Zembra.

I thought it would be unwise to proceed towards Malta as it would involve passing so close to Pantelleria in daylight, and because any air cover from Malta would be concentrated upon covering the convoy on its passage. I also considered it unlikely that Malta yard could do much for us in the circumstances existing at the time and also that our presence there might invite further air attacks on the island. I therefore decided if we were able to get under way at all, to attempt the passage to Gibraltar.

I had been torpedoed a year previously in MANCHESTER in the vicinity of Galita Island in a previous Malta convoy. On that occasion one propeller remained available and Admiral Somerville gave me a Hunt class destroyer as escort. After a three day passage with the assistance of my escort in beating off air attacks by torpedo bombers, and later with an escort of four destroyers from Gibraltar, I was able to get back into harbour.

Although my present condition was considered worse I was hopeful of being able to do so again if I could get out of the narrow swept channel and clear of Zembra Island before daylight.

The time was 0215, and the damage, repair and rescue parties were trying in the darkness to locate the limits and extent of the damage, correct the list and rescue survivors from the flooded compartments.

Sunrise was at 0630 and dawn at 0530. Actually first light occurred at 0500.

As we were so close to the shore I was confronted with the risk of getting into shallow water and grounding in one direction, or of drifting into that minefield in other direction. This latter risk was increased by the fact that the paravanes were then suspended below the ship.

I could hear E-boats to port and on the starboard, bow, and a further attack had to be anticipated momentarily together with its possible consequences.

The thought uppermost in my mind at that time was the possible consequences of receiving further damage so close to shore, vis the risk of grounding and of the ciphers, signal publications and confidential books becoming compromised by falling into other hands. I therefore ordered them to be destroyed and this was done.

I was then beginning to receive reports of damage. The port outer shaft alone remained intact, though steam was not then available, but it was thought [by Captain Drew] that we should be able to get it going in time, possibly in three hours.

The after engine room was flooded, the four-inch magazine was flooded together with adjacent compartments but the limits of the damage had not been finally established. Conditions below were naturally difficult, darkness, fumes and some wrecked machinery impeded works. The water in the after engine room was beginning to boil as a result of escaping steam and rescue work was urgent. The main W/T office was flooding slowly. Two dynamos were out of action and power was off the steering gear, but emergency leads were being rigged. Turret hoists were not working, and one turret which had been damaged the year before ['X' Turret] was suspect. One gyro compass was out of action. There was not much ammunition in the 4-inch ready use lockers after firing at E-boats, and this together with the flooded magazine, put a limit upon the further use of this armament. The port pom pom had been reported as temporarily overheated.

At about this time HMS PATHFINDER came alongside to see if he could be of any assistance. I decided to get away as many people as I could no longer use, such as the 4-inch personnel. About three hundred men were sent, as many as PATHFINDER could take. Before he left I informed him that there was an E-boat ahead to starboard. I saw him engage it and the next morning I found it aground and damaged.

I continued to review the situation and to consider how best I could extricate the ship from this situation, and ensure above all that she did not run aground or fall into the hands of the enemy or sink in water so shallow that salvage operations of any sort would be possible. It seemed to me that I must prevent this at all costs.

The risk of it lay in our close proximity to the coast line of Tunisia and the existence of the minefield, and the probable result of further attacks. I formed the opinion that to save the ship for the time being from this immediate risk depended upon time and being able to get clear of the coast into open waters before daylight, unless I could have an escort who could if necessary sink the ship to prevent her from grounding in the event of her being damaged whilst still in the channel.

The information available to me about our own forces was that FOH [Flag Officer Force H] had withdrawn to the westward covering INDOMITABLE which I had seen about 1000 heavily on fire as the result of a dive-bombing attack. NIGERIA and CAIRO had both been torpedoed that same evening to the northern end of the Skerki Channel. KENYA had received underwater damage right forward, but was not apparently seriously damaged. CHARYBDIS, detached by FOH to help CS10 was making a rendezvous with him but I had not sighted her. CS10 in ASHANTI, KENYA and three destroyers with sweeps, and two ships of the convoy had proceeded ahead of me towards Malta after I was torpedoed. PATHFINDER I sent on to join CS10 at about 0250.

I know that CS10 hoped to make the return passage through this swept channel at high speed the following night and hoped to be clear of Galita Island by daylight. I could not therefore expect to see him for about 24 hours. Two more ships of the convoy passed me steaming slowly to the south about this time, one of them a tanker [inexplicably Captain Drew felt that it was OK for damaged straggler merchant ships to continue to try and get through to Malta but not for his 12-knot cruiser!]. That accounted for four ships of the convoy. Seven had been sunk as far as I could remember and there were another three unaccounted for, and I assumed they were somewhere between me and Skerki Channel if they were still afloat.

I therefore expected no assistance from Fleet units as CS10's force had already suffered considerably and what remained was fully occupied trying to get the convoy to Malta. I concluded from this that anything I did must be done alone as I had no escort. I recall that I considered the situation I was in as being the same as if an enemy cruiser lay damaged and stopped two miles from the north coast of Devon in the Bristol Channel with a minefield close to the north of her.

The situation confronting me was, (a) That if I were able to turn the ship round, and go ahead soon enough, I might be able to get clear of the coast and past the island of Zembra before daylight during darkness. (b) That if I could not get clear of the swept channel before daylight and were subjected to air attack close inshore in these narrow waters, with a damaged and probably unescorted ship, effective avoiding action would be extremely difficult and the probability of grounding would be considerable. (c) That at the moment I could not steam at all.

I considered them each in turn. As regards (a) it was obvious that a damaged ship without escort or air cover, in this open area, Zembra – Cani Rock – Galita Island, would be subject to heavy air attack. (24 hours later CS10 on his return through this area at high speed, was heavily attacked from the air.)

I was prepared to accept this course with its unavoidable risk, as in those more open waters it did not improve the possibility of so valuable a ship falling into enemy hands through grounding. She could but be sunk by the attacks if they were successful, and might proceed towards assistance if they were not. I considered that (a) should therefore be attempted if it were possible.

As regards (b) I found it impossible to reduce the problem to so simple an issue. In the event of my being confronted by (b), I had to decide finally and alone, if I could reasonably expect to get clear of the coast in daylight or not. If in my judgement, the consequences of failing to do so meant that the ship would certainly fall into enemy hands then I was bound to accept the responsibility of sinking her myself. I decided I must get clear before daylight or not at all, because if she received further damage before getting clear, I would have no time to ensure that she did not ground or sink in shallow water.

I formed the opinion that so large a ship should not be allowed to be caught close inshore and damaged in daylight with no escort.

I pondered this very carefully, and it appeared to me that I must therefore think of situation (a) and decide the latest moment at which I should go ahead if steam became available. The correctness of my decision to sink the ship if that moment passed would then depend upon whether I was right in assuming that air attacks at dawn were a certainty. The subsequent arrival of torpedo bombers at first dawn confirmed this assumption [this seems academic as he issued the Emergency Stations order in such haste virtually no options were left open to him!].

I estimated that I should have the ship turned and pointed north and go ahead by 0245 to clear Zembra one hour before sunrise. I could not do so later unless I were to ask CS10 for assistance. I was not prepared to do this, and deemed it my duty to do nothing which could embarrass him in his fulfilment of our main objective of getting help to Malta.

I had sent PATHFINDER off by then to rejoin CS10. I estimate that the time by then was 0250. The ship was still heading 160, and would take a considerable time to turn to the northwards with only one propeller, even if the original estimate of three hours required to make steam available could have been improved upon.[16]

Steam was not available and the moment to go ahead had already passed. With great reluctance I therefore decided that I must accept the responsibility of sinking the ship.

At 0300 I told the Commander to clear the lower deck and get everyone on the flight deck. At 0320 when the ship's company were assembled there in the darkness I came down from the bridge and spoke to them. I explained the situation as I saw it, and told them of my decision to sink the ship and with what reluctance I had reached it. After I told them the steps that I wanted taken including the destruction of RDF sets and the launching of rafts, I warned them to carry out the work silently as we could still hear E-boats and there might be a reasonable chance of their not finding us for a while longer.

Their loyalty to me however rejected the precaution of silence and they gave me three very hearty cheers together with expressions of sympathy and friendship.

I instructed Commander (E) and Torpedo Officer to make the necessary arrangements for sinking. Shortly after I told the Commander to start getting the men away, leaving the short range weapons crews until the last.

Towards 0500 I told the Commander (E) to take the necessary action. Sea cocks were then opened and charges over the condenser doors fired. I then left the ship together with the three senior officers and about 30 ratings, in a whaler. The time was a little after 0500 and the early dawn light had commenced.

As we pulled away from the ship she was listing to starboard and down by the stern. At that moment an Italian torpedo bomber appeared from the direction of Cape Bon flying at a height of about 200 feet. It was quickly followed by another flying much lower over the water. This second machine fired two torpedoes at the ship at a range of about 100 yards but our boat must have interfered with his aim as they missed just ahead. The ship then sank.

The last thing I did before leaving the ship was to make a signal to CS10 by short range, giving him my position, the depth of water, and wishing him luck. I have since seen him in Algiers and learnt that he received the message but in a rather garbled form.

By about 0545 there were about six torpedo bombers flying low over the water in our area examining the rafts. Two of them flew south towards a steamer the tops of whose masts and funnel we could just see from the whaler. I believe this was the GLENORCHY. They torpedoed her and she sank. She blew up after she had sunk and a large column of black smoke and flame rose to a height of about 3,000 feet. An Italian E-boat which was cruising inshore then came and examined the rafts. They took one of my lieutenants and a midshipman off one of the rafts and asked them where I was.

They were subsequently released by the French authorities. There were altogether three E-boats inshore, one anchored and possibly damaged, one aground and damaged and a third cruising about. They and the aircraft appeared to be using the coast as their own.

The progress of the rafts and boats towards the shore was naturally very slow. The whaler in which I was had a small wooden raft in tow and it took us nearly three hours to reach the shore. The majority of the men landed by 0830. I landed a little nearer to the village about 0900, by which time the main party had walked around to the same point. Some rafts remained to be brought in.

Later on whilst sitting in a room where I had been put by the French I heard the fire of automatic weapons and learnt that two destroyers had been sighted steaming north. The time was then 1000. They were able to pick up a number of our men still out there on rafts. I discovered recently that these destroyers had been sent by CS10 to sink two ships of the convoy to prevent them falling into the hands of the enemy.

His report was completed by an approximate timetable of events (Captain Drew was nearly an hour in disagreement with *Pathfinder* as to her arrival and departure):[17]

0130	Torpedoed. Swinging slowly round one circle and then planing round to 160°.
0200	Ordered destruction of secret protocols and confidential books.
0215	Receiving first reports of damage.
0230	HMS PATHFINDER came alongside. Decided to transfer a number of men to her.
0250	HMS PATHFINDER left to join CS 10.
0300	Cleared lower deck.
0320	Spoke to ship's company.
0340	Work in hand placing charges.
0400	Rafts started to leave ship.
0500	Ordered sinking.
0510	Left ship.
0900	Landed.

In his attached appreciation of the sinking Commander Gill essentially supported Captain Drew, noting that it was about 02.15 hours that he started receiving different reports from Commander Hammersley-Johnston, Commander Robb and the Lieutenant Commander Duff as to the state of the ship from a steaming and fighting point of view. He had estimated that the ship could not have been out of the narrow restricted waters between the minefield and the Tunisian coast before full daylight.[18]

It was now Captain Drew's turn to give his evidence. The Prosecutor asked, 'have you or any of you anything to object to in the narrative just read to the Court or anything to lay to the charge of any officer or man with reference to their conduct on the occasion of the loss of HMS *Manchester*?' To this Engineer Commander William John Robb replied that he objected to the part of the narrative which deals with three hours delay before steam would be available.[19]

It must have seemed to Captain Drew that his worst nightmare had just begun. The battle lines had been drawn and would result in some acrimonious exchanges between Captain Drew and Commander Robb and his team of Engineering Officers.

Chapter 12

Captain Drew's Evidence

Captain Drew was taken through the events leading up the torpedoing of his ship by the Prosecutor, along with the commands that he gave up to the time that the ship came to a stop. Captain Drew observed that he did not expect assistance from any other ship and that the chance of fighter cover from Malta was limited. It was also understood that he had received information referring to the presence of some Italian cruisers and destroyers at sea that might be going to attack the convoy. He had been given the positions of relevant minefields off the Tunisian coast.

Captain Agar asked: 'What were the ship's standing orders regarding action to be taken in the event of a breakdown of the rudder?'

Drew replied: 'I do not think that were any standing orders, in fact I should consider it to be very wrong to lay down beforehand what was to be done if a mechanical breakdown occurs in the ship. We had frequently practised breakdowns of the steering gear … the ship's organisation followed the usual practice of the Fleet in that we had parties trained to deal with every form of breakdown and emergency which experience had taught us to anticipate.'[1]

Drew was questioned in detail about the centring or not of the rudder after the damage had occurred. He eventually admitted that he assumed the rudder had been centred and only later noticed the rudder indicator on the bridge [the indicator lights were out]. He could not remember the position of shaft indicator or if the rudder indicator lights ever came on again.[2]

The Prosecutor then began to explore the order 'Emergency Stations' and its implications, asking Drew what it meant in his ship? 'The principal thing,' said Drew, 'was to get the ship in to a state where an emergency could be met and it also included the destruction of CBs, ciphers and SPs.[3] This was an organisation which we had on board had frequently practised.'

Drew agreed that he had ordered the destruction of CBs and SPs within thirty minutes of the ship being hit but was unclear as to whether or not he had actually ordered 'Emergency Stations'. When pressed on this point he admitted that he could not remember when or how he gave this order and could not recall the actual standing orders regarding 'Emergency Stations'. He said that it did not include RDF for example.

The examination then proceeded as follows:

> Agar: How did it for instance affect the crew of the ship?
>
> Drew: Well, most of them by virtue of the fact that we were already at Action Stations were with the stuff they had to destroy.
>
> Agar: As far as the crew were concerned was there any relation between Emergency Stations and Abandon Ship Stations?
>
> Drew: I am afraid I cannot remember, it is a question of remembering Standing Orders. I do not think anybody can.
>
> Agar: What was the state of the ship's company when you gave this order 'Emergency Stations'?
>
> Drew: We had been at Action Stations almost continuously day and night for about two days and we had adopted a system of stand down, or stand to, in order to try and give people some little rest. It meant for instance, in a gun's crew, they could sit down in the vicinity of their gun, leaving one or two standing up and the telephone manned, and as regards officers, some officers were able merge duties that were carried out close to each other during the period of stand down.[4]

The Prosecutor then produced a document headed '*Manchester* Damage Control Orders', which had been deposited with the Director of the Damage Control School, and asked Captain Drew to turn to the relevant section before asking:

> Agar: In the light of these orders is there any relation between Emergency Stations and Abandon Ship Stations?
>
> Drew: Yes, I see that it refers to the cooks, stewards and supply ratings. When any of the above are completed they fall into stations for abandon ship, that is, after putting out galley fires and evacuating patients from sickbay.
>
> Agar: Will you read out the last part of the paragraph before the one you read regarding engine room ratings? My question was the relationship between Emergency Stations and Abandon Ship Stations?
>
> Drew: Any ratings not with stations detailed above proceed on deck and fall in at their Abandon Ship Stations.[5]

After exploring how Captain Drew had ascertained the position of his ship and the depth of water beneath it, the Prosecutor explored the damage reports received on the bridge, their timing and their content. Captain Drew eventually admitted that he had received the first reports about half an hour after the ship was torpedoed:

Agar: What were these reports?

Drew: I think that the first one was that the steering gear was defective, because the lower steering station reported that the rudder had not gone amidships. I rather imagine that the next report came from the Gunnery Officer but cannot remember the sequence in which I received these reports. They were coming through sometimes verbally and indirectly. The Commander (E) came on the Bridge, I should say a little bit later than this time, not very much, but a little later and told me that the Port outer shaft alone remained intact, but that steam was not at that moment available. I discussed this with him, and asked him how long he thought it would take. My impression is that he said something like this, 'I think we shall be able to get it going again,' and he told me he was waiting for a further report, and as a result of that I had an impression that this might take as much as three hours, but of course he had not had his report. I think that the position was that speaking with his experience as an engineer officer he suspected something, just like a Doctor might make a diagnosis and was waiting to have it confirmed. Other reports were that the turrets were not operative, they had no power. The two 4-inch Directors were out of action, that is, they were not usable at that time. I am not sure whether they were permanently out of action. One dynamo was out of action and a second one was nearly out of action because it apparently kept on slowing down. The after engine room was flooded, the 4-inch magazine, the Paymaster's store and I think the Electrical Spare Parts store on the starboard side.[6]

The Prosecutor now drew Captain Drew's attention to the damage sustained in July 1941 and was answered by a detailed account and also information about the speed available after that damage had been suffered. Next the Prosecutor explored the paravanes and their possible recovery to facilitate passage through mined waters, before addressing the issues of E-boats and the destruction of CBs etc.

Agar: Were any steps taken to recover the paravanes?

Drew: No

Agar: In your paragraph 25 you refer to the presence of E-boats on your port and starboard bow. Were any steps taken to counter them by starshell or searchlight?

Drew: No[7]

Agar: Did you order any specific signal book, cipher or charts to be withheld from destruction, temporarily or otherwise?

Drew: Only charts and anything such as the orders for Operation *Pedestal* which were under the control of Commander (N) who was with me on the bridge. He went down later on, an hour or so later, to destroy the relevant charts. The point I am trying to make, is what was actually in our hands on the Bridge we kept in our hands.[8]

At this point the Prosecutor turned to a more detailed exploration of reports made to the Bridge in an attempt to establish the sequence and import of the reports received by Captain Drew. The latter reported that the events were now too distant [actually six months] for him to remember with precision but he felt that many of these were verbal reports. He agreed that the initial reports were made before the arrival of *Pathfinder*.

Captain Drew said that he had received a report that the 4-inch magazine had flooded and estimated that he still had about 300 rounds of 4-inch shell in ready use lockers, mainly on the starboard side because of a long-running battle with E-boats just before being torpedoed. Questioned about the offensive capability of *Manchester* at the time that *Pathfinder* came alongside he stated that the main turrets had no power, the 4-inch guns had no control and little ammunition, some compartments were in total chaos and rescue parties were doing what they could. Captain Drew said that he had not received any reports as to what steps were being taken to restore power.

Regarding the restoration of power to the main armament, the Prosecutor asked: 'Did you expect your turrets to be in action again power-operated?'

Drew replied: 'Well, I do not know that I can say that I expected them all to be, because the situation so closely resembled my previous experience of that sort when only the forward turrets were usable. With ships of that type the structural damage is apt to distort the structure and jam turrets so that they are intractable or stiff and that is what happened to us before; so my opinion to that extent may have been coloured by previous experience.'

Turning to the arrival of *Pathfinder* alongside, which was reported to Captain Drew by Commander Hammersley-Johnston, the Prosecutor asked what action Drew took:

> Drew: I told the Commander to get as many people who were no longer usable, including the wounded, into *Pathfinder* and as far as I remember I told him that I had no intention of retaining the *Pathfinder* as I felt she should press on and support CS10.
>
> Agar: How many people did you want to get rid of?
>
> Drew: I had to leave it to them to decide; it must have been with so much of the ship and equipment no longer usable, the men who were no longer usable would go. In my opinion it would be far better to disembark them as soon as there was an opportunity and they could go on and carry on with the war.
>
> Agar: Did you give a guide to the Commander what it was you wanted, one third, a quarter, an eighth, or part of a watch or a watch; did you give any guide as to how many men you were to send to the

Pathfinder?

Drew: I say the only thing said was to get in as many men as you did not want.

Agar: You further state in paragraph 30 with regard to personnel you sent to the *Pathfinder*, you stated as your aim to get as many people away as you could no longer use, such as 4-inch personnel. Did you send the 4-inch personnel to HMS *Pathfinder*?

Drew: I don't think so, I really don't know who went to the *Pathfinder*; it is very difficult under those conditions to say this or that.

Agar: Did you send your 6-inch personnel?

Drew: I don't think so, actually I don't know.

Agar: Will you more clearly define to the Court the term 'unusable'?

Drew: I do not think that I can make it much clearer, if you have, for example, a piece of machinery that can only be used ...

Agar: I said 'personnel.

Drew: I am coming to that ... the personnel who would work that machinery are no longer usable, their services are no longer required for that machine.

Agar: Would you apply that term to the magazine and shell room guns crews?

Drew: Yes, certainly, if their machinery or weapon was out of action. I will put it another way. I felt that here, or rather there, was a ship in a precarious position; there was no doubt that at some time in the very near future, in such a position as that, the southern end of what is known as 'bomb alley', that she was going to receive some very active attention from the enemy. My natural instinct was, if there are any men who need not remain to go through that experience that I ought to send them away if I could do without them. I should not only save their lives but would return to the Service highly trained men to be back in appointments with the Fleet. That is a question of motive.[9]

Captain Drew said that as far he as he could remember there was no material change in the condition from the time *Pathfinder* arrived and the destroyer left. Asked if he felt that there was any prospect of getting his ship underway again at the time that *Pathfinder* left Captain Drew said that he was awaiting reports.

At about this time in the proceedings there was considerable discussion regarding the timing of key events. Once a timeline had been established the Prosecutor explored the possibility of getting *Manchester* underway again:

Agar: Now I am referring to the time that HMS *Pathfinder* left, and by agreement this is 0220, namely one hour ten minutes after the ship was hit: seventy minutes. What prospect did you estimate you had of getting the ship under way?

Drew: Well, it all depended on having steam. Do you mean physical prospects or tactical prospects?

Agar: Physical prospects?

Drew: Well, I had been told that we expected to get things going on the port outer shaft.

Agar: Who told you?

Drew: In my previous reply I said that the Commander (E) told me that he was waiting for a report to confirm what he thought the trouble was and when I returned to my review of the thing at this time that the situation had not changed.

Agar: I would like to ask you, observing the time interval was seventy minutes after the ship was hit, had the Commander (E) or any other officer confirmed those reports that you had first received?

Drew: I do not quite understand the question; he had not said anything else.

Agar: I will put it this way: it has been established that this phase was seventy minutes after the ship had been hit; how many reports had you received from the Commander (E) up to that time?

Drew: I don't really know.

Agar: At what time, taking as a basis 0220 as the time HMS *Pathfinder* left the ship, can you tell the Court about your appreciation of the situation?

Drew: I think so, that is what we were trying to do just now.[10]

Captain Drew clearly had trouble relating this to the timing of events and after an adjournment attempted to address this issue:

Agar: How did you know that your ship could not steam at all: you have stated that your ship could not steam at all?

Drew: At that time.

Agar: How did you know this?

Drew: Because steam was not available.

Agar: What was the last report you had regarding steam?

Drew: That it was the opinion of my Commander (E) that he would be able to get it going again.[11]

The questioning then turned to the consideration of Captain Drew's definition of 'clear of the coast', which he had put in his written statement and the time taken to achieve that aim. Captain Drew was of the opinion that *Manchester* would have had to travel forty-two miles while the Prosecutor suggested that the actual figure was thirty miles. In essence both were right it being a matter of judgement as to exactly when the ship would be clear of the coast. However, the Prosecutor was trying to show that by opting for the greater distance Captain Drew may have inadvertently brought forward the last possible time for the cruiser to get underway so as to clear the coast by daybreak. Captain Agar then explored the timing of the decision to scuttle *Manchester* as well as Captain Drew's understanding of the condition of his ship at the time that the decision was made:

> Agar: I now refer to paragraph 47 of your narrative. In this paragraph you state first that steam was not available and secondly that you had decided to sink the ship.
>
> Drew: Yes.
>
> Agar: Will you tell the Court at what time that decision was made?
>
> Drew: I should say a little before three (i.e. 0300)
>
> Agar: On what information did you base your decision with regard to the steam that was available?
>
> Drew: I am afraid I do not understand that.
>
> Agar: What reports had you by that time received regarding the steam available?
>
> Drew: I don't think that I had received anything further.
>
> Agar: Before that decision was taken how many reports had you received from the Commander (E) ?
>
> Drew: I should say only one.
>
> Agar: Had you received, before that decision was taken, any further reports from the Gunnery Officer regarding the state of the ship's armament?
>
> Drew: No I do not think so.[12]

In response to a subsequent question about additional reports from the torpedo officer, Captain Drew stated that the events concerned had happened too long ago for him to remember the minutiae of exactly who had reported what:

> Agar: Was a conference held prior to making that decision [to scuttle]?
>
> Drew: As far as I can remember I expressed growing anxiety about being still there at day light, first of all to the Commander and then again later to the Navigator and on another occasion, if I remember rightly, I said the same thing to Commander (E) and the torpedo officer because I wanted it realised that time might be important. Those remarks were not a conference. Later on I should imagine just before I made the decision I did ask the Commander and I cannot remember who the others were (one or two other officers) ... and I think I told them I wanted to explain what I had in mind. I rather think I quoted precedent and what chances seemed to me to weigh up as. I am afraid that is rather clumsy end to a sentence. If that is a conference, then there was one.

Agar: Can you say if any material progress had been made?

Drew: Yes, I think power was being restored at the fore end of the ship; I am not sure about searchlights. I know that an upper deck lead of power to the steering motors was being run, I don't think I can say more.

Agar: What instructions were given to the ship's company as to their future action after the ship was abandoned?

Drew: I told them that I wanted them to proceed towards the light, that is Kelibia Light, and wanted them to go about their preparations quietly and not to waste time because I did not want them to be in the water over the side about daylight, where, if a further attack were made, the explosion of a torpedo would kill very large number numbers of men.[13]

At this point the Prosecutor concluded his examination of Captain Drew and the Deputy Judge Advocate informed Captain Drew that he was going to be cross-examined by Commander Douglas Hammersley-Johnston, Commander (E) William John Robb, Lieutenant Commander Daniel Alexander Rawson Duff and Lieutenant Russell.

Cross examination by Commander Hammersley-Johnston

After exploring several issues Commander Johnston asked Captain Drew to address the issue of 'Emergency Stations' aboard HMS *Manchester* and in particular the consequences of ordering 'Emergency Stations':

Hammersley-Johnston: Will you read to the Court the paragraph about the closing of watertight doors?

Drew: When the order is passed 'Close Watertight doors' or 'Collision Stations' or 'Emergency Stations', it can be understood that the safety of the ship takes precedence over the fighting efficiency of the ship below decks. All compartments, therefore, are to be evacuated, closed and fully clipped except for the Watchkeepers in the following:

Engine rooms, boiler rooms, steering gear, diesel dynamo room, telephone exchange, No.1 lower power room, HACPs, main switchboard, lower steering position, main and auxiliary wireless offices.[14]

After addressing other issues Commander Hammersley-Johnston turned to the question of damage reports:

Hammersley-Johnston: Do you remember what my movements were immediately after the torpedo hit the ship?

Drew: As far as I can remember you went below.

Hammersley-Johnston: Do you remember how long afterwards it was before I returned?

Drew: I think that it was about the time of *Pathfinder*. I am not really certain.

The Prosecutor then expanded the subject by asking: Were any compartments ordered to be evacuated before the lower deck was ordered to be cleared? Drew replied: 'I think I have already mentioned the shell rooms and magazines and the 6-inch quarters, from which personnel were brought up to the lobbies after the torpedo explosion.'[15]

Cross Examination of Captain Drew by Commander (E) William John Robb

Commander Robb had clearly disagreed with his Captain that steam would not be available for three hours. Consequently, his cross examination was aimed at establishing that the port outer engine was available and that the notion that steam would not be available for three hours arose because of a leading question asked by Captain Drew himself. As the cross examination proceeded, Commander Robb clearly became frustrated by his commanding officer's inability to recall critical events in what must have been the most dramatic and stressful few hours of his life.

Robb: After the ship was hit, by what means was the order to stop engines given?

Drew: So far as I know I said 'Amidships, stop both' and the Officer of the Watch repeated that order to the lower steering position.

Robb: Did you receive a report from the lower steering position that this order had been obeyed?

Drew: I think I was informed that the wheel had been put amidships, but that the rudder had not responded.

Robb: As regards the engines, Sir?

Drew: No, I do not remember being told, but it is not customary to report back to me on the bridge the compliance of such orders, but rather to report to me if they have not been complied with. It may help you, however with your question if I were to repeat what I stated at the beginning of this answer. There was a period when I was under the impression that a port engine was still working, and so far as I remember during that period, I must have expressed the opinion that this was so and said 'Get that engine stopped'. My reason for doing this was that having heard that the rudder had not replied to the wheel, I knew that the correct action must be ensuring that the rudder would be centred if it were possible, and that if that happened and I was right in assuming that the engine was running, the ship would then have either steamed on into a minefield or onto the shore. I recall, however, that the ship did come to rest, and I afterwards assumed that it must have been an illusion and that I was mistaken in thinking that the engine was still running.

Robb: You have stated in your reply that you did not expect a report of compliance with your order if this was carried out, but only if it were not carried out. Was such a report made to you by the officer of the watch?

Drew: I think if I am not sure it would be fairer to ask the Officer of the Watch, and actually I am not quite sure about that.

Robb: You will recollect Sir, that when asked by the Prosecutor, I questioned a statement in your narrative to the effect that you concluded from my first report that steam might not be available on the port outer engine for about three hours?

Drew: Yes, I do recollect that.

Robb: Is it possible that a mistake arose as the result of the question which you put to me asking whether it would take up to two or three hours if the trouble was not what I thought it was, because it is my recollection that you did ask me that question?

Drew: Yes, I think that such a thing is quite possible, knowing my usual method of approaching questions of that nature; I usually say to whoever I am questioning if he has not given me an approximate forecast something of this sort: 'Can you tell me, is it a matter on hour, or two or three hours, or merely a matter of minutes?' The purpose of such a remark as this is to try, without pinning you down to an opinion which you probably cannot make, merely to try and persuade you to give me some idea of the sort of delay that I might expect. If that occurred I should think that might be a possible explanation if you did not say anything which would clear my mind on that point.

Robb: I would suggest to you, Sir, that my first report made it clear that there was every possibility of the port outer engine being ready very shortly, that is as soon as the main circulator was restarted. Would you agree?

Drew: I am afraid I can see nothing in that that enables me to contradict my previous statement in paragraph 28 of my report where I said 'Though steam was not then available, but it was thought that we should be able to get it going in time, possibly three hours'. I really think that in the absence of any other statement from you other than expression of opinion, that it is a very fair comment. I would like to add that, that I do not wish it to be thought that I had any doubts about ability in the matter.

Robb: No, Sir. In view of the interval which occurred before you received any further report from me, did you consider that something might have happened to me, and in consequence, in view of the situation did you consider the possibility of making an enquiry from the forward engine room to find out when the port outer engine would be available?

Drew: I think that this is a difficult question at this stage, because I cannot recollect whether you immediately left the bridge after making your report and did not come back for a long time or not. I cannot recollect that I was comforted by the thought that you personally were attending to what was necessary.

Robb: Do you recollect meeting me at the bottom of the ladder to the bridge after there had been some cheering?

Drew: No, I would not like to say 'Yes' or 'No' to that. You remember it was a very dark night and I saw you on that night on one or two occasions or even more, on the bridge. I think if the answer to that question is vital, I might be able to help you more if you go on a bit further.

Robb: May I recall to your mind, Sir, the fact that you did meet me and that I made a second report to you?

Drew: No, I do not think I can agree there. If you mean as regards steam what I do recall is that somewhere about the time that I made my decision to sink the ship, I seem to recall that the Commander said, 'Oh here is Robb', and you spoke to me about what I thought was some suggestion for further adjusting the trim. But I certainly do not remember any report at all on steam.

Robb: May I remind you, Sir, that I reported to you on that occasion that the after engine room was flooded, and I had a rescue party under way, that one engine was definitely correct, and leads were ready to connect to the steering motors, and I asked you if there was a chance of going on. This is when I met you at the bottom of the ladder to the bridge after there had been some cheering.

Drew: No I do not think that is correct. The report you made to me about the outer shaft being intact and engine room flooded and so on, was when you first came to the bridge. I am not sure that I remember you reporting leads to the steering engine, and my impression was that the torpedo officer made that report to me, but that probably is of no importance at this stage. I seem to remember that when I finally made my decision we were on the bridge, and the Commander, the Commander (N), and I certainly thought you were there, and I made other junior officers withdraw because I wished to speak to you all. I think that point I must develop further for the benefit of the Court when I have an opportunity myself of cross-examining other witnesses.

Robb: Do you remember, Sir, my accompanying you to the bridge after the cheering?

Drew: Well I was not aware that anyone accompanied me. It is a ladder that only one person can climb at a time, and in the dark there were several people going up and down this ladder, so that I should not be aware that anybody was accompanying me after speaking to the Ship's Company and when I had finished, it would inevitably occur that a large number of people would be moving about in that particular area.

Robb: May I further recall the incident, Sir, by asking if you remember me telling you that I should require the ammunition and shell rooms opened if you finally decided to flood, and that you asked the torpedo officer to see to it?

Drew: I cannot recall that I remember that conversation, but it strikes me as a thing that might quite easily have happened.[16]

The Prosecutor then asked Captain Drew about his opinion as to the state of his ship at that time and he replied that it was the same as at 01.54 hours [i.e. when *Pathfinder* came alongside] with regards to moving the ship.

In his brief cross examination Lieutenant Commander Duff asked Captain Drew why he accepted 01.54 hours as the time *Pathfinder* came alongside and was told that this was time agreed by the Court. At this point the President of the Court intervened and pointed out that 01.54 hours was the time stated in *Pathfinder*'s certified deck log.

The next stage in the proceedings was that Captain Drew was cross-examined by Lieutenant George Vincent Blakely Russell RN:

Russell: Do you remember, Sir, whether I was included among those officers you called on one side to tell them of your decision to sink the ship?

Drew: No I am afraid that I cannot remember.

Russell: You do not remember, Sir, my asking you on that occasion whether we could not at least see what we could do in speed?

Drew: Yes, I certainly remember that, although I do not recollect it sufficiently clearly to say on what occasion that was. But I said to you that as soon as the engines were ready we would see what we could do.

Russell: Is your memory sufficiently clear, Sir, to say definitely whether or not the steering motors had been reported as ready before you made your decision to sink the ship?

Drew: No, I am afraid that it is not Russell. I do know that you or somebody told me they were going on well. I rather think you described using some shore connections to run your leads along the upper deck instead of between decks.[17]

On completion of his testimony, Captain Drew, who had seemed to become increasingly vague and somewhat evasive during his cross-examination withdrew, to await the testimony of his officers and ratings.

Chapter 13

Statements by Key Witnesses

Once Captain Drew had given his evidence, the Prosecutor then called other key witnesses to build a comprehensive picture of the last few hours aboard *Manchester*.

In particular he was trying to establish the exact condition of the cruiser after the torpedo exploded, the timeline of events and decision making, while at the same time probing for evidence of failures in communication and of a possible lack of resolve.

Evidence of Commander Harold Britton Clifford Gill RN

Commander Gill had joined *Manchester* on 4 June 1942 as Squadron Navigating Officer when she was flagship of CS 18. During the night of 13 August he had formed the opinion from the conversation he had overheard on the Compass Platform that the extent of the damage was such that 'we should be able to steam on the Port Outer Shaft, at about 10 knots in 2 to 3 hours' time'.

It was then between 02.00 hours and 02.15 hours and he went to the chart table with the intention of forming a plan ready for the Captain. About half an hour after the explosion *Pathfinder* came alongside, starboard side aft. He heard the Captain order the ciphers to be destroyed about the time *Pathfinder* came alongside and consequently Commander Gill removed all charts with SECRET marked on them and these were incinerated along with all operation orders, etc. Gill kept the local chart which they were working on and also the Mediterranean passage charts on the bridge–these were burnt later as he left the bridge for the last time. After *Pathfinder* shoved off he discussed the navigational situation with the Captain who then held a conference on the Bridge but excluded Gill. Captain Drew cleared the fore end of the bridge for this. A discussion took place, but he did not personally tell Gill of its outcome, though Gill gathered that Drew had decided to sink the ship saying 'I must make the decision myself'. Thereafter the lower deck was cleared and hands mustered on the Hangar Deck. Gill did not hear what Drew said to the hands.

In his evidence Gill said that 'the ship came to rest only fifteen to twenty minutes after the torpedo hit and that the compass was undamaged and he was able to get an accurate bearing on Kelibia Light but that the Gunnery Officer was unable to provide a range using RDF'.

Gill said that he attempted to ascertain the depth of water but the sounding machine was non-operational. He sent for the Chief Quartermaster to take soundings by line but this was not done. Therefore he estimated the depth at twenty fathoms with reference to the ship's estimated position on the chart. The Prosecutor and Captain Drew both asked detailed questions about the navigational situation. The President of the Court later got Commander Gill to report that the bearing to Kelibia Light was 250 degrees and this remained unchanged over a period. He said that there was no drift despite earlier attempts by Captain Drew to try to get Gill to admit to strong offshore breezes which had sprung up by midday on 13 August.[1]

Evidence from Temporary Instructor Lieutenant Ian Leslie Summerton RN

Lieutenant Summerton, who had joined *Manchester* on 10 April 1942, served as Plotting and Meteorological Officer. He recorded the time of the torpedo strike as 01.10 hours on Thursday, 13 August 1942.

In his written statement he said that about five to ten (later amended at his own request to 'at least' thirty) minutes after the hit Sub-Lieutenant Preshaw came down with a message from Commander (N) to collect what documents he had, and destroy them. He did this by burning them in the incinerator. About five minutes after that he and the Schoolmaster were asked by Commander Hammersley-Johnston to report to the quarterdeck and ordered to join *Pathfinder* which left about five minutes later (at 01.50 hours).[2]

At this point Captain Drew questioned the proceedings pointing out that lack of prior knowledge of the evidence being given especially with regard to times could result in witness incriminating one another especially with regard to prepared witness statements. The Court President replied that the witness statement was but one aspect of their evidence and that the Court was keeping an open mind as regards timings. The witness reaffirmed that the torpedo struck at 01.10 hours by his own watch which was within two minutes of the Plot clock.[3]

Evidence from Lieutenant Bryce Harben Clinkard RN

He had joined *Manchester* on 15 February 1942. His action station was in 'B' Turret and he reported that at 00.50 hours the Type 273 radar detected E-boats on bearing approximately Red 50 (i.e. port).

At 01.12 hours by the clock on the chart table one torpedo was sighted approaching on a bearing of about Green 30 (i.e. starboard). The first torpedo passed about ten feet from the ship which had turned ten degrees to starboard, at a speed of thirteen knots when a second torpedo was

133

sighted on a similar course as the first but about 200 feet nearer the stern. This torpedo struck on the starboard side. The Captain ordered 'Midships' and 'Wheel amidships' but the rudder indicator still showed 'hard-a-starboard'. Very shortly afterwards the Captain ordered 'stop both'.[4]

In his written report Clinkard wrote: 'I remember, but I am not sure at what time, the Captain ordered "Everyone up from below". About ten minutes after we were hit Commander (E) came up and reported to the Captain on the Bridge. I heard him tell the Captain that we had been hit in the after engine room and that that compartment and some compartments abaft the engine room on the starboard side had flooded, and that the ship would certainly remain afloat. Commander (E) then left.'[5]

Evidence of Petty Officer Samuel Edward George Phillips

Petty Officer Phillips joined *Manchester* in September 1938 and was Chief Quartermaster at the time of her loss. His action station on board was the Lower Steering position. After being requested to describe the events of 13 August he was asked:

> Agar: You have stated that you received the order twice to 'come up' from the lower conning tower. Can you say who gave that order?
> Phillips: No
> Agar: Can you say how you received the order?
> Phillips: It just came through the voice pipe 'Come up'.
> Agar: What action did you take when you received that order?
> Phillips: The wheel was already amidships and I ordered everyone up out of the compartment.[6]

Phillips was then cross-examined by Commander Hammersley-Johnston as follows:

> Hammersley-Johnston: Did you report to the bridge that the wheel in the lower steering position had no effect on the rudder.
> Phillips: I cannot remember.
> Hammersley-Johnston: Did you receive the order from the bridge 'Stop both engines'?
> Phillips: No.[7]

When cross-examined by Commander Gill he was unable to give an estimate of how long it was after the explosion that he reported to the charthouse. In response to a question from Lieutenant Malim, Phillips stated that a Leading Stoker and a Stoker were down in the Lower Steering position with him but could not remember if they left that position with him.

Phillips was next questioned by Engine Room Artificer Third class John Wilfred Desmond: 'Did you as Chief Quartermaster receive any specific orders with regard to the lower steering position after you had vacated the compartment?' Phillips' reply was that, 'When I was on the bridge and reported to Commander (N) he told me I might have to close up again'.[8]

He was then asked by the President of the Court if he had taken any precautions about the watertightness of the ship before leaving this compartment. Phillips replied, 'next to the steering, there was the main switchboard and we all had to go through the same manhole and there was still a switchboard watchkeeper down there'.[9]

Evidence from Able Seaman William Conlan

He had joined *Manchester* on 10 April 1942 serving as her helmsman. He confirmed the order, 'Come up' but did not recognise the voice which had given it. Thereafter he had carried large numbers of books, etc. to the incinerator room. He was cross-examined by Lieutenant Malim:

> Malim: When you received the order to come up from the lower steering position who was present within the compartment?
> Conlan: I do not remember.
> Malim: Do you remember a Leading Stoker and a Stoker in the lower steering compartment?
> Conlan: They were attending the Damage Control Switchboard.
> Malim: Did they show any signs of leaving when you were ordered to come up.
> Conlan: No.[10]

By now it was becoming clear that the after steering position may have been abandoned prematurely and possibly without proper authorisation as a consequence of the order 'Emergency Stations'. Consequently, the Court recalled Petty Officer Phillips who wished to add to the evidence given the day before, explaining that the time taken to come up from below from the lower steering position included time taken to go the Captain's flat and back again and then report to him in the charthouse. He added that the whole of the after part of the ship was in darkness.

Captain Drew then asked him about timings and received the vague reply: 'Well, Sir, it is rather a job to think of times. I am trying to stress that I went aft and came forward with the ship all in darkness. It must have taken some time.'[11]

Evidence of Yeoman of Signals Thomas Henry Cardiff

Thomas Cardiff, whose action station was the Flag Deck, had joined *Manchester* in July 1938 but was on the Compass Platform at the time of the torpedo strike.

At about 00.15 hours he had heard two explosions ahead of the ship which he presumed were two mines exploding in the mine sweeping gear of the destroyers ahead. Cardiff confirmed that the torpedo hit at about 01.15 hours and that the order 'Emergency Stations' was given about twenty minutes later. Commander (E) Robb was concerned about events on the bridge and asked:

> Robb: Regarding the Captain's request for the Commander and Commander (E) to report to him on the Bridge, can you remember how long after the hit that request was made?
> Cardiff: I should about forty minutes, Sir?
> Robb: Do you remember my arrival on the bridge?
> Cardiff: No Sir
> Robb: Did you see me on the Bridge?
> Cardiff: No Sir. Actually sir, after that I was down getting people along for the books so I would not have seen you go up.[12]

Evidence from Lieutenant John Haddon Akam, Royal Marines

Akam had joined *Manchester* in May 1942 and his action station was in the 6-inch office in fore DCT.

Akam provided first-hand evidence of the debilitating effect of the order 'Emergency Stations' on *Manchester*'s fighting ability, saying that 'after Emergency Stations were broadcast round the ship by pipe the crew of the DCT left the DCT and that was the last I saw of them'.[13]

Evidence from Gunner David Turner RN

Turner, who had joined *Manchester* on 2 April 1941, reported that whilst on the quarterdeck, a Stoker reported to him that the hand steering was ready and could he have some hands to work on it. He said, 'I detailed four hands accordingly', but when questioned by Commander Robb was unable to relate the timing of this event to the arrival or departure of the destroyer *Pathfinder*.[14]

Evidence from Midshipman James Leonard Gaythorne Carson Parker

Under cross examination by Commander Robb, Midshipman Parker, who had joined *Manchester* on 30 April 1942, remembered the Coxswain getting up the Confidential Books and speaking to Robb. He could not remember anything that the Coxswain said but said that the incident occurred after *Pathfinder* had come alongside.[15]

Evidence by Lieutenant Commander Daniel Alexander Rawson Duff RN

Duff had joined *Manchester* on 4 January 1941 as First Lieutenant and was the Gunnery Officer when *Manchester* was lost. He reported that the 6-inch turrets had suffered power failure, the 4-inch guns were in local control and that the 2-pounder guns and Oerlikon guns were 'alright'. Furthermore, that at the time *Pathfinder* left 'A' and 'B' turrets had regained power while

'X' and 'Y' turrets did not regain power. No reports had been received from the 4-inch Directors starboard and aft, and Duff said that Commander (E) came up on the bridge to see the Captain but was not sure when and could not say that he heard anything definite as to what was said between Commander (E) and the Captain. After revealing that the radar equipment was still operational he went on to estimate that about 280 4-inch rounds remained available.[16] The Prosecutor then explored what this meant in terms of the volume of AA barrage fire:

> Agar: Assuming that was the case can you tell the Court in terms of fire against enemy aircraft the value of that quantity?
>
> Duff: Yes I can.
>
> Agar: Will you do so.
>
> Duff: 288 rounds represents thirty-six rounds per gun and at the rate of fire which was in use in the ship for AA targets this would have been just over three and half minutes firing.[17]

Having established that *Manchester* would only be able to use her 4-inch HA armament for a relatively short time, the Prosecutor turned to the question of how and why the forward 6-inch gun armament was reduced to local control:

> Agar: Now I come to the point where you state that on your own initiative you ordered the TS crew up from their stations. What was your object in this?
>
> Duff: The object was to carry out the policy of preventing possible but unnecessary loss of life. As already stated in my Captain's narrative we had brought the shell room and magazine crews of the 6-inch armament up to the ammunition lobbies whenever there was no immediate prospect of them being employed. I had received a report from DCT as from the TS that they had no communication with the turrets. I had received a report from the Captain of 'B' Turret that 'A' and 'B' turrets had no power. I fully expected either 'A' or 'B' turret to lose power but I did not expect both of them to do so in view of the fact that they were supplied normally from opposite sides of the ring main. I concluded that both sides of the ring main were temporarily dead. I did not expect power to be renewed in 'X' and 'Y' turrets for some time and therefore I ordered the Director to tell the TS crew to come up to the mess deck above which was their normal waiting position when not required below. They were told to close the man holes.
>
> Agar: When you gave this order to whom did you intend that to refer?
>
> Duff: The whole 6-inch TS crew.[18]

The Prosecutor now turned to the vexed question of just what Captain

Drew knew about his ship's remaining armament and what reports had been made to him by Lieutenant Commander Duff:

Agar: Now I refer to your statement as to the power failure to all turrets. You stated that you expected one, at least one section of the ring main to be dead but not both sections. Was it reported to you at any time that power had been restored to either 'A', 'B', 'X' or 'Y' turrets?

Duff: Yes, sir, I said in this statement that power was reported as restored to 'A' and 'B' turrets by the Captain of 'B' Turret and I stated between 15 and 20 minutes after *Pathfinder* left.

Agar: Did you report this to anyone and if so whom?

Duff: I cannot remember whether I reported it to the Captain at that time.

Agar: Did you see any of the TS crew later after you had given the order 'Abandon the TS'?

Duff: No I did not.

Agar: Was any personal report made to you from the officers in the TS or the HACP after the ship was hit?

Duff: No.[19]

Captain Drew was concerned to establish just how much usable armament *Manchester* had left after being torpedoed:

Drew: I would like to confirm that during the time after the torpedoing until I gave certain orders affecting the personnel of the ship, in your opinion, so far as you could see, there was no useful armament at which men were not closed up. I have not put that very well – do you understand it?

Duff: Yes.

Drew: Then will you answer this question: can you confirm that this was the case?

Duff: Yes, sir I can.

Drew: Will you help me for a moment in a little matter of time. You state that fifteen to twenty minutes after HMS *Pathfinder* left, I think it is on page four, 'the Captain of 'B' Turret reported that they had regained power'. Where were you at that time, and where was he?

Duff: The Captain of 'B' Turret was on top of the turret and in order to receive a report from him I had to lean over the front of the bridge.

Drew: You were on the bridge?

Duff: Yes.[20]

He was cross-examined by Commander Robb but could give no information as to the conversations held on the bridge between Drew and Robb or as to the speed that the ship might be capable of once steam became available or even if the ship could be got underway at all. Robb was also interested in the state of the main armament at the time the decision to scuttle was announced by Captain Drew:

> Robb: Do you suggest that after the Captain's address to the ship's company you returned to the bridge and received reports as to power being restored to 'A' and 'B' turrets?
>
> Duff: No, I do not suggest that. I stated that the interval was not very long but I only came to that conclusion because I do not remember anything particular and so many events occurred during that time; but I have already stated that the whole time amounted to some three and a half hours.
>
> Robb: Would you be concerned with receiving reports, regarding the turrets after the Captain addressed the ship's company?
>
> Duff: No, I would not.[21]

This last response prompted a follow-up question from the Prosecutor:

> Agar: With regard to the answer to the last question, why would you not be concerned in those reports?
>
> Duff: When he addressed the ship's company the Captain had already made his decision. The fact that damage had occurred in the after part of the ship indicated to me quite clearly and I felt sure to him as well, that any failure of turrets or other machinery in the fore part of the ship could not be anything other than temporary.[22]

At this point Warrant Officer Reddy decided to cross-examine Lieutenant Commander Duff about the availability of 'X' and 'Y' turrets. The questions asked were of a very technical nature and this episode would come back to haunt WO Reddy the following day.

> Reddy: You have stated that I reported loss of fire to 'X' and 'Y' turrets; did I make any report at that time about main air supply?
>
> Duff: No, I do not think you mentioned it.
>
> Reddy: Was not the subject of using the main air as a means of alternative training to the turrets discussed at that time?
>
> Duff: I do not think it was. You and I were both quite clear in our minds about that, about the possibility of air training after an extensive trial which we had carried out at Scapa Flow in which we found that unless the air from the ship's air main was available it was not practicable to train a turret by air and use the air blast at three guns for more than some thirty broadsides using the air bottle.
>
> Reddy: Can you recollect any mention being made in the course of that report of the after air compressor.
>
> Duff: No, I cannot say that I do remember.[23]

It was agreed that about thirty broadsides could be fired using air training.

Evidence of Commander Douglas Hammersley-Johnston MVO, OBE RN

Commander Hammersley-Johnston, who had joined *Manchester* on 1 August 1940, was cross-examined by the Prosecutor regarding comments to Captain Drew about *Manchester*'s situation. He replied that 'as far as I can remember I remarked to the effect that as the ship's hull would keep her afloat the whole thing boiled down to the time it would be before we were able to steam or get under way'.

When questioned by Lieutenant Commander Duff, Hammersley-Johnston confirmed that he had sent the port watch, less the 4-inch gun crews, to *Pathfinder*.[24] Lieutenant (E) Malim tried to get the Commander to agree that there was still enough steam to drive the port outer engine for twenty-five minutes after the torpedo explosion but Hammersley-Johnston said that he was not in a position to do so.[25]

Under cross examination by Commander Robb, Hammersley-Johnston said that he had made a mental note that 'the damage would be very similar to the previous occasion' but did not remember passing this on to the Captain. He also expressed surprise that Captain Drew had said that the steering motor was not yet ready during the conference some hours after the torpedo hit – especially as repairs of this sort had been practised frequently.[26]

Asked when he knew that the Captain was considering sinking the ship, he replied: 'On my return to the bridge after casting off from HMS *Pathfinder*.' Under further cross-examination he confirmed that this was at 02.30 hours and that this was three and a half hours before dawn, assuming 06.00 hours as dawn. It was agreed by the Court that in practice that day it would have two and a half hours to first light.[27]

Robb referred to Captain Drew's statement that he had consulted officers when compiling his narrative after being released from captivity and establishing the time-table of events, before asking, 'were you included in these consultations?'

The President of the Court informed Hammersley-Johnston that he was not required to answer. Changing tack, Robb asked, 'do you know whether I (Commander Robb) was included in these consultations?', to which Hammersley-Johnston replied 'I do not know'.[28]

Evidence of Gunner Eric Whiteside

Gunner Whiteside revealed that about 350 rounds of 4-inch AA shell were in Ready Use lockers at time of the explosion.[29]

The next to give evidence was Commander Robb, the man who firmly believed that Captain Drew should not have abandoned ship. The real battle over the sinking of HMS *Manchester* was about to begin.

Chapter 14

The Damning Evidence

Commander William John Robb was duly called to give his verbal testimony. His written statement has been included in full in an earlier chapter and, consequently, this chapter deals only with his cross-examination:

Agar: How many officers and ratings were on duty in the after engine room before the ship was torpedoed?

Robb: One Engineer officer, one Chief Mechanician, one ERA, one Mechanician, one Stoker P.O., one Leading Stoker and six ratings.

Agar: Of these, how many were evacuated after the explosion?

Robb: Two stokers and possibly a leading stoker.

Agar: Am I right in that there were 9 casualties, that is missing presumed killed, in the after engine room?

Robb: Yes, Sir.

Agar: Was the ship previously damaged when you were aboard?

Robb: On 23 July 1941.

Agar: Who were the Senior Officers then on board?

Robb: Captain Drew, Commander Hammersley-Johnston, Captain (E) Coleby, myself as Senior Engineer, Lieutenant Commander Clark was the Torpedo Officer, Lieutenant Commander Duff, the Gunnery Officer.

Agar: Can you state briefly the nature and extent of the damage sustained by the ship on that occasion?

Robb: The ship was struck by a torpedo from an aircraft in Y.4 oil fuel tank about 198 port. The deck of 'X' flat, port side was blown up practically to the deckhead overhead. The compartments flooded were the after engine room, the 4-inch magazine, the Midshipmen's chest flat, 'X' magazine, the port Provision room, 'X' shell room. Flooding extended over the lower deck along the lower deck along the port side and when the ship was at its maximum list flooding was halfway up the scuttles.

Agar: Again quite briefly would you state the effect of that damage?

Robb: The list of the ship was twelve to fifteen degrees subsequently

141

corrected. Secondary flooding then occurred over the starboard side and the ship had a list of about one and a half degrees to starboard and the flooding water on the lower deck went across. The effect as regards machinery was very similar to the last occasion; three engines out of action and one available; one turbo-dynamo out of action.

Agar: So far as the effect on the machinery was concerned on that occasion what speed were you able to maintain?

Robb: We maintained twelve knots for the first part of the journey; subsequently the speed fell off for some reason that the Navigator, Lieutenant Commander O'Dair, was not able to explain by any conditions of set.

Agar: To your knowledge, could you say the distance travelled on that occasion, the one with the propeller unit?

Robb: No I cannot Sir, but, I think we got into harbour on the evening of the third day after we were hit.[1]

After discussing the damage sustained in August 1942 the Prosecutor asked:

Agar: On the previous occasion when the ship sustained damage what was the effect, if any, on the steering gear?

Robb: The steering motors failed; the watch-keeper changed to hand steering gear, the ship was not stopped, it circled round and continued back to Gibraltar on hand steering. Within a short time leads were run and steering motors restored at a time convenient to the bridge.[2]

Commander Robb was then cross-examined by Drew who was keen to establish that while the damage suffered on 13 August 1942 was very similar to that incurred in July 1941, the ship's situation was much worse because of the close proximity of the Tunisian coast.

Drew: I will deal with the Prosecutor's last question first of all, he asked you about the ship steering by hand steering about a year before when we were torpedoed in the Mediterranean. Can you re-call if the ship was out of sight of land at the time?

Robb: I don't know, Sir.

Drew: Would you assume that the position, assuming that we were out of sight of land would be materially different from my point of view to the night of 12-13 August?

Robb: Yes, Sir.

Drew: Referring to your evidence that you have read out, page one, are you certain that the order 'Stand down' was passed after the gunfire from our ship to which you refer?

Robb: I heard no 'Stand to' from the last 'Stand down' I heard until the ship was hit.

Drew: That does not really answer my question. I said are you certain that the order 'Stand down' was passed after the gunfire from our own ship to which you refer.

Robb: No, Sir, I cannot be certain.

Drew: How do you know that between midnight and 01.00 there were some alarms with gunfire from our own ship and that manoeuvring of engines took place with 'full ahead' on one side or the other, etc.?

Robb: That is my general impression of the state of affairs at that time. Generally it had been going on all day long, we had had these orders 'full ahead' one side or the other on every previous occasion.

Drew: You have stated on oath that between midnight and 01.00 in the morning manoeuvring of engines took place with 'full ahead' on one side or the other, etc., you are certain of that?

Robb: To the best of my knowledge, Sir.

Drew: Are you aware that during the period we were cruising close inshore astern of the sweeping destroyers with our Admiral in *Ashanti* close astern of us and other ships present and that in their reports there is no mention of any occurrence of this nature?

Robb: I presume, since the reports have been read in Court, that which you state can be borne out.

Captain Drew was asked to revise his question by the President of the Court. He therefore said:

Drew: Are you prepared to believe that during the time you mention, that is midnight to 01.00, no such manoeuvring took place until avoiding action just before the torpedoing of the ship?

Robb: I am prepared to believe it based on the information you have given me, Sir.[3]

The President of the Court pointed out that no witnesses summary after such a length of time could be regarded as absolutely accurate. Nevertheless, Drew reminded Robb that in his written evidence he had stated that he had arrived on the bridge ten minutes after the ship was torpedoed. Drew then asked Robb if it was possible that this time was also unreliable. To this Robb answered that indeed this was quite possible.

Captain Drew's line of questioning now changed to consideration of events on the bridge and the availability of the port outer engine. Drew must have been stunned to learn at the start of the court martial that, contrary to his own belief that steam would not be available for three hours, his Chief Engineering officer thought otherwise. His cross-examination of

Commander Robb produced some heated exchanges as Drew sought to try to establish exactly what had happened that night:

> Drew: I now refer you to the statement you made to the Court before you read your evidence, as to the report of the conversations; would you agree that in fairness not only to me but to other officers that these conversations, which you have stated are not reliable but only a record of the impressions that you had, should be regarded with the very greatest reserve?
>
> Robb: No, Sir. I deny that I said the records were unreliable. I consider that they are reliable.
>
> Drew: You record that when you came on to the bridge to report to me that a telephone call came from Lieutenant (E) Malim and that you asked me to talk to him about shafts, after you had discussed with me what might be the matter with the port outer, I take it you would agree with that?
>
> Robb: Yes, Sir, we were discussing the port outer.
>
> Drew: Yesterday Lieutenant (E) Malim told the Court that he told me that the port outer was alright and could be used. If I am correct in that how do you account for the fact that you and I then go on to discuss how long it will take to get it right again?
>
> Robb: My conversation with you on the bridge fell into two distinct halves with an interruption in the middle. In each half there are certain phases. It is quite possible that the phase of discussing the engines occurred before Lieutenant (E) Malim's report. You did not tell me what Lieutenant (E) Malim's report was.
>
> Drew: From your reply then may I assume that with reference to p.5 [of Robb's statement] as well as p.4 that much of this recorded conversation is not in its proper sequence?
>
> Robb: No, Sir. I have only said that it is possible that Lieutenant (E) Malim's report occurred after the discussion about engines but I am sure it occurred before you explained the tactical situation to me.
>
> Drew: I have so far made no reference to the tactical situation or the *Pathfinder*.
>
> Robb: Yes, Sir, you have referred to p.5.
>
> Drew: Yes, but the sequence of things on p.5 is what I refer to not their context. In this recorded conversation on p.4 was it clear to you that I was under the impression that the port outer shaft was intact but that it was not usable?
>
> Robb: There was no reference to the engine being intact, the question did not arise.
>
> Drew: You stated a few moments ago that in this part of the conversation we were in fact talking about the port outer. Do you agree to that?
>
> Robb: Yes, Sir.

Drew: Do you think in a situation like that, that there was the one thing I wanted to know above other things?

Robb: Yes, Sir and I made it perfectly clear by my reply that it was only a matter of restarting the main circulator.

Drew: Do you agree that you replied, 'I cannot say without seeing what is wrong, but I am confident that it will be alright and can quickly check up on it; if it is no good we shall have to take our chance on the port inner, it was still revolving when I left'? That reply is recorded in answer to my question which read, 'And if it is not [alright] what do you think and how long will take to put it right?' Do you agree that I have correctly quoted your evidence?

Robb: That was in reply to the question 'Will it take two or three hours?'

Drew: Have I correctly quoted your evidence?

Robb: Yes.

Drew: With regard to this having to take our chance on the port inner, in your reply I see you say on p.3 'I knew the after engine room was probably flooding through the shaft bulkhead gland into the forward engine room'. Also on p.3 you say you had been informed by the Damage Control Officer of the state of affairs in the vicinity of the after engine room. Do you think that you were properly informing me of the things I should want to know by suggesting that I could expect to use the port inner?

Robb: I was suggesting that the state of the after engine room required further investigation; what I had in mind was the fact that we had recently been fitted with arrangements for steaming with a partially flooded engine room. My information regarding damage at the time was very vague and I did not feel it would be right at that time to give up all hope of doing something with the port inner.

Drew: Do you remember coming to the bridge to report to me and using the words 'The port inner is intact'?

Robb: No, Sir, I do not.

Drew: To refer again to your p.4, you state, 'I can quickly check up on it', in your evidence; after that you record what looks like a lengthy conversation on Malta and Gibraltar and so on. Do you not think that in that critical time if you had stayed on the bridge discussing tactics that I should have chased you off down into the engine room?

Robb: The position was, Sir, that you did not take up the point about checking up on the engines, you continued to talk to me and you dominated the conversation.

Drew: If I did not take up this question of getting the one and only engine in use why do you suppose I said 'Is the engine you have had to stop ready for use now?' and then later 'If it is not what you think it is, how long will it take?' and then later 'Will it take two or three hours?'

Robb: I had told you, Sir, it was only a matter of restoring the circulator.

I had subsequently said that we could quickly check up on it; as you did not take up that point I assumed that as you used the term and that you were clear that my opinion was that the engine would be all right. If you had not, I assume that you would at once have said 'Please check up on it' or words to that effect. I re-call at the time feeling that it was a strange question to put to me and also remember saying that if the trouble was not what I thought it was I thought that it would be more serious and I could not say how long it would be. Then I followed it up by saying 'I am confident that it will be all right and can quickly check up on it'.

Drew: Yes, that is what I re-call too, but I cannot understand how knowing that I wanted the answer in view of your statement 'If it is no good we shall have to take a chance on something else' I cannot understand how you suggest that instead of checking up on it you and I appeared to have gone on with a very long conversation about matters which are scarcely engineering.

Robb: That is what happened, Sir.[4]

Drew then questioned Robb about his knowledge of the tactical situation, etc., before asking Robb if he had confused the sequence of events as he went from the bridge to the steering via the 4-inch gun deck. Robb replied that he remembered being surprised to find *Pathfinder* still alongside as he had told her to go away when ready.

Drew: If the Court desire it, I could call some witnesses who were with me on the bridge to show that after thanking the *Pathfinder* we stood and watched her steam away without more delay than was necessary for casting off her lines, would you agree that it would be impossible for you then to have visited all those places in so short a time?

Robb: No, Sir, I would not agree, I think that it is well known that I have been in the ship for two and three quarter years and can move very quickly even in the dark. As an officer, I can shout gangway or gently get round people who were in my way and I did in fact move very quickly from one place to another as I was anxious to get back to you.

Drew: Now later on, on p.9, you reported that the after engine room was flooded, rescue parties working there and so on and one engine was definitely correct and leads were ready to connect to the steering motor. Would it be possible that you may have made that report earlier?

Robb: No, Sir, I had no information about the steering gear until I left the quarterdeck.

Drew: But if the ship is torpedoed and the torpedo bursts in the engine room as this one has been stated to have done, would you expect water to come in or not?

146

Robb: Sir! I had no information that the torpedo was in the engine room until I got there and found it Sir. You did not tell me Lieutenant (E) Malim's report.

Drew: On p.3 you describe that you called and saw Lieutenant (E) Malim before your first visit to the bridge and you say then 'I knew the after engine room was flooding by the leak through the shaft bulkhead gland into the forward engine room but not to what extent'. Do you agree to that?

Robb: I agree that I stated that Sir, and that was the extent of my knowledge.

Drew: I have been rather puzzled by the general trend of your evidence and am anxious to have it clear that it was not dictated by any apprehension on your part. Will you tell the Court if I, as your Captain, ever expressed any dissatisfaction with your conduct on this or, for that matter, on any other occasion?

Robb: Not to me Sir, or, to my knowledge to anybody else.[5]

Robb was then cross-examined by Commander Hammersley-Johnston who, after enquiring about engine room registers and, later, hose connections to the forward engine room, turned to the events of 23 July 1941.

Hammersley-Johnston: I refer to the replies given to the Prosecutor's question about the previous damage to the ship in 1941. In that reply you state the speed as twelve knots subsequently falling off; in your evidence you said you told the Captain he could expect to steam between twelve and thirteen knots. Which is correct?

Robb: It is correct that in 1941 we got twelve knots which subsequently fell off. The exact speed on one shaft definitely cannot be forecast as it depends upon the state of the wreckage and drag on the ship.

Hammersley-Johnston: Was there any reason to suppose that on this occasion we could obtain a higher speed on one shaft than on the previous occasion when, as has been already stated, the circumstances concerning the damage were very similar.

Robb: Judging purely by the list being less than last time I assumed that there was a possibility of the damage being if anything less. Further, as Engineer Officer of the Ship on this last occasion, whereas on the previous time I was not, I was prepared to put a degree of overload on the engines if desired and provided that the vibration of the hull was not unacceptable.

Hammersley-Johnston: What time of day was the ship torpedoed in1941

Robb: Around 10 am.

Hammersley-Johnston: Was it daylight?

Robb: Yes.

Hammersley-Johnston: Would it in your opinion take a longer time to connect the emergency leads to the steering motors when working in darkness than it had on that occasion?

Robb: Possibly but not necessarily.[6]

Robb was then cross-examined by Warrant Engineer Allan Frederick Budden RN:

Budden: Do you remember having a report from me in the Damage Control HQ as to the state of the boilers and the action I had taken?

Robb: Yes, I remember a report from you but it was so far as I can remember after my second visit to the Captain.

Budden: Do you remember what it was, Sir?

Robb: As far as I can remember it was that you had shut down in 'B' boiler room, that 'A' was all right and I replied, as far as I remember, that it did not matter now it was not required.[7]

After an adjournment, the President of the Court addressed Commander Robb:

President: Can you estimate how long before you heard the Captain tell the *Pathfinder* to shove off you arrived on the bridge?

Robb: Not very long, Sir, I only remember my report, a little conversation and Lieutenant (E) Malim's report.

President: What was the first occasion on which you reported to the Captain that one engine was definitely correct?

Robb: In my first report I stressed the fact that it looked the same as the last which I think …

President: You must stick to the point. I mean the first occasion on which you reported that one engine was definitely correct.

Robb: In my first report I said that we should have one engine available immediately, in my second report I used the exact words 'One engine is definitely correct'.

President: And the second report was when?

Robb: When I met the Captain returning to the bridge after I heard cheering.

President: Of your knowledge was this report made to the Captain in any other way, that is, 'One engine definitely correct?'

Robb: Not to my knowledge, Sir.[8]

By this stage in the proceedings it must have become clear to all concerned that Commander Robb and his team of engineers believed that *Manchester* had been abandoned too soon and without a proper evaluation of her true circumstances.

There now followed a succession of witnesses from the ship's engineering department and Robb used his cross-examination of them to make that point. In particular he believed that the port inner engine remained intact and might be restarted if the after engine room could be pumped out. That being the case it might be possible to get more speed provided the vibration was not excessive.

Testimony of Warrant Engineer Oliver John George RN

Mr George stated that at about 01.10 hours there was a sudden 'Emergency full speed' order, and that an explosion followed at 01.15 hours. The ship took an immediate list of eleven degrees to starboard:

> Amongst other things, the Port Main Circulator had tripped – this was rectified in about 2 minutes. The gauges in the Forward Engine Room showed that there was between 340 – 350lbs of pressure in both boilers in the Forward Boiler Room. The port outer shaft was still running. I subsequently received, about 10 minutes after being hit, an order from the bridge by word of mouth to stop the port outer shaft. This was done by shutting off the steam and this was made known by way of the reply gong. A turbo-generator in the Forward Engine Room was running and I knew the diesel generators were going as I could hear them. No orders were received on the Engine Room telegraph.
>
> There was no communication with the after engine room and I noticed that there was no pressure showing on the gauges from the after engine room. At this point the time was about 0135 and about ten minutes later the ship got back to a starboard seven degree list.
>
> By this time I was exhausted and Commander Robb told me to take a rest and I proceeded to the flight deck to get a rest. I arrived on the flight deck at about 0150.
>
> At about 0230 the ship's company was called to attention and the Captain addressed the ship's company and then an officer, I think it was Commander Hammersley-Johnston, spoke to the ship's company to the effect that the Captain had decided to abandon ship.[9]

Cross Examination of Warrant Engineer A.F. Budden by Commander Robb

Commander Robb knew that repairs to the damage caused in July 1941 included the installation of fittings to enable the ship's engine rooms to be used when partially flooded. He described the alterations carried out as 'raising of pig's ears, flooding funnels to fit tanks, and fitting certain additional valves to the feed tank – these additions and alterations were instigated by the Admiralty and carried out in the ship with the express purpose of enabling the engine room to steam in a partially flooded condition, assuming that water was not above the gear case bearings. The

149

work also included the breathing pipes from the main circulator'.

Consequently, in his questioning of Mr Budden, Commander Robb was trying to explore the possibility that the flooding in the after engine room occurred because the torpedo hit abaft of that compartment rather than on it. If that was the case then it might well have been possible, after extensive work by the damage control parties, to reduce the flooding in the after engine to a level at which the port inner engine could be restarted.

Robb: Were you in the ship on the previous occasion of being torpedoed?

Budden: Yes, Sir.

Robb: Did you see the state of the flats subsequent to damage?

Budden: Yes, Sir.

Robb: Will you agree that loose gear was thrown about and fittings displaced on the lower deck in the flats, not only by the site that was hit but fore and aft of this?

Budden: We know this to be a fact from subsequent knowledge.

Robb: Would you agree that information regarding gear thrown about in the fan flat, such as hammocks, kit lockers for example, would not necessarily indicate a torpedo [hit] in the after engine room, but there might be a possibility of it being aft of this?

Budden: Yes, Sir.

Robb: Do you agree from your personal knowledge that in the *Manchester* class, the shaft tunnel passages are linked by Plummer block compartments with bulkhead glands which cannot be kept watertight underway due to overheating?

Budden: Yes, Sir.

Robb: And that flooding in any space through which the shaft passes will extend to all compartments the whole length of the shaft through these glands?

Budden: Yes, Sir.

Robb: Do you remember the position of the hit on the previous occasion of being torpedoed?

Budden: Yes, Sir.

Robb: Will you explain what you know regarding leakage into the forward engine room on that occasion?

Budden: Leakage into the forward engine room took place through the shaft tunnel. This would, of necessity, require flooding of either the after engine room or compartments abreast 'B' boiler room. Water could not have entered the forward engine room by this hit without flooding the after engine room.

Robb: Would you say it was necessarily total flooding, or would partial flooding give that effect?

Budden: Partial flooding would have that effect.[10]

Chief Engine Room Artificer Edward Miller James was then cross-examined by Commander Robb:

> Robb: Can you recall the incident when you came to ask me if it would be alright to put steam on the port engine to try it when the circulator was started; can you recall where I was?
>
> James: Yes, Sir, I think you were about amidships, there was a group around you and I sort of butted in.
>
> Robb: Can you recall the interval after having started the circulator and tried the engine before I came back to the engine room and you reported the port outer engine was correct?
>
> James: Well, in my statement I assumed this to happen in about twenty minutes and you came down at the end of that time, and it would be about twenty minutes after the explosion as far as I can recollect.
>
> Robb: Can you recall how long I was away from the engine room having left it after you asked me if it would be alright to start the port outer engine?
>
> James: No, Sir, I remember you having been down the engine room at three different times but the intervals I cannot remember.[11]

Commander Robb also cross-examined Engine Room Artificer 3rd class John Wilfred Desmond and established that Commander (E)'s standing orders made it quite clear that in the event of rudder control being lost while the wheel is over, the rudder was to be brought back to the midships position by opening the bypass valve connecting the pipes to the two cylinders driving the rudder and that the duty of the watch-keeper in these circumstances was to 'place the pins in position for mechanical control and when the lower conning tower are ready to take over steering insert the pins in the correct place'.[12]

The next two witnesses were from *Manchester*'s gunnery department who were examined about the availability of the 4-inch HA guns and their control systems after the torpedo struck.

Statement made by Temporary Lieutenant John Daniels RNVR
In his statement, Lieutenant Daniels wrote that he had been:

> In MANCHESTER 8.40 – 13.8.42 as HA control officer and AA Divisional Officer. My action station was officer in charge of the starboard HA Director. At midnight on 13.8.42 I was at my action station. The director and communications were correct. Just before dark on 12.8.42 we were ordered to carry out sweeps for E-boats. We picked up land echoes on RDF set 285 which made it hard for RDF operators to distinguish these echoes from ship or E-boat echoes.

Later I saw what I thought was the wreck of the HAVOCK. Later the port 4-inch guns opened fire, searchlights were burnt on the port side only. I received no orders for the starboard 4-inch guns and these did not open fire. As the director had been told to carry out a visual sweep I saw a torpedo pass just close to our bows and gave orders to the Director crew to train to starboard and in the direction in which I thought the E-boat was. We did not see the E-boat by the time the second torpedo hit aft.

Then I heard two 'swishes' and next felt the ship shudder and the ship listed to starboard. The starboard AA Director was turned round by hand. This was a little difficult owing to the list. After we were hit, I phoned the HACP below and enquired if they were alright. They replied they were all right. Shortly after this, about a minute or two later, I tried to get through again to the HACP but could get no reply.

About ten minutes after the explosion, the crew of the Director got out. I then went to the bridge and reported to the Gunnery Officer that training was hard owing to the list and that there was very little the Director could do. I asked him for orders and he said that he would not be manning the Directors for a while. I heard Commander (N) making arrangements for the destruction of secret matter and, whilst I was at the after end of the bridge Commander (E) came up and reported to the Captain (Commander (N) & the Gunnery Officer were present) that the ship could do a possible eleven knots on one shaft and that they were connecting up the hand steering.

I then assisted Commander (N) in getting all the charts and secret books and burning them in the incinerator. Whist doing this I heard a pipe 'Port Watch muster on Quarter Deck, stand fast short range weapons'.

Later, I returned to the bridge just as PATHFINDER was shoving off. The PATHFINDER said that he could not take any more and our Captain told PATHFINDER to carry on and tell them what had happened to us, and in any event get a plane to see what had become of us at daybreak.

Later when within about 1.5 miles from the shore we were picked up by a French boat. We saw two destroyers come up and were keen for the French boat to take us to them. But the destroyers were unidentified at the time, and the nationality of the lurking E-boat was unknown at the time.[13]

The next statement read out to the board was from Sub-Lieutenant John Edward Tabor RNVR:

I joined MANCHESTER on 16.8.1940 as general duty High Angle Control Officer, Port Director, my action station was HA Port Director (hand trained). At midnight on12/13.8.42 I was at my action station. Later in action with an E-boat I was controlling the port 4-inch armament.

Later I saw the wake of a torpedo across our bows and then felt an explosion aft on the starboard side. The ship listed to starboard. I was still in communication by sound power telephone with the High Angle Calculating Position (HACP). They told me that the electric light had gone and they were in darkness. We were also in communication by sound power telephone with the ADO.

I heard by telephone from the HACP that the TS was being evacuated and I therefore may have or may not have ordered the HACP to be evacuated. I could not get through to the guns. I then left the HA. Port Director and stood by the Pom Poms and Oerlikons. I spoke to Paymaster Lieutenant Commander Cope.

I then heard that the port watch was to go aft on the Quarter Deck. Later word was passed to go up to the flight deck. I went there and heard the Captain say, so far as I can remember: 'The convoy must carry on. As we are crippled, he had to make a decision. That we were going to abandon ship and that we were just off Cape Bon'.

The Commander then spoke and told us that we would need warm clothing. Later we started getting rafts away.[14]

Warrant Ordnance Officer Albert Edward Reddy had joined *Manchester* on 21 April 1942, and was in charge of the maintenance of the armament on board. His action station was 'X' Turret. His statement read:

At midnight on 12.8.1942 I was by the door to the cordite gallery of 'X' Turret. I heard an explosion. I then went to 'X' Turret gunhouse. I took up my position in the rear of the right gun. In the course of the following hour we were ordered into action and fired. At the end of this hour, there was an explosion which threw me onto the deck. I found the left rear door open and the lights out. One emergency lamp was switched on and off again because the door was open. The gunhouse was dimly lit by instrument lighting. The turret pump had ceased to run and I assumed that the power to the turret was cut off. There was no communication with the TS.

I went to the roof of 'X' Turret and looked down on the Quarter Deck and saw twenty to thirty men. I also saw tracer coming to the ship. I told the men to lie down. But as no one appeared to be in charge I went down to the Quarter Deck. The men laid down. The ship was by this time listing ten to twelve degrees to starboard. I went to the after Oerlikon gun but found no one manning it.

Sometime after this, I proceeded to the Flight Deck where I was in charge of No.18 Carley Float. I must have been convinced that Emergency Stations had been sounded off as I began to cast off No.18 Carley Float. I was assisted by one Able Seaman and a crowd appeared to be gathered on the Port side of the Flight Deck by the hangar doors. I shouted at them for some assistance and I was joined at this time by Mr Turner. We lowered two Carley floats and took them to the Flight Deck. When I was satisfied that the Carley floats were ready if necessary to use them I went aft.

The next paragraph of his statement was crossed through in the transcript of proceedings and is delineated by square brackets, it reads:

[I tried all the 4-inch guns and found them correct for training and elevation. I then went back to 'X' Turret with the idea of rigging emergency training by air pressure. When I got there, I found that the gauge showing the air pressure from the ring main registered a very low pressure and therefore was unable to rig emergency training. There was no communication to the TS. I proceeded to 'Y' Turret and found the same state of affairs. 'X' and 'Y' turrets were mechanically sound apart from the supply of electrical power.]

When I got out onto the Quarter Deck I found a man sitting on the starboard side with what looked like a pile of books beside him. I spoke to him and he asked if I was an Officer. I found him to be Paymaster Midshipman Cocks with some cypher books which he asked me to guard whilst he fetched the remainder. He was covered in oil fuel and seemed in a weak condition. He declined my offer of assistance and he went to fetch some more books. When he returned I asked him what he proposed to do. He said that he would report to the Captain that he had the cypher books on deck. I told him to remain where he was and I would report to the Captain.

About this time I heard a pipe for Port Watch to fall in on the Quarter Deck standing fast close range weapon crews. Also whilst I was on the quarter deck I heard someone detailing hands to man the hand-steering.

On my way to report to the Captain, I met Mr Williams, Warrant Electrician, who was rigging emergency leads to the steering motors. I proceeded to the Bridge but found no-one there. I have no idea of the time.

I spoke to the Pom-Pom and Oerlikon crews. I found their guns to be correct. They said that they were the starboard watch and were standing fast. I left the bridge and went to the Flight Deck. I found a large crowd of men and heard someone speaking. I pushed my way through the crowd and heard the Captain say in effect that he had no wish to wait for us to suffer the humiliation of falling into Italian hands but that we were very close to the Algerian shore and we were to make our way there where we would be interned. He also said that he wanted us to get well away before dawn. Then I approached the Captain and reported that Paymaster Midshipman Cocks had the cypher books on the deck and requested instructions. The Captain replied, 'ditch them'. I returned to the Quarter Deck and told Paymaster Midshipman Cocks. We sank the books in a kit bag with a 6-inch shell as a weight as we could not get to the Cypher Room for the proper bags.

I then went back to the Flight Deck and met Mr Budden, Mr Williams and Mr George. I made a sling for the Carley float and it was lifted out by the Starboard Crane. At this time, the Commander and the Gunnery Officer were on the Flight Deck. I went over the side and we left the ship.[15]

Cross-examined by the Prosecutor, Reddy admitted that he could not be more precise as to exactly what he did or at what time. However, at the time he went aft he knew that 'A' and 'B' turrets had electrical power and that the 4-inch guns were possibly still unable to be elevated or trained.

He had no recollection of making any report to the Gunnery Officer, had only vague memories of seeing the Gunnery Officer on the Flight Deck immediately before leaving the ship and could not recall any orders from the Gunnery Officer.

Cross-examined by Lieutenant Commander Duff, Reddy said that he had a faint recollection of seeing 'Guns' on the bridge but nothing more. Reddy also admitted that he had no recollection of raising the question of air training for 'X' and 'Y' turrets. He also admitted that no-one had acquainted him with the state of affairs in 'A' and 'B' turrets.

The President of the Court now directed Reddy to Lieutenant Commander Duff's statement, which he then read, stating: 'Mr Reddy came on the bridge about the time *Pathfinder* was approaching the ship. He confirmed that power had failed in all turrets and that the AA Directors starboard and aft had jammed and could not be trained and that the 4-inch mountings were in action in local control.'

The President then pointed out various inconsistencies between Reddy's statement and Reddy's cross-examination of Lieutenant Commander Duff. The President also went on to say that, 'It appears to the Court that you are prevaricating in your evidence. I must warn you that under Section 66 of the Naval Discipline Act you are liable to imprisonment for such prevarication. The Court will now give you an opportunity of making a statement to the Court on this account.'

Reddy's statement in response read:

> At the time Lieutenant Commander Duff gave his evidence to the Court I was surprised to hear definitely that I made a report to him on the armament. I had no definite recollection of making such a report. In questioning Lieutenant Commander Duff I had no intention of misleading the Court. Rather stupidly perhaps I endeavoured to establish in my mind that such a report was made. I am deeply sensitive to my oath. It appears in a very earnest and sincere endeavour not to include evidence anything of which I am definitely not certain I have given the impression that I am lying. That is all, Sir.[16]

Lieutenant Commander Duff declined to follow with questions but the Prosecutor followed and wrung from Reddy the declaration that he believed air training was impossible for 'X' and 'Y' turrets at the time.

Reddy was cross-examined by Master-at-Arms William Edward Terry who was concerned that the after Oerlikon had been unmanned. Reddy was unable to provide any information on this matter.[17]

Evidence of Chief Ordnance Artificer Ernest Millson John St Quinton

St. Quinton was responsible for maintenance of armament in the fore part of the ship and his action station was in 'B' Turret but he was in 'A' Turret when the torpedo hit. The effect of the hit was (i) temporary dimming of lights and (ii) loss of gunnery communication all round (i.e. turrets). Apart from these two effects, 'A' Turret was ready for action in all respects while 'B' Turret was fully operational within ten minutes of the hit. He continued:

> When in the Canteen Flat I found all the TS crew and also both HACP crews lined up in single file. They had been ordered to abandon the TS and both HACPs and remain where they were in the Canteen Flat. I decided to go to the Flight Deck and found it crowded with officers and men who were mostly engaged in unlashing Carley floats, providing provisions and water and getting them ready.[18]

Evidence of Petty Officer Roy Dawkins

Dawkins, who was employed in general duty 'A' and 'B' turrets and his action station was in 'B' Turret, confirmed St. Quinton's account and in answer to a question from Lieutenant Commander Duff confirmed that power to 'B' Turret did not fail.[19]

Evidence of Leading Seaman Douglas William Barclay

Barclay, whose action station was in 'B' Turret, right gun, had been left in charge of the turret because PO Dunning was with the Bofors gun crew on top of the turret. Barclay confirmed that 'A' and 'B' turrets remained operational in local control, not least because the Transmitting Station had been evacuated![20]

Evidence of Lieutenant Harold Duncan McCormick RCNVR

Lieutenant McCormack was the ship's RDF officer and he confirmed that *Manchester*'s RDF equipment at the time of her loss consisted of:

Type 279	Air warning set
Type 284 M1	Surface gunnery set
2 x Type 285 M1	H.A. gunnery sets
Type 273 M Mk.2	Surface warning set
Type 252	IFF
Type 251	Homing beacon

He confirmed that for the *Pedestal* operation they had been ordered not to use RDF (except Type 273) at night and all RDF, except Type 273, was held at one minute's notice. Type 279 was not used at night. He reported that the effect of the torpedo hit on the ship's RDF was limited and that:

> We blew a fuse on the Type 284 which was replaced within one and a half minutes and after that each set was in a high state of efficiency. At the time of the hit the Type 273 was being used to detect targets after which Type 284 would be used for gunnery ranging following acquisition of a target.[21]

Captain Agar's Statement

Towards the end of the court martial the Prosecutor, Captain Augustus Agar, made a statement because he had become concerned about remarks made by some of the survivors of HMS *Manchester* in Court to the effect that some of them felt that their statements had been taken in an irregular manner. He went on to explain that he had been appointed by the Admiralty as Prosecutor on 16 December 1942 for court martial under Section 92 of the Naval Discipline Act to enquire into the loss of HMS *Manchester*. He said that in each case (eighty officers and men) he explained the procedure in detail pointing out his responsibilities and that their statements were being taken without fear or favour and without regard to any person or personality. He stressed that each interviewees statement would be in the form of a narrative of what each one himself saw, heard or did during the period covered by the statement.

A fair copy of each statement would be typed up and would only be signed if the interviewee was satisfied with it. They were only required to give their own statement and nothing else.

The original statement was kept by Agar and no copies were retained by those survivors who had made statements. They were able to amend their statements in Agar's office and were given ample opportunity to read through their statement before giving evidence at the trial. He added that this also applied to Captain Drew whose evidence in part consisted of his written narrative which he had forwarded to the Admiralty and which was regarded as his statement.

Thus, Captain Drew was in exactly the same position as all his officers and men in that his statement was entirely voluntary. The Prosecutor concluded his statement by pointing out that although witnesses were able to change their signed statements, any material deviation or deletion from the original might be a matter for comment by the Prosecution. However, any addition to the statement would be taken as additional evidence given for the benefit of the Court.[22]

The President of the Court then asked the Prosecutor if, in the light of evidence presented during the trial, he wished to amend the list of questions used during proceedings. Agar replied that he would like to do so and would also draw up a list of survivors who would be able to provide more information in response to revised questions. After circulating the revised questions ten witnesses they were recalled for re-examination.[23]

Commander Gill, who was cross-examined by Commander Hammersley-Johnston, explored the issue of when steam would be available.

> Hammersley-Johnston: At the time the decision was made to sink the ship what was your knowledge of how long it would be before steam would be available?
>
> Gill: I thought at the time that we should be able to steam between four and five o'clock in the morning. That is the time I had at the back of my mind.
>
> Hammersley-Johnston: When did you first hear that this length of time was being called into question?
>
> Gill: The first I ever heard definitely of steaming earlier was a remark the Captain made to me about ten days after we got to Laghouat, that would be about the end of August.
>
> Hammersley-Johnston: In what circumstances did you hear this and what was the remark?
>
> Gill: The Captain came into the room that I shared with you and said to us 'I have just had a hell of a shock'. So I said 'What is that, Sir?' thinking it was something to do with the French. He said words to the effect 'I now hear that Robb is saying that we could have got steam earlier.'
>
> Hammersley-Johnston: Did Captain Drew ever discuss this again with you?
>
> Gill: He never discussed it again.
>
> Hammersley-Johnston: What discussion did you have with Captain Drew on the subject to the loss of the ship?
>
> Gill: From time to time we discussed the whole operation particularly the strategical and tactical side at the time we got detached from the convoy.
>
> Hammersley-Johnston: Where and when did you write your appreciation which had been attached to Captain Drew's report?
>
> Gill: In the transport *Arundel Castle* on the way to the United Kingdom, about 20 November 1942 I should estimate.
>
> Hammersley-Johnston: Did you write the appreciation alone?
>
> Gill: Yes.[24]

In view of these disclosures, it was hardly surprising that Commander Robb decided to cross-examine Commander Gill.

> Robb: Did the Captain say under what circumstances 'Robb is now saying we could get steam earlier'?
>
> Gill: No, he did not tell me anything more than that.[25]

Next, Lieutenant Malim was recalled and cross-examined by Commander Robb who was keen to establish just what information had been given to Captain Drew while Robb was on the bridge.

> Robb: On my return from the bridge , during which time you made your
>   telephone report to the Captain, what information did you give me
>   concerning machinery and reports?
> Malim: I gave you the same report as I had given the Captain, that is the
>   one telephoned through to him.
> Robb: Can you state briefly what that report was concerning machinery?
> Malim: I reported that the after engine room was flooding, that both inner
>   shafts and the starboard outer shaft were out of action and that the
>   port outer shaft was still workable. I said that one dynamo was out of
>   action, I reported what counter flooding measures were being taken.[26]

Captain Drew now sought further clarification as to the exact words used by Lieutenant Malim in his telephone report to the bridge on that fateful night.

> Drew: When you state that the port outer shaft was still workable are you
>   sure that you did not tell me it was intact?
> Malim: I do not remember the exact words but I do not think that I would
>   have used the word intact referring to an engine. I said shaft.[27]

Chief Stoker Charles Gibson now asked Lieutenant Malim two particularly pertinent questions which must have confirmed Captain Drew's worst fears.

> Gibson: When was the first time you found out or that you knew the ship
>   could not steam?
> Malim: I did not know at any time that the ship could not steam.
> Gibson: When was the first time you found out there was a doubt about
>   the ship being able to steam?
> Malim: Not until we got ashore, I do not know at what place, sometime
>   after we had landed in North Africa.[28]

Chief Engine Room Artificer Edward James was recalled and cross-examined by Commander Robb who was eager to get evidence that the port outer shaft was still functional.

> Robb: You will re-call that as I went up the ladder to report to the Captain
>   you asked me if it would be all right to put steam on the port outer
>   engine and test it. How long after I went up the ladder did you
>   actually try the port outer engine?
> James: I should say it would be about 10 minutes or something like that.

Robb: You have stated that you informed the boiler room and opened out on the engine, what revolutions did that engine attain?

James: As far as I remember, I remember seeing the Chadburn indicator up to about one hundred revolutions.

Robb: How long was the engine running on that occasion?

James: I turned the engine over to another engine room artificer while I examined the rest of the engines and while I was doing the examinations, or about that time, they had stopped it by order from above, someone shouted the orders down the hatch, the orders came down from the deck above to stop the engine.[29]

The next witness to be recalled was Master at Arms William Terry who, under cross-examination, was able to establish the whereabouts of Commander Robb at a specific time during the night.

Robb: When did you finally leave the neighbourhood of the [quarterdeck] Oerlikon gun?

Terry: I left the quarterdeck [in response to an order given by Commander Hammersely-Johnston] on which the Oerlikon gun was situated just after *Pathfinder* had left from alongside the ship.

Robb: Before you left did you hear any enquiries shouted down the hatch of the Admiral's lobby

Terry: Just after I had finished assisting the regulating of the passage of ratings on board the *Pathfinder* I went to the immediate vicinity of the hatch mentioned and I thought I recognised your voice, Sir, enquiring as to work going on below.

Robb: Could you say when this was in relation to the *Pathfinder's* departure?

Terry: I cannot give a time; it was a short time before the *Pathfinder* left the ship.[30]

Suddenly, Commander Robb had evidence that the port outer engine was 'good' and had also been able to establish his position in the ship at a key moment.

After the collection of evidence by submission of written statements and cross-examination had been completed 'key players' in the saga of the loss of *Manchester* were invited to make personal statements in their defence. Captain Drew and Commander Robb were amongst those who made such statements.

Statement in Defence by Captain Harold Drew

Drew started by explaining the reason why he wrote his report whilst in transit to the UK was to indicate to the Court the nature of the enquiry that lay ahead. He went on to change some approximate times after further consultation and consideration. Then came a key admission:

> There is one unfortunate issue that has arisen of which I had no knowledge; that is the question of steam being available at any time up to the moment when I decided to sink the ship. I had not expected it and heard it for the first time in this Court and I was at some loss to know quite how to deal with it and so I am afraid I can add nothing to what I have said on that point.

He went on to state that he meant to give the order 'Emergency Stations' but could not say that he actually used these words. He observed that he found himself 'in a ship that was a perfect library of confidential matter close inshore in waters which were at the time so much hostile that no passage of them could be attempted by day'. Consequently, he felt it imperative to start their destruction as soon as possible just in case further damage meant that their destruction might be compromised.

'I used an order,' Drew said, 'or meant to use an order, which I knew was familiar to me. My whole training has been that it is not good to improvise orders in time of emergency. As I read them they should not have had the effect of taking anyone away from any part of the armament at which they were already closed up.'

He explained that after the torpedoing he was anxious to prevent the ship running amongst other ships coming up astern and that he was keen to take way off her for fear of running either into land or a minefield. He felt that his Executive Officer and Gunnery Officer did a good job in getting rid of people [to *Pathfinder*] who might have been of no use to us. He felt that as the after turrets were not usable and there appeared to be no power in 'B' Turret it was wise to transfer out some of the ship's gun crews. He continued:

> Some witnesses, perhaps out of a sense of friendship for me have said that I was thinking of saving valuable lives. Much as I would like to be credited with that I am afraid I cannot agree. I have never yet known a precedent for sinking a ship to save life.
>
> The only justification for sinking a ship is to prevent her from falling into the hands of the enemy, or to prevent some major disadvantage that might result from not doing so. I did not think I ought to be found there in a large ship like *Manchester* in daylight in the middle of such an operation as that one. Any further attack on the damaged ship at slow speed must inevitably cause me to try some avoiding action and had that occurred the possibilities would be that the ship would have grounded and then a very difficult situation would have arisen. Under such circumstances resistance to French attempts at internment could have

brought Vichy-France into war against us. Similarly, the ship might have fallen into Italian hands.

It has been shown that destroyers did arrive next day. These destroyers, the Court have since heard, arrived some five and a half to seven hours after daylight [i.e. after first light]. Had we been able to get underway at the latest time which I deemed it to be advisable to try, we should have been round the corner and well out of sight from them. I merely mention that because if the situation I had visualised transpired, that is the arrival of enemy aircraft down the coast, we should either have been in trouble or out of it before these ships could possibly have reached us.

One other question I have to answer relates to the effect of the transfer of personnel from the ship to *Pathfinder*. So far as I could see at the time, and thinking it over after, the morale of the ship's company, even taking into account that sixty-two per cent of the seamen had only been at sea for the first time since April [1942], morale seemed excellent.[31]

Commander (E) Robb then also made statement in defence:

I would like to take this opportunity to rectify my reply to the President's question in which he asked me: 'Did any other Engineer Officer make a report that the port outer was definitely correct as far as I knew?'

I was aware of my mistake immediately but I did not know how to rectify the matter. My reply to the President's question should have been that on my return to the workshop flat after having been sent for by the Captain, Lieutenant Commander (E) Malim informed me that he had reported the port outer engine correct in his telephone report to the Captain. I re-call Lieutenant Commander (E) Malim running through the points on a signal pad as he gave me the update situation.

As this matter to some extent concerns organisation in regard to checking and following up reports after damage I should like to emphasize that Lieutenant Commander (E) Sutton's evidence stated that he was informed that this report had been made to the bridge by 'phone. This checking and following up reports is illustrated by the Damage Control Officer and Heel and Trim parties checking up that machinery compartments were being counter-flooded and all wing compartments [were] in hand although the organisation provided for such action without waiting for further orders.

With reference to my report to the Captain in which I made my diagnosis as fully and accurately as my knowledge then permitted, I am convinced that my report conveyed the impression that the port outer engine would be available as soon as the main circulator was re-started. I also stressed the fact that it looked the same as last time. In my opinion that summed up the situation to the Captain who was in the ship the last time, better than any verbose report. My conversation with the Captain, which was dominated by the Captain (and I did not feel that in the presence of a Senior Officer I could leave without dismissal or an order from him) took us to the point where he gave me orders to make preparations to sink the ship, and he repeated that order to me. At that point I was convinced from the trend of the conversation that the Captain was very dis-satisfied with the prospect of proceeding on one engine and hand steering gear.

I felt that nothing short of a complete survey would be of any use to the Captain and having asked him whether he would wait until I had checked up on the second engine before he made his final decision I made my tour of the ship as quickly as possible. I have referred to the point that when I got to the workshop flat I was informed that Lieutenant Commander (E) Malim had reported to the Captain that the port outer engine was available. I will not say more of that or my tour of the ship, except that I did not get off the engine room ladder: I only ran down the ladder, got the Chief ERA's report and I came straight up again.

I would also like to point out that from the night 12/13 August until the commencement of this trial neither the Captain, nor the Commander, nor the Commander (N) have ever enquired from me as to what was the cause of the alleged three hours delay before steam was available. It was a shock to me to learn that this alleged delay was put forward as part of the Captain's reason for sinking the ship. I had only one conversation with the Captain in the internment camp in relation to this matter and, if the Court desire, I am prepared to give evidence on oath in regard to that.[32]

There can be no doubt that Commander (E) Robb did not agree with his Captain's decision to scuttle HMS *Manchester*. Furthermore, one gets the distinct impression that he was unhappy to the point of feeling betrayed by Drew's use of an alleged three hour delay in the availability of steam as a factor in the loss of the ship. It really is quite extraordinary that they only had one conversation about it in the internment camp. One could be excused for thinking that they would have talked of nothing else!

Chapter 15

The Verdict

After three days of exhaustive deliberations the Court issued its findings, which were highly detailed.[1] The Court found that *Manchester* was damaged at around 01.10 hours on 13 August 1942, when approximately seventy degrees and two to three miles from Kelibia Light. This was at around four hours before first light and five hours twenty minutes before sunrise.

The cruiser's side was penetrated in the neighbourhood of 175 station in the vicinity of the after engine room. With regard to the main armament, there was an initial power failure to all turrets; 'X' Turret filled with fumes and the after 6-inch DCT was put out of action. The effect on the HA armament was that the starboard and after 4-inch DCTs were reported as stiff in training and the 4-inch magazine flooded. Fire control communication in the fore part of the ship in all probability remained intact, except for some breakers coming off, but some damage must have occurred to the circuits leading aft.

The after engine room flooded thereby putting out of action the port and starboard inner shafts, whilst the after boiler room suffered from controllable leaks and [boiler] fires were put out because of seawater in the fuel oil. With regard to the forward engine room, the starboard outer shaft was probably damaged but the port outer turbine and shaft were in working order but the port circulator tripped. A full head of steam of 344lb was maintained at all times in the forward boiler room in both boilers. The fire main fractured in the office flat about station 170 starboard. Number 4 steam dynamo situated in the after engine room was put out of action by flooding but the remaining three dynamos were not affected. Power failed on the port and starboard after section of the ring main. In the case of the steering motors, they remained mechanically sound but power failed to the steering motors.

The Type 279 air warning radar was probably put out of action because of the destruction of generators, while the Type 284 main armament set blew a fuse which was replaced quickly. The surface warning Type 273 radar remained in action.

Turning to internal and external communications, the Court reported that there was some loss of lines internally but the damage control HQ remained in contact with the bridge. External communications were still intact despite the loss of main W/T office.

There was ingress of about 1,900 tons of water which caused a ten and a half degree list but except for the damaged compartments, the watertight integrity of the ship was not affected and *Manchester* would not have been in danger of sinking except in very bad weather. The list was countered quickly by counter flooding, transfer of fuel oil and jettisoning of starboard torpedoes.

The Court found that *Manchester* was not under control of engines or steering gear immediately after the torpedo hit and that no proper steps were taken to re-establish communication between the bridge and the engine room via the lower steering position. As regards the steering, the correct action was taken by the watch-keeper in the tiller flat to centre the rudder. Unfortunately, no action whatsoever was taken to establish communication between the bridge and the after steering position. Although emergency leads were run to the steering motors about one hour after the damage, no steps were taken to start the motors and connect the steering gear.

The port circulator was restarted quickly and consequently *Manchester* was able to steam at 01.25 hours on one shaft giving a speed of ten to thirteen knots depending on whether the brake could hold the starboard shaft at that speed. Furthermore, *Manchester* was able to steer by rudder at 01.20 hours by hand pumps and by electric motors at 02.25 hours.

'Emergency Stations'

The order 'Emergency Stations' was given by Captain Drew and the ship's orders for 'Emergency Stations' state clearly that they cover the action to be taken in the event of the ship receiving damage from mine or torpedo *when not closed up for action stations*. The Court was unclear as to what this order meant when given under action conditions. Consequently, the Court felt that 'Emergency Stations' was *not* a proper order to give in the circumstances prevailing at the time at which it was given. The Court ruled that Captain Drew evidently intended it to be used as a handy means of conveying the order to destroy confidential books. This in effect it did, but it also caused confusion by giving the impression that various compartments were to be evacuated and by attaching undue importance to making preparations for abandoning the ship.

As a consequence of this instruction the following positions were evacuated with or without orders between the time the ship was hit and at the time part of the ship's company were ordered to muster on the quarter deck: Lower steering position, TS, the HACP, both 6-inch DCTs, all three 4-inch HA.DCTs, 'X' and 'Y' 6-inch gun turrets.

It was not known who, if anybody, ordered the evacuation of the lower steering position at 01.20 hours while Lieutenant Commander Duff ordered the evacuation of the TS at that time. The originator of the order to evacuate the HACP remained unknown while the forward 6-inch DCT was evacuated by Captain Akam RM on hearing the 'Emergency Stations' order. The starboard HA.DCT was evacuated by Lieutenant Daniels at 01.20 hours and the port HA.DCT was evacuated by Sub-Lieutenant Tabor at 01.30 hours. The originators of the orders to evacuate the after DCT, the after HA.DCT and 'X' and 'Y' turrets remained unknown but, these were the only orders that the Court considered to be proper.

The consequence of the improper evacuation of lower steering position and the TS was the severance of vital communications and was a forerunner of similar orders to the other positions. Improper evacuation of 6-inch DCTs put the main armament into local control while the evacuation of the HACP had a similar effect on the 4-inch HA armament.

The Court noted that the general effect of all of these improper evacuations was to hinder the re-establishment of communications and delay the completion of repairs and, in particular, prevented vital information regarding the port engine from reaching Captain Drew.

Attempts to Counter or Minimise the Damage
Turning to steps taken to counter or minimise the effect of the damage the Court found that no action was taken to restore the armament, torpedoes and paravanes. With regard to machinery, boilers and electrical machinery, the port circulator was restarted and port outer engine made serviceable. Minor defects in forward engine boiler room were rectified quickly and steam maintained. No effective action was taken to restore power to the after sections. Various breakers were remade in the forward section. In the case of the steering gear the hand pump was manned and emergency leads were run along the upper deck to the steering motors.

Apart from remaking some breakers, no repairs were effected in the internal communication system, nor was it retested and, although the main W/T Office was evacuated no attempt was made to man second and auxiliary offices. The Court felt that the time taken to supply power to the steering motors was unduly long. Furthermore the co-ordination and direction of repair work, especially electrical, was handicapped by various communications being untended and, as a consequence, it was impossible to repair and carry out the necessary tests. Repair work in the Engine Room Department was well organised and well carried out.

With regard to Special Publications and Confidential Books the Court reported that Captain Drew ordered their destruction at about 01.40 hours, but went on to observe that some of this material would have been subsequently required if the ship had got underway. The Court also felt that some of the secret or confidential matter which was destroyed would have improved the chance of HMS *Manchester* being brought into a British port.

Overall, the Court felt that the order to destroy secret material was a proper order but some secret and confidential material should have been retained for a longer period.

The Court was unclear as to who ordered *Pathfinder* to proceed alongside *Manchester* and consequently, the purpose of the order could not therefore be deduced. However, the Court was adamant that the decision to transfer a portion of *Manchester*'s company to *Pathfinder* gave the impression to some members of the ship's company that the ship might be abandoned. This was not a proper order to give in the circumstances and was given by Captain Drew.

Furthermore, the loss of these 172 officers and men meant that it would be impossible for *Manchester* to regain her full fighting efficiency.

Turning to the loss of *Manchester*, the Court noted that the cruiser was sunk by scuttling charges on the order of Captain Drew. The order to abandon and prepare to scuttle was given at 02.50 hours, abandoning started at 03.45 hours and the order to scuttle was given at about 04.45 hours.

Manchester's Capability at 02.50 hours

The Court determined that at the time of the order was given to abandon ship at 02.50 hours on 13 August 1942, *Manchester* could have:

> Steamed at ten to thirteen knots on one shaft.
> Steering normally except that only the port outer shaft was available.
> Was able to fight the HA armament fully and main armament with one watch.
> 'A' & 'B' turrets could be fought normally (apart from manning).
> 'X' & 'Y' turrets could probably have been operated from emergency electrical supplies.
> 'A' & 'B' turrets could have been controlled normally from fore DCT and TS
> 'X' & 'Y' turrets probably could not be controlled from TS.

The after DCT could probably not have been used because the sight appeared to be jammed and hand training was very stiff. The 4-inch HADCTs and HACP could have been used, but no evidence whether control circuits to all 4-inch guns were serviceable or could be made so. All 4-inch guns were serviceable and could have been used in local control, if not with normal control, but only 350 rounds of 4-inch ammunition were available. All close range weapons were serviceable. All gunnery radar sets were serviceable. The port torpedo tubes were loaded and serviceable. All searchlights were out of action, ASDIC was unserviceable due to a near miss, no information on depth charges.

The Court find no evidence that *Manchester* would have been unable to communicate with other British forces, although communication could only have been in plain language because of premature destruction of codes and cyphers.

The Court was quite clear that *Manchester* could have withstood another torpedo in any position other than the forward engine room and that she was capable of reaching a British port. Although she could have provided limited assistance to the convoy, *Manchester* was capable of further action against the enemy. Unfortunately, her Commanding Officer was not entirely aware of the real condition of his ship at the time that the order to prepare to scuttle ship was given. The Court believed that there was a negligible risk of the ship being captured by the enemy.

The Court recorded that *Manchester* sank at 06.47 hours on 13 August 1942 in a position two to three miles and seventy degrees from Kelibia Light.

Conduct of the Commanding Officer, Officers and Men of HMS *Manchester*

The Court noted that proper order and discipline was generally maintained on board *Manchester* but in some cases a lack of direction and co-ordination resulted in some places being evacuated unnecessarily.

Furthermore, not all officers whose duty it was to make reports to the Captain made adequate and proper reports about the progress in restoring steaming and fighting efficiency. However, the Court felt that the Commanding Officer did not take proper steps to acquaint himself with the condition of his ship.

Responsibility for the Loss of HMS *Manchester*

Finally, the Court addressed the key question of whether or not the loss of *Manchester* was caused 'by the wrongful act, neglect or default of the Commanding Officer, and/or any other officers or men of HMS *Manchester*, if so, who?'

The answer it delivered was that the cruiser was indeed lost due to a wrongful act, and that the person responsible was its Commanding Officer, Captain Harold Drew, DSC, RN. The Court then moved on to consider a second question:

'Did the Commanding Officer or any other officer or man of His Majesty's Ship MANCHESTER in any way fail in his duty and/or is such person in any way to blame for his conduct or behaviour on the occasion of the loss of HMS MANCHESTER. If so, who and in what way?'

The Court attributed blame as follows:

To Captain Harold Drew, DSC, RN: In that he negligently performed the duty imposed upon him when acting as Commanding Officer whereby he gave orders on 13 August 1942 for HMS MANCHESTER to be abandoned and scuttled when having regard to the conditions prevailing at the time it was his duty to stand by the ship and do his utmost to bring her into harbour.

To Lieutenant Commander Daniel Alexander Hewson Duff RN: In that on 13 August after HMS MANCHESTER had been torpedoed he negligently performed the duty imposed upon him as Gunnery Officer, whereby (a) he ordered the transmitting station to be abandoned without due cause, (b) he permitted the other gunnery positions to be evacuated without due cause and (c) he failed to take proper steps to restore the fighting efficiency of the gun armament.

To Temporary Lieutenant Allan John Daniels RNVR: In that about 01.20 on 13 August 1942 after HMS MANCHESTER had been torpedoed he negligently performed the duty imposed upon him as HA Control Officer by leaving his action station at the starboard HA Control Tower without due cause.

To Temporary Sub Lt John Edward Tabor RNVR: In that about 01.30 on 13 August 1942 after HMS MANCHESTER had been torpedoed he negligently performed the duty imposed upon him by the HA Control Officer by leaving his action station at the Port HA Control Tower with due cause.

To Mr Albert Edward Reddy, Warrant Ordnance Officer RN: In that on 13 August 1942 after HMS MANCHESTER had been torpedoed he negligently performed the duty imposed upon him as the Warrant Ordnance Officer of the said ship by omitting to take sufficient steps to ascertain and report to the Gunnery Officer the state of the armament and to effect the necessary repairs. -

To Petty Officer Samuel Edward George Phillips, Official Number: P/JX.127153: In that about 01.15 on 13 August 1942 after HMS MANCHESTER had been torpedoed he negligently performed the duty imposed upon him as Chief Quartermaster in charge of the Lower Steering Position by leaving the wheel and telegraph in the Lower Steering Position unmanned, without reporting to the Navigating Officer that the port telegraph was showing full speed and the starboard telegraph half speed ahead.[2]

The Court found that conduct of each of the six above defendants amounted to an offence under Section 9 of the Naval Discipline Act and that a charge of this nature under that Section had accordingly been proved. The Court also found that:

Commander Harold Britton Clifford Gill, DSC, RN, as Navigation Officer, failed to maintain communication with the Engine Room and re-establish communication with the steering position or positions after HMS MANCHESTER had been torpedoed.

Commander (E) William John Robb RN as Engineer Officer failed to keep the Commanding Officer informed as to the state of readiness of the Port Outer Engine with sufficient promptitude after HMS MANCHESTER had been torpedoed.

John Wright, Able Seaman, Official Number P/JX.183499 as Starboard Telegraph man he left the Starboard Telegraph in the Lower Steering position at half speed ahead when he abandoned that position at about 01.15. The Court is of the opinion that his omission should have been rectified by P.O. Samuel Edward George Phillips who was acting as Chief Quartermaster in charge of the Lower Steering Position at the time.

William Conlan, Seaman, Official Number P/X.20292 RNR as Port Telegraph man he left the Port Telegraph in the Lower Steering position at full speed ahead when he abandoned that position at about 01.15. The Court is of the opinion that his omission should have been rectified by P.O. Samuel Edward George Phillips who was acting as Chief Quartermaster in charge of the Lower Steering Position at the time.[3]

In the case of these four defendants, the Court, however, found that their conduct did not amount to an offence under the Naval Discipline Act and formally acquitted them.

The Court noted with dissatisfaction the tendency for officers and men to order positions throughout the ship to be prematurely abandoned *but wished to record with satisfaction the fact that this did not occur in the Engine Room where a high state of discipline was maintained.*[4]

The Court went on find the conduct of the remaining officers and men satisfactory and that no blame was attributable to them for the loss of *Manchester* and therefore acquitted them of the same.

The Sentences

Petty Officer Samuel Edward George Phillips was brought before the Court and on being asked if he wished to make a statement in mitigation replied: 'My conscience is clear. I have done my duty.' He did not wish to call evidence in mitigation and was sentenced to be reduced in rank to Leading Seaman.[5]

Mr Albert Edward Reddy was brought before the Court and asked the Captain and Gunnery Officer to speak on his behalf. Reddy was found guilty and severely reprimanded.[6]

Sub-Lieutenant John Edward Tabor was brought before the Court and stated in mitigation that: 'I considered that at the time that when I left the

Port Director it was of no further value at that moment and I considered that I could be better employed elsewhere.' In support, Captain Drew said that 'he (Tabor) showed himself to be a man of courage under fire'. Sub-Lieutenant Tabor was sentenced to be reprimanded.[7]

Lieutenant Daniels was brought before the Court and stated in mitigation: 'I was the Control Officer of the Starboard HA Director and at the time I and the crew left the Director it was not serviceable. My crew remained on the Flag Deck where I knew I could find them again. I then reported to the Gunnery Officer to find out if I could be more useful elsewhere. My action I considered was better than sitting at a useless weapon.'

Captain Drew, in support, said that 'Lieutenant Daniels was a very fine officer with all the qualities that one could wish him to have'. Lieutenant Daniels was sentenced to be reprimanded.[8]

Lieutenant Commander D.A.R. Duff was brought before the Court and made the following statement:

> I realise now from the evidence that has been laid before the Court that my order to the Transmitting Station crew to leave their station was an error of judgement. That this order would be passed on to the 4-inch H.A.C.P's crew and that they too would leave their stations never occurred to me at the time.
>
> I feel now that I was indirectly responsible for the HA Director Control Officers – Lieutenant Daniels and Sub-Lieutenant Tabor – ordering their Director's crews to leave stations. As they had no possible means of controlling their guns from those positions, they would naturally think of finding some other and more useful employment. I feel that the consequences of my order to the Transmitting Station crew, intended as it was as a temporary measure only, was very much enlarged in ways that could not be foreseen.
>
> My duty as Principal Control Officer (PCO) on the bridge or as PCO ready to direct any part of the armament on any suitable target, [meant that] I remained on the bridge. I was confident in the ability of the ordnance and electrical repair parties to effect, as speedily as possible, the necessary repairs and I did not think it advisable to send a succession of messengers to hunt for officers and men in charge of these repair parties. I had no doubt that I should be receiving a report that 'A' and 'B' turrets had power again very soon, and it was only because I knew that we had been unable to fire 'X' and 'Y' turrets after very similar damage the year before that I agreed that we could send one watch of 6-inch gun's crews in the PATHFINDER.
>
> The Court will remember from the evidence of Mr Burnett, Gunner,- that when he reported to me that my confidential books had been

destroyed, and asked me what I thought we were going to do, I told him that I thought we were going to fight the ship. That was not an idle phrase. I thought at that time that was what we should be doing, as soon as we should be going ahead and steer. Without making excuses for my error of judgement, I wish to say that the strain of the previous two days and nights with little sleep and irregular meals, cannot but have failed to have had some effect on my judgement.

Captain Drew speaking in support of Lieutenant Commander Duff said, 'I feel that I cannot speak too highly of the character of Lieutenant Commander Duff. He shares with some few other officers in the service the title of perhaps the most "shot over" man in the war. I myself have seen him under fire and it seems to me quite fantastic that an officer of his character and reputation should be standing here today at all.' Duff was sentenced to forfeit six months seniority as a Lieutenant Commander and to be severely reprimanded.[9]

Finally Captain Drew was brought into the Court and made the following statement:

> When I came down to attend this Court, I was under the impression that I would have to satisfy the Court as to my actions on a matter of judgement – a decision made under most unusual circumstances. The nature of this Court under Section 92 of the Naval Discipline Act, of course means that it is only at the end that you discover what you are accused of and now I find that I am charged with negligence. It was so remote from my recollection of that night that I am afraid that there is nothing further that I can say.

Captain Drew was sentenced to be 'dismissed from His Majesty's Ship VICTORY and to be severely reprimanded'. The Court dissolved that day (20 February 1943) and the following day C-in-C Portsmouth notified the Admiralty of the outcome.[10]

Criticism of the Procedure

The court martial drew criticism from the Prosecutor, Captain Agar, and the Judge Advocate of the Fleet who were concerned that it was not the best way to ascertain the facts behind the loss of the ship and because the standards were not really up to those in civilian courts. In particular the processes of examining, cross-examining and re-examining were questioned, it being pointed out that the procedures were based on those given by the then Judge Advocate of the Fleet in 1917.

Captain Agar wrote an unofficial letter to the Admiralty about the *Manchester* trial saying:

In the case of *Manchester*, the ship was a large and important one, and the number of surviving officers and men also were numerous. This fact combined with the relatively long interval of time between the loss of the ship and the Trial made it necessary for the Prosecutor to interview a large number of survivors – as everything was based on memory – of whom the majority were called as witnesses. It took me six weeks to prepare the case, during which time the survivors had to be collected from various appointments or jobs which they were doing. The actual Trial lasted three weeks, so in all, from the date of my appointment to the conclusion of the Trial, at least two months passed during which time some eighty officers and ratings (mostly key ratings) were immobilized from war service.

As regards the Court, seven senior officers were occupied for three weeks with this duty, which must have interfered seriously with their normal work.

Section 92 of the Naval Discipline Act has the peculiarity that all survivors are not only potential 'accused' but also potential 'witnesses'. As 'accused' they have to be present in Court throughout the proceeding and as 'witnesses' they have the right of cross examination, of which right in fact a substantial number of witnesses availed themselves. It is obvious, therefore that the proceedings themselves must be prolonged and more cumbersome than the ordinary procedure under Section 29. This partly accounts for the long duration of the trial.

At the outset of the Trial, there was a feeling amongst the survivors – both officers and men – that advantage had been taken of them because each had given the Prosecutor a statement (of which they did not have a copy) and they were unable to compare their statements before the Trial. This feeling was dispelled in the course of the Trial when it was pointed out that their written statements were their evidence, and given voluntarily, and that they were at liberty – if they chose – to alter these at a late stage if they wished but of course the Prosecutor was bound to point out to the Court any material alteration if made during the course of the Trial.

Summing up these points for what they are worth I would remark as follows:

That Section 92 as it now stands, should only be used if the number of survivors is relatively small, or if the ship is small.

That in the case of a large ship, or a long interval between loss and Trial, a full Board of Enquiry should take the place of Section 92, followed if necessary, by a Court Martial under Section 29.

That where Section 92 is used, the survivors as a whole should have the help and advice of a qualified officer to watch over their interests from the date that the Court Martial is ordered.

Finally, there was one particular feature which disturbed me. The position of the Captain of the ship tried under Section 29, is that he is only cross-examined by the Prosecutor. Under Section 92, however, he is liable to cross-examination by any officer or man of his own ship and we then get the spectacle – as happened in this case – of a Captain being cross examined by his own Engineer Officer in front of his own men, and the same applies to a lesser degree to the other officers of the ship. I feel that this is bad for the Service, though others may not take this view.[11]

Captain Drew also wrote to the Admiralty commenting on Section 92:

In my own particular case I attended the court martial expecting to have to justify to them that my judgement and reasoning in deciding to sink an immobile and damaged ship if she did not become mobile before a certain time, was justified, having regard to her position and the circumstances then prevailing.

The evidence of one of the witnesses, which was quite unexpected by me, and of which I had no inkling before I heard it in court [a surprising admission having spent months with his officers in a Vichy French internment camp] must have presented a very different picture to the Court. It was very different indeed to the one that night in August [1942]. A very vigorous and well-prepared defence would have been necessary to re-establish in the minds of the Court, the situation as I saw it at the time. The result for me was, that a question of judgement seemed to have become one of conduct.

I feel too that insufficient attention is paid in these cases to the fact that people, who at this time had had no sleep for nearly three days and nights and who had been steadily bombed, machine-gunned and attacked with torpedoes, and had seen ships sunk, burned or damaged, and then finally got torpedoed themselves at one o'clock in the morning, are not well able to think and act with the clarity and balance that can be achieved under normal conditions.

Neither can they when giving evidence (6 months later), cast their minds back into the state they were in then, from fatigue and strain. They cannot recapture the stress of the moment with the result that what might have been and probably was a fine example of self-discipline, in evidence and under examination becomes a lame and halting tale.

At times such as these, officers and men alike react instinctively to training, tradition and any ideas that they may have set themselves prior to sailing on any particular operation rather than to deliberation and unhurried thought.[12]

The Judge Advocate of the Fleet, J.G. Trapnell, entered the fray on 7 May 1943:

This enquiry appears to have been held in accordance with Section 92 of the Naval Discipline Act and King's Regulations and Admiralty Instructions.

As a method for ascertaining with as much accuracy as possible what happens on such occasions this sort of enquiry is, no doubt, of great benefit but as a machinery for deciding whether a man should be convicted of an offence with justice, it leaves a lot to be desired.

The statements of witnesses are obtained by question and answer without caution and are or may be read to the Court. They are not in the legal sense voluntary statements. It is of little value to caution a witness who has already given such a statement when he comes to the book to be sworn. It will be recognised that he is unlikely to make an objection; advantage is thus obtained of a statement which as to the part would not be, at any rate, admissible on a charge before the civil courts. Moreover the statements are of all these persons who may turn out to be accessories but no regard appears to be paid to the requirement of independent corroboration.

In all other respects the system of naval justice as administered by Courts Martial is of such a high standard that the continued used of this procedure seems regrettable.

The supposition that time is saved is doubtful. Enquiries in the present case could easily have limited possible Courts Martial to half a dozen or so. The vast majority of the survivors who made statements were obviously not likely to be charged with any offence and had Court Martial proceedings been adopted in the present case it is submitted that a large number of officers and men would not have been immobilized for many days and the time of the Court would have been saved.

In addition, the officers and men 'convicted' would have had (what every man should be entitled to) proper and sufficient notice of the charge, the opportunity to prepare and put forward a defence and, in particular, to obtain evidence that might have affected the result.

The view that the real mistake was an error of judgement might well have been supported by the evidence and I am bound to say that in a properly defended case it might have been entitled to succeed. The danger of a decision or such topics where the case is not properly defended and the procedure really precludes it, is obvious. I respectfully submit this procedure should be discontinued except as a machinery for ascertaining what actually took place.[13]

However, the Head of Naval Law, Mr Lawson countered:

The custom of holding a court-martial to try the survivors of a lost ship has a tradition of centuries behind it. It is recognised that the procedure is not entirely in accordance with modern ideas on criminal procedure, but in ordinary criminal cases it is never necessary to proceed except on a specific charge. The nearest approach to a section 92 court-martial is a formal inquiry under the Merchant Shipping Act in which the court has the power to take away an officer's certificate.

In 1939 the Board decided that the best way to ascertain the facts about the loss of a ship in war-time was a Board of Inquiry, a court-martial only being convened if there was prima facie evidence of blame; and A.F.O. 3700/40 states that it is not the intention to hold section 92 courts-martial during the war. Apart from the *Manchester* there have been only three such courts-martial since the beginning of the war, - two in small craft in which the convening authority overlooked A.F.O. 3700/40, and one, the *Punjab*i, which was convened by C-in-C Home Fleet, with Admiralty concurrence because the witnesses were readily available for a few days and there was no time to hold a Board of Inquiry as well as two courts-martial. It may well be that the occasion for holding another section 92 court-martial will not arise before the end of the war.

In the case of *Manchester* the Board decided that it would save time to proceed by section 92, and in spite of the Judge Advocate's remarks it is thought that the object was achieved. No one could have foreseen the length of time taken by the trial (one would probably have to go back to the days of Admiral Byng and Admiral Keppel to another so long), but in any case the alternative would certainly have taken much longer. It would have been necessary to hold a second Board of Inquiry after the survivors were released from internment (one already had been held when the few who had not been interned returned to this country), and as ten officers and men were finally convicted, or blamed, it might have been necessary to hold that number of courts-martial. Apart from anything else, it would have been difficult to convene so many different courts.

With regard to the Judge Advocate's suggestion that what the court found to be negligence might only have been error of judgement, one can only say that this question must have been very much in the minds of the court and that their decision was not lightly reached. Apart from the thought they gave during the hearing of the evidence they took four whole days to consider their findings.[14]

The Vice Chief of the Naval Staff, writing on 1 June that year, observed that:

It is unfortunately clear that the *Manchester* was scuttled unnecessarily and that except as regards the Engineering Room complement there was a lack of leadership and dogged effort to save the ship.

From his statement that his officers and men were physically worn out, there appears to be some doubt whether Captain Drew fully appreciated his responsibility for husbanding the physical resources of his men by arranging periods of rest even at the expense of some risk. This possibly comes under the heading of 'Lessons Learnt'.

As regards the conduct of the trial under Section 92 of the Naval Discipline Act:

(a) In the light of experience it seems possible that a second Court of

Enquiry to ascertain the facts and to frame charges, followed by six to eight Courts Martial to deal meticulously with these charges would have interfered less seriously with the war effort of the larger number of officers and men involved as the Court of the Accused as so forth.

(b) That the procedure was not fully understood by those taking part is obvious from the frequent explanations by the President and Deputy Judge Advocate which proved necessary.

(c) That the Captain of one of H.M. ships should be cross-examined by his own officers and men in the presence of a large number of others tends to weaken naval discipline and this procedure seems to lend itself unnecessarily to this.

(d) As the Judge Advocate states, our system of Naval Justice as administered by Courts Martial is of a very high standard. The fact that a procedure is openly criticised by the Judge Advocate, the Prosecutor and the Senior Officer amongst the accused is a sufficient reason for its discontinuance to be seriously considered. Naval Justice should be like Caesar's wife, above suspicion.

I consider therefore:

(a) That the sentences should be allowed to stand.

(b) That Captain Drew should not again be given the Command of one of HM Ships.

(c) Commander Gill and Commander (E) Robb were formally acquitted and under ordinary Court Martial procedure nothing would have been recorded against them. I therefore think that nothing should be recorded in their case, particularly in the case of Commander (E) Robb since the higher state of discipline in the Engine Room as compared to the remainder of the complement should be credited to him.[15]

The Second Sea Lord did not concur with the Vice Chief, feeling that neither Commander Gill nor Commander (E) Robb were entirely blameless being in his opinion coming under the heading of 'officers implicated to a lesser degree'. The Second Sea Lord also felt that while the Section 92 procedure worked well in the case of HMS *Punjabi*, in which there were only two officers implicated, it was not suitable in cases where the conduct of a large number of officers and men was under investigation. He felt that a review was needed – probably in peacetime.[16]

On 14 June 1943, the First Sea Lord, Dudley Pound, after agreeing with the Vice Chief's objections to this form of trial, wrote:

There is no doubt that the trial was very thoroughly carried out and much time was spent in deliberating on the Findings, and I consider, therefore, that in spite of the fact that the officers feel that the trial was conducted in an unfair manner:

(a) that the sentences should stand;

(b) that Captain Drew should not again be employed afloat in Command and that a note should be made accordingly in his record;
(c) that no notation should be made in the records of Commander Gill and Commander (E) Robb.[17]

Four days later the First Lord signalled his agreement with the First Sea Lord's note.[18]

With Captain Drew no longer able to command a ship, he was placed in charge of Maintenance at Scapa Flow, being based in HMS *Prosperine* at Lyness, from March to August 1943.

Subsequently he was given a staff appointment in Bombay working with the Indian Navy from late 1943 until late 1945. By April 1946 he was back at the Admiralty serving as Director of Naval Recruiting. He also served as Chairman of the Victory Celebration Committee for which he was awarded a CBE. During January to August 1948 he was Naval ADC to HM King George VI.

In late 1948 he returned to India where he served until 1951 as Deputy C-in-C of the Indian Navy with the Acting rank of Commodore 2nd Class and was involved in the restructuring of the Indian Navy. He retired in 1952 and died in 1987 in his ninety-second year.[19]

Chapter 16

England Expects

HMS *Manchester* was a modern, large and powerful 6-inch gun cruiser which would have been considered an important unit in any fleet of the period. Her sinking, under what can only be described as difficult circumstances, generated considerable controversy, not least because many of her survivors considered that Captain Drew was in an impossible situation. They argue that because his ship was apparently immobile and had no worthwhile armament, he scuttled his ship to avoid its capture and thereby saving the lives of his crew. To add insult to injury, they believed that Captain Drew was a victim of a miscarriage of justice when the subsequent court martial severely reprimanded him and dismissed him from his ship, never again to be employed afloat.

Inevitably, such controversy all too often generates more heat than light and the time has come to shed some light on the whole business by addressing the six questions posed in the introductory chapter.

1. Why did the combination of enemy action and the decisions made on board after the ship had been torpedoed reduce a hitherto effective fighting unit to little more than a helpless hulk?
The damage done by the torpedo was serious but not fatal. However, it is easy to argue that the orders given subsequently finished the job by doing as much if not more 'damage', thereby ensuring that *Manchester* could not be saved. The evidence given at the court martial demonstrated clearly that the hasty and premature orders from Captain Drew and Lieutenant Commander Duff reduced a battle-worthy, if damaged, ship into a state of chaos from which there was no recovery. Thus, Captain Drew's order 'Emergency Stations', given within about ten minutes of the ship being torpedoed, did as much to sink the ship as the torpedo.[1]

This order had the effect of causing all those not engaged in damage control and repair to go to their abandon ship stations thereby suggesting to one and all that that was the chosen course of action by their commanding officer. Furthermore, instead of trying to restore *Manchester*'s damaged capability they started to prepare Carley floats for use. Lieutenant Commander Duff's order to the TS effectively disarmed *Manchester* while at the same time causing yet more disruption to vital internal communications. The abandonment of the HACPs created yet more chaos all of which was to the detriment of those trying to recover the ship.[2]

2. Was HMS *Manchester* as helpless as actually claimed?

The short answer is no. Mr Andrew, a Constructor from the Director of Naval Construction's department, who gave evidence at the court martial in February 1943, said that *Manchester* was capable of ten to thirteen knots on the port outer engine.[3] Commander Robb was hopeful of getting the port inner shaft, which was powered from the after engine room, underway provided the after engine room was only partially flooded. He knew *Manchester*'s engine rooms had been modified to enable this to occur but that is in the realms of speculation rather than what 'should have been'.[4]

The torpedo struck at about 01.10 hours and evidence presented to the court martial showed that from 01.25 hours *Manchester* was capable of steaming at ten to thirteen knots on the port outer engine with hand steering. The rudder had been centred by then using hand pumps. By 02.40 hours power steering using the wheel in the lower steering position was available as well – the Court believed that it should have been available fifteen to twenty minutes earlier. Commander Robb was confident of obtaining thirteen knots and said that he was prepared to 'push' the port outer engine to its limits provided the vibration was not excessive.[5]

Manchester's watertight integrity was satisfactory and she could have survived another torpedo hit as long as it wasn't in the forward engine room.[6] She was in no danger of sinking except in exceptionally heavy weather. Furthermore, the cruiser would have had at least half her 6-inch and all 4-inch HA guns under normal control but, unfortunately, the Gunnery Officer neglected to inform Captain Drew of the real situation. All the ship's radar was working normally except for the Air Warning Type 279 which was 'probably' out of action.

Sadly, Captain Drew seems to have given up his attempt to get his cruiser back to Gibraltar by about 02.45 hours, telling his crew that he believed that his badly damaged ship was unable to make significant headway and, in his opinion, was slowly sinking. Prior to this Drew had already received and ignored a report that the port outer engine was 'good' and he should have known, been told or have asked that power had been restored to the steering motors.[7]

3. What options did Captain Drew have to choose from?

Captain Drew's knowledge[8] concerning British forces was that Vice Admiral Syfret had withdrawn Force Z to the westward to cover the aircraft carrier *Indomitable* which had last been seen about 18.00 hours on 12 August

1942, heavily on fire as a result of a dive-bombing attack. The cruisers *Nigeria* and *Cairo* had both been torpedoed that same evening near to the northern end of the Skerki Channel. Another cruiser, *Kenya*, had received underwater damage forward, but was not apparently seriously incapacitated. The AA cruiser *Charybdis* and the destroyers *Somali* and *Eskimo* had been detached by Vice Admiral Syfret to help CS 10 and were attempting to rendezvous with him but had not been sighted. Rear Admiral Harold Burrough (Flag CS 10) in the destroyer *Ashanti*, accompanied by *Kenya*, three destroyers with sweeps and several ships of the convoy, had proceeded towards Malta after *Manchester* was torpedoed. At 02.20 hours the destroyer *Pathfinder*, which had come across the crippled cruiser, was sent by *Manchester* to join CS 10.

Captain Drew knew Rear Admiral Burrough intended to make the return passage through the channel within one and a half miles of the Tunisian coast at high speed during the night of 13/14 August and hoped to be clear of Galita Island by daylight. The information available to those aboard *Manchester* concerning the enemy surface forces was that a force of cruisers was to the NW and constituted a potential menace. E-boats were at sea and a further attack was anticipated at any moment. It is most unlikely that Captain Drew knew that the Italians had abandoned the planned cruiser strike.

Captain Drew stated that he thought it would be unwise to proceed towards Malta as it would involve passing close to Pantelleria Island, with its Italian E-boat and bomber bases, in daylight and that any air cover from Malta would be fully employed covering the convoy and its passage. He also believed that it was unlikely that the heavily bombed Malta Dockyard could do much for *Manchester* in the circumstances then extant. Furthermore, he felt that the *Manchester*'s presence might invite further air attacks on the island.

The distance along the track towards the west was fourteen and a half miles to Cape Bon, twenty-five and a half miles to Zembretta Island, and thirty miles to Zembra Island. This route passes within one and a half miles of the coast until clear of Zembretta Island. Captain Drew therefore decided that if he was to get underway in time to get clear of Zembra Island before daylight, he would attempt the passage to Gibraltar. Quite correctly, he wanted to ensure that *Manchester* did not run aground or fall into the hands of the enemy or sink in water so shallow that salvage operations of any sort would be possible.

Manchester could expect no assistance from Force X which had suffered grievously already and Drew rightly assumed that what remained was fully occupied trying to get the convoy through to Malta. Correctly, he recognised that this was the primary object of Operation *Pedestal* and therefore anything he did would have to be done alone. He decided that the latest moment at which he could proceed towards Gibraltar was 02.45

hours, assuming he was able to get underway and have the ship pointed North by that time. Thus, he hoped to clear Zembra one hour before sunrise (i.e. by 05.30 hours). He considered that he could not do so later without asking Rear Admiral Burrough for assistance. Captain Drew was not prepared to do anything which could hinder CS 10 in his fulfilment of the main objective of resupplying Malta.

At the time that Captain Drew informed his ship's company that he had decided to abandon *Manchester*, the badly damaged ship could, and should have been if Drew had tried to sail on with the limited engine capacity available to him, more than ten miles away from the position in which she was scuttled.

Another question that could be posed at this stage was whether HMS Manchester could have escaped?

Evidence given to the court martial strongly suggests that HMS *Manchester* was capable of moving on one shaft with hand steering from about 01.25 hours on 13 August and that power steering would have been available from 02.40 hours.

One can argue that the suggested speed of thirteen knots is optimistic with ten knots being plausible in view of the likely drag caused by the damaged starboard shafts and the need to avoid straining damaged bulkheads and of course her damage and additional weight. Maintenance of electrical power would be essential to defend the ship as well as ventilating machinery spaces and any breakdowns of turbo generators and diesel engines could become a critical factor in the ship's survival. *Manchester* would have had at least half her main armament and all her HA guns available to defend herself. That being the case, what options did Drew have if he had decided to try and escape?

Option 1 would be to head west for Gibraltar and, assuming that she had started this journey by 02.00 hours, she should have been well clear of Zembra Island by 05.30 hours. Initially she would be unescorted but Rear Admiral Burrough detached *Eskimo* and *Somali* to find her at about 07.00 hours (though, of course, Drew was unaware of this). Assuming that Captain Drew broadcast *Manchester*'s position as soon as she was detected by Axis aircraft that morning, the two destroyers would have joined him at about 13.00 hours on 13 August. *Manchester* would certainly have been found and attacked by Axis aircraft that day but if she survived she would have been overtaken by the remnants of Force X on 14 August. Until then, she would have been extremely vulnerable to the Italian submarines known to be operating in the sea between Sardinia, Tunisia, and Sicily and he would have no air cover. Had *Manchester* survived to be overtaken by Force X it is a moot point as to whether Rear Admiral Burrough would have ordered her to be sunk so as to avoid further damage or loss to his already shattered force.

On the morning of 13 August an Italian aircraft reported that a torpedo-damaged 'aircraft carrier' was stopped fairly close to Bizerte in position 37°30'N, 9°45'E. A substantial air strike was sent to finish her off, only to discover that the 'aircraft carrier' was a small island[9]. The implications for a lame cruiser such as *Manchester* are all too obvious, but any aircraft attacking her would not be attacking the ships of the convoy. Thus, although unable to support the convoy directly, by acting as 'live bait', she would still have been performing her fundamental duty as an escort. It should also be noted that air power is a wasting asset during operations mounted over several days against defended targets. Thus, their attacking potential is diminished by losses of aircraft and crew, damage to aircraft and exhaustion of the aircrew themselves.

Option 2 would have been to head for Malta which was about 180 miles from the position in which *Manchester* was torpedoed but only forty miles from the airfields of Pantelleria. At first sight this option seems to be highly unfavourable because of threat of attack by aircraft, E-boats and even a scratch Italian 'surface action group' consisting of the destroyer *Malocello* and two torpedo boats. This group had been hastily cobbled together to hunt down stragglers after Parona's cruiser force was withdrawn from the fray. The previous night *Malocello* had laid a temporary minefield, using mines fitted with soluble plugs to sink after seventy-two hours, in Vichy waters off Tunisia. The French were informed confidentially but for some unknown reason the mines were ineffective.[10]

Once again, assuming that *Manchester* was underway by 02.00 hours, she would have been passing Pantelleria no later than 06.00 hours by which time she could have received some air cover from long range Beaufighters based in Malta. This option would have also benefitted the surviving merchant ships in the *Pedestal* convoy by providing Kesselring's aircrew with an attractive target. *Manchester*'s presence some miles astern of the main body of the convoy and its escorts might have helped the merchant ship *Dorset* to get to Malta.

Option 2 would have also brought *Manchester* closer to escorting warships and away from known submarine positions. In this scenario, it is likely that the cruiser would have met the destroyers *Somali* and *Eskimo* by 08.00 hours at the latest, though to be fair to Drew he did not know that the destroyers were coming.

At this point it is worth noting the experience of Force X and the remaining ships of the convoy which benefitted from air cover provided by Beaufighters and long-range Spitfires based in Malta from 09.30 hours onwards. By 12.30 hours Force X and the convoy were then in range of the island's short-range Spitfires and consequently were unmolested thereafter. By this time, the RAF fighter force in Malta had achieved an effective level of air superiority over the island and consequently none of the merchant ships was attacked after arriving in Grand Harbour. Assuming that

Manchester survived long enough to get to Malta it is possible that she would have remained more or less unharmed. It is certainly possible to argue that Drew would have had a better chance of saving his ship if he had steered for Malta.

4. Why did Captain Drew choose to scuttle his ship?

Captain Drew's reasoning was that *Manchester* was in a very unfavourable tactical situation which was quite different from when the ship had been torpedoed on 23 July 1941. On that occasion *Manchester* was hit in a position about 38°N, 9°E south of Sardinia and once she was underway she was sailing westward and thereby pulling slowly away from enemy air bases. Consequently, she had only to survive the rest of daylight to be reasonably sure of getting back to Gibraltar.

The air threat was confined to the Regia Aeronautica and its torpedo bombers. In comparison, on 13 August 1942, *Manchester* was almost surrounded by enemy air bases, the Luftwaffe was out in force, there were enemy submarines at the western end of the Sicilian Channel, and a large Italian cruiser force was reportedly poised to enter the area. *Manchester* was in a narrow channel with the Tunisian coast on one side and a minefield on the other and there was a risk, albeit slight, that the ship could fall into enemy hands.

Worse still, Pantelleria was just forty miles away and would have to be passed to reach the 'safe haven' of Malta which was about 180 miles distant. One can well imagine Captain Drew thinking 'Oh no, not again' when his ship was torpedoed at 01.10 hours that morning and one can also understand the sense of pessimism that must have overwhelmed him. Evidence presented to the court martial suggests that his decision-making ability was paralysed by the tactical situation and that, in all probability, made the decision to scuttle his ship at about the same time that he ordered 'Emergency Stations' i.e. within ten minutes of the torpedo strike.

5. Why did the Admiralty decide not to employ Captain Drew afloat ever again?

The evidence presented at the Court of Enquiry in September 1942 suggested that there had been a lack of dogged determination, even a lack of will, to try to recover *Manchester* with a view to getting her underway. This equated to a lack of leadership from the man at the top. The First Sea Lord (Dudley Pound) was particularly insistent that the ship should have been fought to the end and that any ship with one gun remaining could still damage the enemy. Even before the court martial in February 1943 the Admiralty had added a notation to Captain Drew's service record to the effect that he never be allowed to command any Royal Navy ship again.

There can be little doubt that the tame scuttling of HMS *Manchester* does not compare well with the fate of cruisers such as HMS *Exeter*, HMAS *Perth* and USS *Houston* which were sunk by superior Japanese forces. All three cruisers were in appalling tactical situations and were fought until they sank - as were the armed merchant cruisers *Rawalpindi* and *Jervis Bay*. While the details of the loss of both *Exeter* and *Perth* would have been unknown to the Admiralty in 1942 and 1943, the fate of *Manchester*'s half-sister, *Edinburgh*, must have been fresh in the minds of Their Lordships.

On 30 April 1942, whilst proceeding off North Russia at nineteen knots *Edinburgh* was struck by two torpedoes fired by a submarine. The first struck abreast the foremast on the starboard side causing flooding of all compartments in the immediate vicinity. The second struck the after steering compartment on the starboard side. Later the stern broke off and the ship had to be taken in tow with all 6-inch gun turrets reduced to local control. Later, thanks to the heroic efforts made to recover the ship, *Edinburgh* was able to proceed under her own power at two knots which was later increased to eight knots and steered by her surviving main engines. On 2 May *Edinburgh* was turning in circles while engaging enemy destroyers when she was torpedoed again. At this point *Edinburgh* was abandoned and torpedoed and sunk by the destroyer *Foresight*.[11]

Manchester's sister *Liverpool* had been crippled by an Italian 17.7-inch aerial torpedo which exploded abreast the starboard side of the after engine room on 14 June 1942, while escorting the *Harpoon* convoy to Malta. Clearly, *Liverpool*'s tactical situation was much better than that of her sister but it still required leadership and determination to get the crippled ship back to Gibraltar.[12]

Rear Admiral Burrough's own flagship for Operation *Pedestal*, the Colony-class cruiser *Nigeria*, suffered severe damage when torpedoed on the port side abreast the foremast. The forward boiler room was flooded and all electrical power was lost and the steering gear jammed amidships. The ship was underway within thirty-five minutes and limped back to Gibraltar. *Nigeria*'s tactical situation was similar to that of *Manchester* on 23 July 1941.[13]

Given that the nation was in the middle of an existential war, the Admiralty must have expected Captain Drew to do everything possible to get his ship underway and then use it as an escort or a sacrificial lamb to ensure that as much of the convoy as possible arrived in Grand Harbour. That being the case they would probably have preferred him to sail his crippled ship to Malta, even at a speed not dissimilar to the relatively unarmed stragglers.

6. Was the court martial fair?
The short answer is 'yes' and there can be little doubt that the verdict was correct as well. However, there was a perception of unfairness, to modern eyes in particular, in the procedure which could mean that witnesses self-incriminate. Furthermore, because it was a Section 92 Court Martial under

1917 rules, senior officers could be cross-examined by the lowest seaman and this was perceived as possibly deleterious to naval discipline.

In addition, because it was a combined Board of Enquiry/Court Martial a witness could arrive in Court, give evidence and then some time later find out that they had been found guilty of a charge. This indeed happened to Captain Drew and undoubtedly gained him some sympathy. The Judge Advocate of the Fleet even argued that if a normal Board of Enquiry had been held it was possible that Captain Drew might not have been found guilty of negligence at a subsequent court martial.

However, having studied the transcript of the proceedings, it is clear that this was a very fit-for-purpose approach which got to bottom of the matter and, to modern eyes at least, was very democratic in that those in positions of responsibility could be asked to explain their actions by their juniors. That senior officers were discomforted by the procedure is irrelevant.[14]

Did the damage inflicted on 23 July 1941 influence the outcome in August 1942?

Captain Drew was appointed to command *Manchester* on 31 May 1941, and joined the ship on 3 June. Although he had served as the Executive Officer of the cruiser *Amphion* in the mid-late 1930s, *Manchester* was his first command and thus his first experience of the 'loneliness of command'. Furthermore, he had no first-hand operational knowledge of the war at sea as it had developed since 1939. On 23 July of that year, a mere fifty-one days after joining *Manchester*, she was torpedoed and very badly damaged while escorting a Malta convoy. The relatively inexperienced Captain Drew demonstrated skill, leadership and determination in getting his crippled cruiser back to Gibraltar.

The damage inflicted in 1941 was remarkably similar to that suffered in August 1942 but, on the latter occasion, Captain Drew seems to have opted unconsciously to scuttle his ship within ten minutes of being torpedoed when he ordered 'Emergency Stations' rather than fighting her through to the end. Yet just thirteen months earlier, albeit in a tactically more favourable situation, the same man had brought *Manchester* back to Gibraltar after a struggle lasting three days. Obviously, in August 1942, *Manchester* had been crippled in much closer proximity to enemy-held territory but the expected determination to try to save the ship seems to be missing. Why?

To return to the events of 1941, after getting *Manchester* back to Gibraltar Drew remained with his ship while she was patched prior to sailing to Philadelphia for permanent repairs. Drew was the most senior British officer in that port at the time. He was therefore without a more senior officer to monitor his psychological condition while at the same time providing a metaphorical shoulder to lean upon should the need arise.

Furthermore, the absence of a more senior officer meant that there was no-one with the authority to report to the Naval Secretary at the Admiralty to recommend his reassignment to a less demanding post. He therefore remained in *Manchester* and was quite soon faced with a similar situation to the one from which he had successfully extricated the same ship just thirteen months earlier. It is not entirely unexpected that faced with what must have seemed to him to be a repeat of an earlier experience, his decision making skills and determination may have deserted him.

The big difference between the two occasions was that in 1941 *Manchester* was torpedoed much nearer to Gibraltar and so getting her back to safety was very much easier. On the second and fatal occasion with the ship southeast of Cape Bon the return passage was much more risky. Sadly, at an early stage in proceedings Drew seems to have dismissed the possibility of making for Malta which was much nearer although not exactly a safe haven. Perhaps he assessed the prospect of getting there as nil. Clearly, this was not an option to the merchant stragglers loaded with a mixture of foodstuffs, petrol and high explosives who were expected to make for the besieged island come what may.

A lack of firm and energetic leadership

There is a distinct possibility that Captain Drew had been a less than decisive leader for some time and that well before that fatal night of 13 August, some of his officers had begun to doubt and question his leadership. Interacting with a man who has become inadequate but not disastrously incompetent is very difficult and 'when such a man is in charge of the whole shooting match it leads to a slack ship which is always an unhappy one. His subordinates begin to believe that there is no point in sticking one's neck out because the man in charge will not take any notice and consequently a kind of general apathy sets in.'[15] This could explain why Commander Robb did not stand up more decisively to his Captain. Instead, he allowed Drew to continue a monologue about the ship's appalling tactical situation without politely reminding him about the need to get the engines going.

It can be argued that Robb's failure to communicate the true state of *Manchester's* capability was a contributory factor in the ship's loss because a more energetic intervention on his part might have stopped Captain Drew's headlong gallop to scuttle. However, to criticise Commander Robb for not standing up more decisively to his Commanding Officer is more than a little unfair because in that era there was not the expectation that junior officers would question their senior's attitudes.

It is also entirely possible that by the time that Commander Robb was able to make the claim that *Manchester* was capable of moving under her own power, events on board had taken such a catastrophic path that he must have felt that it was simply not worth pursuing the issue. This also could explain why Commander Gill was not more proactive with regard to reporting that power steering had been restored. An alternative explanation is that Captain Drew was an unapproachable sort who didn't invite input from others and his subordinates knew it.

Because the tactical situation was uppermost in his mind, Captain Drew seemed to lose sight of the fact that he needed to get the machinery and steering back on line as soon as possible while at the same time restoring *Manchester*'s fighting ability. Instead, he channelled all his energy into peripheral issues such as the burning SPs and CBs, getting 'spare' crew onto *Pathfinder* and having an inappropriately long monologue with his Engineering officer about the tactical situation when he should have been chasing Robb to get his ship moving.

In effect, Drew was busy doing things related to his situation but did not want to address the real issue of getting underway and so either didn't hear, understand or take in key reports about the ship's machinery. Because he was unwilling to address the issue of getting underway, he therefore wasn't concerned about armament. This is classic displacement behaviour and suggests he had mentally made the decision to scuttle the ship very early on and probably at the same time (about 01.40 hours) as he gave the flawed order 'Emergency Stations' when he could have been underway fifteen minutes earlier. Almost certainly the pressure exerted by the adverse tactical situation resulted in a hasty and premature decision, while the announcement of 'Emergency Stations' had an unstoppable domino-like effect which ensured that *Manchester* could not be recovered.

Clearly, firm leadership is decisive to the whole business of extricating a ship from circumstances that could, under less energetic direction from the top, result in its loss.[16] During the court martial it became clear that Drew was loath to chase up those attempting to recover the ship. His comment that 'it is not customary to report back to me on the bridge the compliance of such orders, but rather to report to me if they have not been complied with'[17] is that of an administrator rather than a thrusting warrior. To save his ship he needed to energise his subordinates and give them a sense of purpose and direction. One can hardly say that Captain Drew tried everything, or even anything, possible to keep his ship afloat and get away.

In a letter to the Admiralty sent after the court martial, Captain Drew wrote that 'at times such as these, officers and men alike react instinctively to training, tradition and any ideas that they may have set themselves prior to sailing on any particular operation rather than to deliberation and unhurried thought'.[18] That this is obviously true is borne out by the time and money the military devote to training so that when placed under difficult and dangerous circumstances people instinctively know what to do. That being the case one needs to ask why, with the exception of the Engineering Department, this was not always true aboard *Manchester* on that fatal night? Once again it comes down to leadership and the direction and discipline that it imposes. Sadly, Drew's order 'Emergency Stations' gave too many of *Manchester*'s men a false impression of the situation.

It would seem that discipline aboard *Manchester* was breaking down from an early stage in what should have been an attempt to recover. That more than 150 officers and men were offloaded into *Pathfinder* well before there should have been any thought of abandoning ship must have had a deleterious effect on the determination of those remaining on board to try to save her. In comparison Robb's engineers were well-motivated and very determined to try to save their ship to the extent that many had to be ordered to give up their recovery work after it was announced that the ship was to be scuttled.

While the immediate blame can be placed correctly on Captain Drew it is possible that the seeds of the disaster lie in the events of July 1941. It is likely that he had become a casualty of overstrain bordering on mental breakdown well before the events of the night of 13 August. Assuming that to be the case, I have no doubt that as the *Pedestal* convoy was passing Gibraltar en route for Malta Captain Drew's degree of anxiety had begun to rise to an almost intolerable level. This may appear to be hard on Drew but such things happen in war which is a brutal, messy and unforgiving business. Put simply, by August 1942 Captain Drew had become the wrong man in the wrong job at the wrong time and his superiors must take the some of the blame for leaving him in post for which he had become unfit.

Appendix I

Particulars of HMS *Manchester*

Ordered 3/1935
Laid down by Hawthorn Leslie 28/3/1936
Launched 12/4/1937
Completed 4/8/1938

Displacement: 9,400 tons (light), 11,500 tons full load.

Dimensions: 591 feet 6 inches (overall) x 62 feet 4 inches (beam) x 17 feet 5 inches draught light/ 21 feet full load.

Machinery (by Hawthorn Leslie): Four Admiralty 3-drum boilers; four sets of Parsons geared turbines; four shafts; 82,500 shaft horse power = 32.5 knots (designed maximum)/31 knots full load.

Oil fuel: 1,950 tons.

Endurance: 12,300 miles at 12 knots; 7,100 miles at 20 knots; 2,600 miles at 31 knots.

Protection: Belt 4.5 inches; upper deck (over boiler rooms & forward engine room) 1.5 inches; lower deck (forward & aft of boiler rooms) 1.25 inches & 1.25 – 1.5 inches over steering gear; box citadel protection to magazines 3.5 – 4.5 inches; 6-inch gun turrets 1 – 2 inches; barbettes 1inch.

Armament: Twelve 6-inch (4 x 3); eight 4-inch AA (4 x 2); eight 2pdr AA (2 x 4); eight 0.5-inch AA (2 x 4) guns; six 21-inch (2 x 3) torpedo tubes.

Aircraft: One athwartships catapult and three Walrus amphibians.

Complement: 800 (815 as flagship & 980 in wartime).

As completed in 1938 *Manchester* was fitted with a HF/DF aerial at her foremast head. This sensor had become relatively common in the Royal Navy by 1939 but no other navy used it. Royal Navy cruisers were equipped with HF/DF to enable them to detect raiders beyond the horizon.

Modifications after completion:

(1) On completion of refit on Tyne 27/3/1941: Eight 0.5-inch AA (2 x 4) machine guns were landed. One 40mm AA gun mounted on top of 'B' turret and five single 20mm AA guns added.

(2) On completion of refit at Portsmouth on 1/5/1942 : *Manchester*'s close range AA armament included eight 2pounder AA (2 x 4 – as built), one 40mm AA on 'B' Turret and eight single 20mm AA (8 x 1 – one in each bridge wing, four on aft superstructure, one on 'X' Turret and one on quarterdeck) guns. Her radar fit included: SR.RDF Type 284 fitted on the low-angle Director Control Tower (DCT) for 6-inch guns on the bridge, SW.RDF Type 273 (Surface Warning) fitted aft of the LA.DCT on the bridge, AR.RDF Type 285 (AA gunnery radar for 4-inch guns) fitted on HA.DCTs (High Angle Directors) in bridge wings but not on the aft HA.DCT, AW.RDF Type 279 (long range air warning) fitted at the mastheads.

(3) In late 7/1942 or early 8/1942, two single Army pattern 40mm AA guns were added amidships prior to serving as an escort to the *Pedestal* convoy operation.

Appendix II

HMS *Manchester* Torpedo Damage, 23 July 1941

The following is taken from Director of Naval Construction Damage Report DNC 4B/R81 (Copy No. 2 in the author's possession).

Manchester was torpedoed in the Mediterranean on 23 July 1941 and proceeded to the USA for repairs. Consequently it was not possible for the damage to be inspected by a representative of the Director of Naval Construction in according with Confidential Admiralty Fleet Order (C.A.F.O) 2972/39, paragraph 2.

The report of the incident as forwarded by the Commanding Officer (Captain Drew) through Rear-Admiral Commanding 18 Cruiser Squadron and Commander-in-Chief, Home Fleet (Admiral Sir John Tovey) was therefore reproduced for circulation from SV Goodall (later Sir Stanley Goodall, Director of Naval Construction) on 27/2/1942. The Engineer-in-Chief and the Director of Electrical Engineering concurred in this decision.

From: Rear Admiral Commanding 18th Cruiser Squadron
To: The Commander-in-Chief, Home Fleet (copied to the CO HMS MANCHESTER)

It is considered that credit is due to HMS MANCHESTER for the care taken in compiling this comprehensive and valuable report.
A glance at the extent of the flooding reveals how seriously the stability of the ship was affected and how much greater might have been the consequences had the weather been bad. Viewed from this angle it would have been better if the pumping out of A2, A4, B8, B10 etc., to correct the list had not been done.
The successful use of gas masks by rescue and repair parties on this occasion should not be allowed to obscure the dangers attending their use when reference in the Medical Section to a number of cases of (carbon) monoxide poisoning. Personnel should be trained to use the Salvus and Type 23Q equipment and

only resort to the use of gas masks during salvage and rescue operations if this equipment is unavailable.

HMS MANCHESTER's recommendations are concurred in general, subject to the following remarks:

Communicating Doors
This, it is understood, is already being done in ships of modern construction.

Miners' Lamps
It is agreed that a form of lamp which need be held in the hand is necessary. Head harness would be different to wear in conjunction with breathing apparatus and some means of suspending the lamp around the neck or securing it to the chest would possibly be better.

Air Test Plugs
An order is being issued to the 18th Cruiser Squadron for this to be done.

Emergency Ring Main
The difficulties of passing a centreline emergency Ring Main through such compartments as the Magazines, Shellrooms, Boiler Rooms and Engine Rooms would appear to preclude this suggestion being put into effect. Although the emergency ring main as at present fitted is liable to damage, the damaged portions can be readily isolated or replaced.

Electrical Vertical Supplies
The fitting of further vertical supplies is concurred in but again it is doubtful if further piercing of the armoured deck is warranted.

Warning Telephone
This system has proved itself such a valuable means of passing information about the ship that duplication of the system together with the adaptation of the S.R. equipment for passing orders through the ship is worth consideration.

Fuse Boards
An increase in the number of fuse boards supplied is recommended but, owing to the congestion already existing between decks, it is not recommended that the additional number should exceed six.

Electrical Stores
A number of ships have already taken steps to distribute essential stores throughout the ship.

Steering Motor Supply
A change over switch in the steering compartment which could be operated by the watch-keeper has obvious advantages and the recommendation is concurred in.

HMS Manchester – Torpedo Damage Report

From: C-in-C Home Fleet to Admiralty, copied to Rear Admiral Commanding 18th Cruiser Squadron:

Forwarded for information, concurring generally with the Rear Admiral Commanding, 18th Cruiser Squadron.
2. With reference to the Rear Admiral Commanding, 18th Cruiser Squadron's remarks, paragraph 2, the handling of stability problems in a severely damaged ship calls for considerable knowledge and judgement; and whilst the discharge of "ballast" from A2, A4, B8, B10 low down in the ship adversely affected stability and may be questionable, the final test must be the safe return of the ship to harbour.
3. The general handling of the damage control repairs, etc. was good.
4. The adoption of butterfly nuts to air test plugs, although convenient in certain circumstances, involves a considerable amount of work in all ships, and in view of the difficulty of supply and fitting these plugs, further changes appear undesirable. The adequate supply of spanners for repair parties is most necessary.
5. The primary and vital factor enabling the hit to be sustained was undoubtedly the watertight subdivision; some 2,000 tons of water remained in the ship on entering harbour. X and Y 50-ton pumps could not be worked, and the portable pumps again proved invaluable.
6. It is recommended that the allowance of portal electric pumps in this class of cruiser should be increased to at least 6, the pumps being supplied complete with equipment and starting resistances (A.F.O. 3315/40 refers). The diesel-driven portable pump authorised in A.F.O 5303/41 should be additional to these 6 pumps. In my letter 1843/H.F.729/11 dated 20th December 1941, an increase in the allowance for pumps for capital ships and aircraft carriers has been similarly recommended. There is always the likelihood that some of the portable pumps will in any case be

damaged by the hit. I regard the supply of pumps as of the utmost importance and request I may be informed when they may be expected.

7. The failure of the warning telephone system is noteworthy, although there was not loss of power in the ship.

8. The flooding of the gyro room through holes in which no cable glands were fitted was a serious matter. Flooding due to a similar cause was also reported by H.M. Ships NELSON, RESOLUTION and by other ships. The air testing of compartments is a laborious process and its importance cannot be over-emphasised.

9. With reference to the recommendations contained in Appendix V of HMS MANCHESTER's report:

Miner's Lamps. It appears that the lamps authorised by A.F.O.4515/40 may not have been demanded. The attention of the Commanding Officer, HMS MANCHESTER is invited to this Order.

Emergency Ring Main. It appears that the alterations and additions ordered by C.A.F.O.307/40 had not been completed in HMS MANCHESTER at the time of the damage. It is considered that these arrangements when completed will be satisfactory.

Model Ring Main. This would be of value to ships not included in C.A.F.O.1038/41. It is considered that a suitable model could be made by the ship's staff.

Jack Tovey
Admiral
Home Fleet
2nd January 1942

HMS Manchester, Report on Torpedoing 23 JULY 1941

This was introduced by a brief narrative, explaining that at 09.46 hours on 23rd July 1941, when to the southwest of Sardinia *Manchester* was struck by a torpedo port side aft, below the 'X' Flat. The weather was Force 7, with the wind from the northeast. The depth was 1,100 fathoms:

The immediate effects of the torpedo hit were that the ship lost speed, listed rapidly to a maximum of 12.5° to Port, and trimmed 7 feet 6 inches by the stern. Lower steering was reported out of action and steering from after steering assumed, one steering motor being in action. At 09.58 hand steering had to be resorted to, but at no time was the ship out of control.

By this time reports had been received on the Bridge that the After

Engine Room was flooding rapidly and was being abandoned, that various compartments aft of that position had flooded or were flooding and that the starboard engine only was available.

Speed was gradually increased to 12 knots and course set in accordance with instructions.

More accurate information with regard to damage sustained was shortly received, while the ship was being brought upright by the transference of fuel and shifting Army stores to Starboard, also by discharge of Port torpedoes.

Enormous quantities of oil fuel had been driven up through the flats one spout of oil spraying the top and side of 'X' Turret through a hole made in the Ward Room Ante Room deckhead.

Although dense smoke filled the compartments immediately affected there was no fire. The ship entered harbour at 00.55 on 26th July, with a calculated amount of 2,000 tons of water in the After Engine Room and compartments aft of that (from bulkheads 155 to 227).

Difficulty was experienced in berthing alongside (in Gibraltar) this was due to the Port outer screw resting on the bottom. The shaft, which had broken away with most of its 'A' bracket, had to be lifted and secured to the After Capstan before the stern of the ship could be brought alongside.

Damage Control Headquarters Reports. Before the ship was struck, hands were closed up at Action Stations, and all normal reports had been received.

At 09.46 a heavy shock was felt, and the ship began to list to Port. In approximately one minute, 10 degrees was registered, and a maximum of 12.5° degrees was reached in about 3 minutes.

Steering in the lower steering position went out of action immediately and was taken over in the After position.

Efforts to establish communication with the after section H.Q's (No. 5 party) were unsuccessful. It was then known that all ratings in 'X' flat were casualties.

No. 4 party in the Workshop flat shortly reported the seat of the damage, and a little later a more detailed report was received from No. 6 party in the Keyboard Flat.

At 09.53 a general appreciation of the situation having been formed, orders were passed to the Heel and Trim Party to sluice down from A2 and A4 to A1, B1 and X1, also to be ready to start counter flooding in the Starboard W/T compartments abreast the For'd Engine Room, and "A" and "B" Boiler Rooms. A report by this time had been received that the After Engine Room was flooding seriously, steam ejectors being in use and main circulators on bilge suction.

The After Engine Room was reported flooded, abandoned, and shut down at 09.58. Orders were then passed to Heel and Trim Parties to pump out A2, A4, B8 and B10 tanks. Also orders were broadcast to shift all moveable gear from Port to Starboard.

Counter flooding was then cancelled. This had been contemplated in order to lessen the list in as short a time as possible to give the 6-inch guns a larger field fire against low flying aircraft.

Later, oil fuel was transferred from 'X'4 to 'A'1, and the Port forward fresh water tank pumped out. By 12.20 the ship was brought upright, but a slight list to Starboard developed later, due to secondary flooding. This was corrected by pumping out.

Fire and Repair Parties – shoring. The torpedo struck at 202 station in Y4 oil fuel tank, completely wrecking the port lower compartments between stations 179 and 209, driving the port side deck of 'X' flat to the upper deck and putting out all lighting in 'X' and Gunroom flats.

Unfortunately, the After Section Damage Control Headquarters was situated in 'X' flat. There were few survivors here, and they were unable to resume duty after rescue, thus there was some little delay before concerted action was taken. The majority of the After Medical Distributing Section were also immediate casualties or else rendered unconscious soon after by oil fuel gas and explosion fumes. The number of casualties was increased by the fact that all Fire and Repair Parties, Magazine crews and Medical Parties were backed up by Military other ranks who were embarked for the operation.

There is no direct evidence of fire other than dense white smoke. This, together with foul air, complete darkness and sloping oil-covered corticene [linoleum type decking], made first investigations difficult. The seat of damage was quickly found however and the following details established.

'X' Flat: Most of Port side deck blown up to deckhead. All compartments beneath, missing with reflected sunlight showing up over a considerable area. Ship's side intact to well below the waterline.

Of the two midships hatches, the one to the Compressor Room was open with oil fuel flooded up to coaming level, the hatch to 'X' Magazine trunk holding. Starboard Forward and after communication doors (2 clips and fully clipped) shut and clipped, but forward door distorted and not watertight. Bulkheads and deckhead soaked in oil fuel, and remainder of deck awash with water and oil fuel. Starboard side littered with damaged tins thrown up from Port provision store together with a portion of the deck from the Port side. Flat in complete darkness and air very foul. Several unconscious survivors on starboard side. This flat has no direct access to upper deck except through Magazine embarkation hatch which is a vent hatch and which was blown up. GUNROOM FLAT (Forward of 'X' Flat): Port after communication door (Fully Clipped) sprung open and distorted. Bulkhead in vicinity slightly cracked and badly distorted. Manhole door in hatch to Midshipman's chest flat open and distorted, (E.R.A. had shortly before gone down to stern gland compartment), remainder of doors and hatches closed, clipped and holding with exception of embarkation hatch (vent hatch) above four-inch Magazine trunk blown open, and manhole door in hatch above ladder to Gunroom flat (access hatch to Gunroom Flat). Water pouring into flat over coaming of port after door and oil welling up through manhole in hatch to Midshipman's Chest flat.

Gunroom flat soaked in oil fuel with depth of 5 feet in ship's side to port. Flat in darkness, the air would not support unaided breathing long while thick white smoke prevented the useful employment of torches. A considerable number of casualties covered in oil, most of whom were collected in a heap at the foot of the ladder.

'Y' FLAT: Secondary and emergency lighting in operation. Port forward communication door (2 clip) bottom distorted with water and oil pouring over coaming, hatch to No. 6 Breaker Room, clipped and holding, but badly distorted and leaking, with deck in vicinity distorted. Remainder of doors and hatches closed, clipped and holding. Water and oil 2 feet at ship's side to Port, and a number of casualties due to shock.

ACTION TAKEN: In the Gunroom Flat, the Port after communication door was secured by one clip and then securely shored, leakage into the flat through cracked bulkhead, being stopped with soft wood wedges. Similarly the manhole door to Midshipman's Chest Flat was shored down, and soft wood wedges employed to stop leakage of oil fuel.

The manhole door through the hatch to the Main W/T Office was opened and the oil fuel level observed to be four feet below hatch level. Two casualties were observed floating, and these were rescued. Further rescue was prevented by the rapid increase of level. The manhole door was shut, clipped and shored down. The main hatch above the gunroom ladder was opened up to assist ventilation, all local fans being out of action. The flat cleared itself fairly quickly so portable blowers were not required. Casualties were completely evacuated, this work having started simultaneously with shoring. The trunk to the 4-inch Magazine was tested, and then the hatch opened, survivors were found clinging to the ladder, oil fuel being half way up trunk. These survivors were rescued and the hatch closed and clipped.

A portable pump suction was led into the flat and a good suction obtained. The port after corner of the flat was then heavily shored as vibration here was very marked.

In 'X' flat, as free water was washing across from the port side, little could be done for the time being. Any hope of rescue for 'X' Magazine's crew was out of the question as the trunk proved to be full. This applied similarly to any ratings remaining in the Compressor Room. Accessible casualties were taken out and the Starboard side cleared of debris. A second portable pump was rigged ready for use here. No permanent suctions could be used as these were all fractured.

In 'Y' flat, the port forward door was opened in an effort to straighten it. This proved impossible, but two casualties were extricated from the wreckage in 'X' flat. The door was then shut and clipped and softwood wedges driven in and the bottom made partially watertight in this way. The hatch to No. 6 Breaker Room was shored down and made watertight. Test plugs were then examined to determine the extent of the flooding. Hatches were opened up when this was considered safe.

The 'X' Shellroom crew had already left their shellroom, closing the trunk upper hatch, evacuating casualties from the flat.

'Y' Magazine and Handing Room Crews were brought up. It was established that in 'Y' flat all compartments on the Port side were flooded. Amidships, the Warhead Room was flooded but not 'X' Shellroom underneath it, while 'Y' pump space was leaking slightly and "Y" Magazine and Handing Room underneath almost dry. 'Y' Magazine and Handing Room were closed and clipped, the pump space above shored up, and then closed down.

On the Starboard side, No.5 Breaker Room and adjacent compartments were dry.

In 'X' flat, all compartments beneath were flooded except the Starboard provision room, which was leaking slightly.

In the Gunroom flat, all compartments beneath were flooded except the Slop Room and adjacent compartments on the Starboard side.

By this time, the After Engine Room had been flooded, abandoned and shut down due to both shafts stuffing boxes being torn from the port after bulkhead by the force of the explosion.

The limits of flooding were found to stretch from station 155 to 227.

Immediate measures having been taken it was possible to assume a general plan of action. Also lighting had been re-established and better working conditions prevailed.

A heavy programme of shoring was undertaken throughout the lower deck and in all other compartments which were not flooded, between stations 155 and 234. This was considered necessary due to severe vibration and panting.

On the 23rd, as soon as Shipwrights were available from immediate shoring requirements, a wooden bulkhead of 1.5-inch tongue & groove was built between 'X' barbette and the forward bulkhead of 'X' flat.

In spite of many obstructions on deck and bulkhead this made very nearly watertight and the suction of the second portable pump employed on the starboard side of 'X' flat. Later, when the Starboard side was nearly cleared of water, a second dam was built. This formed a coffer dam which was pumped out as necessary.

The wedges driven in round the lower portion of the Port forward door of 'Y' flat not proving very satisfactory, a dam was eventually built and filled with cement. This set in 1.5 hours and proved very satisfactory.

Throughout the passage (back to Gibraltar), as panting became more pronounced, further shoring was undertaken. Among bulkheads shored up was the after bulkhead of "B" Boiler room.

Two portable pumps were in constant use. Endeavours were made to bring a third into service but were unsuccessful as a third starting resistance was not held and could not be improvised successfully in the time.

The compartments subject to slow flooding beneath 'Y', 'X' and Gunroom flats were, No. 5 Breaker room, Starboard provision store and Slop room compartments. These all required constant attention.

On the 24th, the hatch to 'Y' pump space was re-opened and an emergency supply led to the 50 ton pump. 'X' shellroom trunk had been opened up some time before and found to be flooding due to distorted door of Warhead Room in trunk, allowing water to leak down trunk through lower which had been left open by shellroom crew when evacuating.

When the 50 ton pump was started suction on 'X' shellroom could not be obtained through flexible suction. This latter was then transferred to 'X' flat and the portable pump brought from there to 'Y' flat and employed on 'X' shellroom. Great difficulty was experienced at first in obtaining suction here, due to the head of water. Unfortunately the loose water in 'Y' pump space then gained access to the coils of the 50 ton pump motor which burnt out. Further shoring was then put up in the pump space, and the space closed down. The lower and upper hatches to the trunk were closed and clipped with 'X' shellroom about a third full.

The gyro room was also opened up and partially pumped out, but when the extent of the leak was ascertained (leaking through cable holes, no glands fitted) this was abandoned, as it would have required the constant service of a portable pump which was more urgently required elsewhere. Instead the bulkhead was shored up across the Slop room passage.

On 24th a collision mat was rigged to Port of the dam in 'X' flat. This was made as neat a fit as possible and was provided to absorb the surge of free water surface and prevent damage to the wooden bulkhead should heavy seas be encountered.

As the weather was deteriorating, the Starboard forward door of 'X' flat, was replaced by a sound one and 'X' flat was isolated, work being continued by means of 'X' Magazine upper deck embarkation hatch. No really bad weather was encountered however.

Bailing parties were employed in all three flats during passage. The Military detachment supplied most of these, as hands were closed up (at Action Stations) most of the time on passage, further attacks being expected, though only one of these materialised.

ENGINEERING: (Prior to being torpedoed) the ship was steamed at 124 revolutions, in units with two boilers connected in each unit. The hands had been closed up at first degree of readiness since dawn. The usual action reports were received in the Forward Engine Room regarding machinery and damage control parties. The following narrative is not chronological owing to varying time lags between events, and between answering orders and completion of execution.

At about 09.46 the ship received a severe shaking from an explosion, but this was no worse than that which recently had been experienced as a result of a near miss, by a heavy bomb, indeed, in the interval before reports were received, it was thought that this had occurred, and that the list, which was being assumed, was due to resulting minor damage and heel under full wheel.

The first report received was that the Port telemotor lead had failed, one steering motor had stopped, and that the ship was steaming by mechanical wheel in after steering compartment.

No. 3 (Starboard) diesel had to be stopped owing to failure of electrical pump. As this pump could not be restarted either on dynamo or ring main supply, the diesel was started on Fire Main Circulation. Later, the electrical defects were found to be that the

202

explosion had caused minor internal defects to the starter, and that the brushes had jumped clear of the commutator.

In the after compressor room, a centreline compartment, all lights went out, oil fuel gushed in from Y.4 oil fuel tank from a large hole in the port bulkhead, the hole was made by the projection of a piece of 'F' plummer block.

In the C.O.2 compartment the watchkeeper had started the 50 ton pump on the fire main, and 20 ton pump on turret cooling. He had stopped the machine and was closing the gas circuit valves when the concussion from the explosion caused the safety disc to burst. Large escape of gas was saved by shutting all valves on the gas circuit.

After the explosion the Port outer shaft tended to speed up and was checked. Reports were received that there was damage aft, and that the After Engine Room was making oil fuel rapidly.

In the After Engine Room all emergency lights and half the main lighting went out, all supply and exhaust fans stopped. The Lower Power Air Compressor stopped and smoke issued from the starter box. The starting handle hand jumped round half a turn, and a certain amount of burning took place before the handle could be returned to the 'Off' position. Both fire and bilge pumps stopped, and the after one was being splashed with oil fuel.

The after plummer block on the port outer shaft had been torn off the inner bottom and shaft was bent. Oil fuel, followed by water, gushed into the engine room from port shaft bulkhead glands, which had been blown in.

On loud bumping being heard, the Port inner shaft was eased, but when it was discovered that the outer shaft was damaged, the inner shaft was re-started and 124 revolutions were obtained with approximately the same receiver pressure as before. It can only be assumed that the damaged plummer blocks and bulkhead glands were acting as brakes.

The bilge suctions of the main circulators were opened, main sea inlets closed and speed of circulators increased. The steam bilge ejector was also opened out and the High Power (E) party commenced rigging emergency leads to the forward fire and bilge pump.

Within ten minutes however the flooding was already above the starting platform, port side, the ship being listed 12.5 degrees.

It was clear that the circulators and steam ejectors were not overcoming the flooding which increased rapidly. With no ventilating fans running the unpleasant fumes from the oil fuel made breathing very difficult. There was no hope of continuing to steam this engine room, although it was appreciated that it was desirable to steam as long as possible even at the risk of some pollution of lubricating oil and feed water. With the list on the ship and the oil covering the steering platform it was difficult to stand or move about, and personnel were affected by the fumes, so it was decided that the after engine room would have to be abandoned.

The turbine regulating valves were shut, but the main bulkhead valve was not closed as this would stop the main circulators and bilge ejector and it was hoped, at least, to prevent maximum flooding by keeping these in use. The Master valve to No. 4 dynamo and steam to other auxiliaries, except forced lubricating pumps, was shut and engine room abandoned. The auxiliary exhaust system was isolated, shutting off the after engine room, and exhaust from "B" auxiliaries was led to the forward engine room. Meanwhile the brake had been put on the port outer shaft, and this left the ship steaming on the Starboard outer engine only. The ship's organisation of Red Diamond valves (to be kept shut when not in use) and Green Triangle valves (to be shut in the event of an emergency) should have prevented the contamination of feed water in 'B' boiler room overflowed with oil fuel which was later replaced by spurts of water.

The only way in which this could come through from the After Engine Room is by the common drain valve to the overflow tank. This valve is controlled from the boiler room, and had been shut by the valve wheel and drains opened to reserve feed tank.

Subsequent examination on return to harbour showed that the valve pintle was just too long, and prevented the valve from seating. This valve is of course always open on service and there is no necessity to shut if except in such an emergency. There is no record of it having been examined since first fitting when the ship was built. The fault in the pintle has now been rectified. The matter was dealt with at the time by breaking two joints in the low level drain system and inserting wooden plugs, but unfortunately a certain amount of contamination took place in the reserve feed tanks, and thence to the boilers.

'B' 2 boiler was then shut down, and 'B' 1 banked with main stops and main bulkhead valves shut, saturated stop open to supply the steam fire extinguisher and auxiliary superheated stop open to supply fan, oil fuel pump, auxiliary feed pump on reserve tank suction, and if necessary the boiler room bilge ejectors. The intention was that, in the event of further damage including 'A' boiler room, the forward engine room could have been supplied with steam from 'B' boiler room.

In 'B' boiler room, the port feed heater drain pump stopped with the explosion, and feed heater drain had been changed to reserve feed tank. Emergency electrical supply had been led to the drain pump, which was re-started and feed water drain changed back to the pump.

About 11.00 hours, heel being substantially decreased, it was decided again to try the effect of the steam bilge ejector in the after engine room, an early report having suggested that originally no suction was picked up when oil fuel had to be handled.

'B' 1 main stop and the bulkhead valve were opened, boiler fed by auxiliary feed pump on reserve tank suction, and ejector worked from the lower deck position. It was kept in use for 20 minutes and this time it gave a good discharge, but made no impression on the level in the after engine room as both feed tanks emptied during this time, starting with 19 ton in each, the ejector was shut down and "B" boiler room reverted to the banked condition, topping up with feed water as required through the cross connection line from 'A' boiler room.

The bulkhead between the after engine room and 'B' boiler room stood the strain very satisfactorily and no bulging could be discerned. The ramming stay from the steam drum proved a very effective shore. Minor leakage took place from bulkhead flange adjacent to the main bulkhead valve, main cross connection valve and the auxiliary exhaust bulkhead valve, this being easily dealt with by the fire and bilge pump.

No damage took place to any machinery in 'B' boiler room, apart from contamination of feed system and boilers.

Sometime after the engine room had flooded up, the main stop valve drains in 'B' boiler room were observed to pass salt water, the main steam pipes presumably having flooded via turbine glands and a leaky manoeuvring valve and bulkhead valve.

In the forward engine room, the temperature rose to 140° F, due to stoppage of Starboard supply and exhaust fans, which obtain power from the after engine room.

After the after engine room was abandoned, a call was received from the Bridge for all possible speed, and the Starboard engine was worked up steadily to 260 revolutions. At this, the L.P. relief lifted. Speed was reduced to 220 revolutions to ease the pressures and reduce vibration, which was excessive and especially violent in the after part of the ship. Eight sprayers at 100 lbs pressure indicated just under full power for this shaft.

The closed feed system in the forward unit worked perfectly throughout, and the purity of the feed water was maintained.

The speed attained was 12.5 knots to commence with but this fell away to 11.5 knots for no apparent reason after 1 hour.

Shortly after the change to mechanical wheel was completed, the second steering motor stopped owing to No. 6 (Starboard) ring main breaker opening on overload.

The watchkeeper immediately changed over to the hand steering pump unit, and the ship was steered from this position until supply to one steering motor became available. Mechanical wheel was then brought into use again, fire main supply to the V.S.G. pump cooler was obtained by hoses over the upper deck, as fire main was thought to be fractured.

Subsequently, when all branches to the damaged portion to the ship, "X" Magazine spray, etc.) had been shut off, the fire main itself was found to be intact. A short creep test was put on the starboard telemotor lead, which was found correct, and steering was then reverted to the lower steering position.

Minor leakage into shaft passages, plummer block, and gland compartments took place through the shaft bulkhead glands. These glands gave trouble through overheating during the contractors trials, and are the subject of correspondence. They were only loosely packed in order to avoid overheating at high speeds, it being considered that they could be tightened up if required to produce watertightness. In the event, however, only those glands accessible in the forward engine room could be and were tightened up to stop the leakage from the shaft passages into the engine room.

The shaft passages under the diesel rooms and lubricating oil store were kept pumped out down to the level of the plummer blocks. The 6 bulkhead glands in the after engine room were, of course, not accessible.

ELECTRICAL: The model ring main indicated the position of the damage as being in the Port After Section, i.e. No. 12 section and Port Ring Main extension to the steering motors.

No. 6 ring main breaker Port had opened on overload and therefore the following group of breakers had failed:

XII A1	Main W/T Office.
XII A2	Air Compressor.
XII A3	'X' and 'Y' turrets Lighting.
XII A4	Important Lighting and Power.
XII A5	After Capstan (not closed).
XII C1	No. 1 Steering Motor (not closed).
XII C2	No. 2 Steering Motor.
XII B1	'X' Turret Pump.

No orders were given to close these breakers on account of possible electrical fires, also the extent of the damage had not been reported. It was assumed that the changeover switches to the Starboard side of the Main W/T Office and 'X' Turret pump had been operated. No. 1 Steering Motor X1 C1 was still running on the starboard ring main extension. 'X' and 'Y' lighting are duplicated. The after gyro alarm bell was ringing, and orders were low power to change over the balancer change over switch to forward compass. This was reported as having already been done and that damage to the Port and Starboard H.A. Tables was being attended to. At this time a list of 12.5 degrees to port was observed.

At 09.50 No. 3 diesel Dynamo Room phoned, asking to be taken off the board immediately. This was done and No. 4 ring main breaker (Starboard) closed, leaving the Starboard side supplied from No. 1 dynamo.

At 09.52 the 6-inch Transmitting Station phoned that power had failed on 'X' and 'Y' turrets. As no communication had been received from the after repair party, a messenger was sent with a written order to make the change over switch for the after for the after turrets.

At 09.53 No. 4 dynamo ammeter was fluctuating around 1800 amps and the voltage was low. The after engine room repair party were phoned for information. Reply "We are flooding" was received, Damage Control Headquarters also reported that the engine room was being abandoned.

No. 4 Main Supply Switch was then opened, No. 4 at this time was only supplying X.A group of branch breakers for the after engine room and owing to the flooding, No. 5 ring main breaker was not closed.

Shortly after this, the messenger returned with the information that 'X' Magazine and after compressor room were flooded and that he could not find any of the after electrical repair parties. Orders were passed by phone to No. 2 Diesel Room to prepare to supply the lower deck emergency ring main and await orders.

The 6-inch Transmitting Station was then phoned and informed that power to the after turrets could not be supplied as the Compressor Room was flooded. Further information was received that there had been a failure of high power on the auto-selector switch, when No. 4 dynamo off the board, because this switch had failed to operate fully and all the generators, i.e. 50 volt, 50 cycles, 120 volt 333 cycles, and the firing generators had stopped. The matter had been quickly dealt with as follows.

As No. 1 8 kilowatt generator was running, No. 2 8 kilowatt circuit breaker was unlocked and No. 1 made, restoring low power. The auto-selector was operated by hand and brought to No. 1 dynamo position, restoring high power. Approximately 20 seconds was taken to complete this.

At 10.01 No. 1 dynamo ammeter suddenly showed 1800 amps, then No. 6 ring main breaker (starboard) opened on overload. This immediately affected the following breakers:

X1, C1, X1, C2	- steering motors
X1, B1	- 'Y' Turret pump
X1, A3	- 'X' and 'Y' turrets lighting
X1, A4	- Important lighting and power

Information was then received from Damage Control Headquarters that we had been struck below 'X' flat by a torpedo together with an estimate of the damage.

Written orders were then sent to the emergency cable party to run the lower deck emergency cable from No. 2 Diesel Room, changing over to Starboard side in the Pay Office Flat to steering motors aft. No. 2 Diesel Room was instructed to supply verticals from the emergency supply switch. The after engine room being abandoned, No. 5 ring main switch (Starboard) was opened, and the after engine room repair parties instructed to take over the duties of casualties in the after repair parties.

When No. 6 ring main breaker (Starboard) opened, hand steering had been reverted to. Instructions were now given to prepare emergency supply to the steering motor starters.

At 10.13 No. 3 Diesel generator was placed on the board and No. 4 ring main breaker opened, this gave the generator a small load from the ring main, and left a good margin for emergency.

Repairs to H.A. Tables were now reported completed. Defects had been:

Port H.A. Table:

(a) Red pointer on 'Follow Angle of Sight' jammed
(b) Sensitive valve spring rod dislocated in the Director setting Hunter Unit

Starboard H.A. Table:

Oldhams coupling in fuse and firing interval clock starting handle (vertical shaft) had jumped out of the clutch and jammed handle At about 10.30 emergency supplies were ready for the steering motors but these could not be made as the oil cooling system was out of action, and temporary fire main hoses were being run forward of the damaged section. Power steering was resumed at 11.50.

Temporary lighting which had been supplied to 'X' and Gunroom flats was backed up, and yard arm groups supplied, also power supplies for 3 portable pumps. During the whole period up to docking, emergency supplies were successfully maintained.

Three ratings from the forward repair parties were ordered aft to back up the repair aft. Of the latter party, four had been rendered immediate casualties by the explosion, three in 'X' flat and one in the Gunroom Flat.

During the refit, January – March 1941, the ring main switch gear and branch breakers were modified in accordance with Admiralty Fleet Order 1255/40, and all switch gear concerned functioned correctly (NB the changes suggested in AFO 1255/40 had come about as the result of earlier damage reports on a variety of RN ships since the outbreak of the Second World War).

Warning telephone system failed due to the flooding of the Main W/T Office and public address equipment was brought into action by utilising the microphone on the Bridge. Telephone communication was generally good.

The failure of the auto selector switch can only be assumed due, at present, to concussion from the explosion.

GUNNERY: The sequence of events with regard to damage sustained by the explosion was as follows:

After H.A.D.T. put out of action due to shock to instruments. Crew reported ready to relieve forward H.A.D.Ts as necessary.

Communications between Transmitting Station and 'X' and 'Y' turrets mostly destroyed. In 'Y' Turret, all communication dead. In 'X' Turret multiphone to T.S. still in action, orders being relayed to 'Y' Turret by shouting.

Primary and secondary lighting in 'X' and 'Y' turrets extinguished and Oldhams lamps brought into use.

Port and Starboard H.A. Tables affected by shock, repairs quickly carried out.

'X' Shellroom evacuated and 'X' Magazine flooded, arrangements made to supply 'X' from 'Y' with Military Draft assisting.

4-inch Magazine, reported flooded, evacuated and closed down.

6-inch Transmitting Station – High and Low power failed for short period. 'X' Gunhouse and Cordite gallery evacuated for a few minutes while thick smoke and fumes were cleared.

'X' and 'Y' turrets power supply failed, turrets shortly reporting 'Ready' with everything in hand.

After Director Control Tower reported training failed and Rangefinder out of action. Training in Hand.

'Y' Magazine and shellroom evacuated due to danger from adjacent flooded compartments and panting of decks.

It was then considered inadvisable to bring 'X' and 'Y' turrets into action due to the danger to adjacent structure already severely damaged. These Quarters were shortly fallen out and used to back up hand steering parties and fire and repair parties.

MEDICAL: The After Medical Distributing Station was situated in the Warrant Officers Mess in the Gunfire Flat. This compartment is immediately forward of 'X' flat under which the torpedo struck. The Medical Officer and two Sick Berth Attendants were rendered unconscious inside a minute by carbon monoxide while two of the stretcher party outside the Warrant Officers Mess were killed and the remainder rendered immediate casualties. This was unfortunate as all casualties had to be brought to the forward distributing station situated in the Chief Petty Officers mess.

The first casualties arrived in a few minutes and quickly developed into a stream that threatened at first to become overwhelming. The rate of arrival made it possible to give only the roughest treatment at first, and distribution became an urgent question. This was solved by laying a line of stretchers along the alleyway. This line soon stretched far down the well deck. When the rush eased, sorting became feasible.

Those already dead were carried away and covered, the wounded and unconscious being carried into the Sick Bay and the Chief Petty Officers Mess, both of which had been cleared of lighter cases. By this means it was possible to keep the more serious cases under supervision.

Circumstances were favourable. Most of the injured suffered from blast and monoxide poisoning, and the weather allowed these to be taken to the well deck for artificial respiration.

The number wounded was small and mostly not severely so, one case only urgently requiring operation.

By the afternoon 15 dead had been collected, 21 being missing and assumed trapped in flooded compartments. Those suffering from blast and monoxide poisoning gradually recovered and were up and about by 22.00, with the exception of 8 who recovered the next morning.

In all, 74 casualties received treatment. One of the ten wounded died. Three Military Officers, two Military other ranks, and two ratings were landed for treatment on arrival.

DAMAGE: Generally between Stations 186 and 213 inclusive on Port Side.

Port Strakes – A, B, C, D, E, F of outer bottom together with transverse and longitudinal frames torn away and crumpled over a length of 40 feet, and depth of 25 feet, platform and lower decks thrust up to upper deck. Upper deck buckled and holed above seat of damage.

'X' gundeck holed.

Port transverse bulkheads buckled and split.

Port longitudinal bulkheads buckled and split. The compressor room bulkhead abreast the point of contact perforated by a piece of plummer block projected from below.

Internal armour abreast 'X' magazine and shellroom slightly buckled with magazine port bulkhead set in towards centre line.

Port outer shaft 'A' bracket both arms broken off 1 foot from plating.

198 bulkhead below platform deck shattered and two internal armour plates dislodged.

213 bulkhead torn in wake of bent inner shaft.

Port shafting – one tail section badly distorted, one bent. One intermediate section badly bent, two slightly bent.

Starboard shafting – Plummer bearings out of alignment.

Port bearings – 4 plummer bearings and 4 bulkhead glands fractured, or missing in their entirety.

Plummer block compartments and contents (200 Port) missing.

Port propellers, both damaged.

Port outer stern gland casting fractured and stiffeners bent and torn away, shipbuilder's tube extensively damaged.

'X' Turret supporting structure slightly distorted.

4-inch magazine – 50% bottle rack stowage buckled and beyond repair.

Installations in After Engine Room, after Gyro Compass Room, Main W/T Office, After Compressor Room and No. 5 Breaker Room submerged in oil fuel and water, also complete outfit of Electrical spare gear submerged in oil fuel and water.

GENERAL REMARKS:

Except those in the vicinity of the explosion, the concussion suggested nothing worse than a near miss. A number of these have been experienced which have given the ship a greater general shock.

Some reports contain evidence of a second explosion, but these reports are conflicting with regards to time interval, and are not substantiated by any who did not become a casualty.

It is quite remarkable that the 4-inch Magazine Crew together with 'X' Handling Room Crew, who had to negotiate the obstructions in the after compressor room, all escaped. They have no clear idea as to what happened between the explosion and recovering consciousness on deck.

Evidence with regard to initial conditions and rate of flooding in the damage compartments is not available. Shock and gas so affected survivors that their memories of the event are hazy and unreliable. Two instances of uncertainty relate to the Main W/T Office manhole door and the 4-inch Magazine trunk hatch, both of which were found shut. Four casualties were recovered from the Main W/T Office, but two of these appear to have been taken out before the first investigations were made in the Flat. How they were taken out by whom, is not clear. Rescue conditions were almost impossible due to darkness, thick smoke, explosion fumes and sloping decks made treacherous by oil fuel. One of these casualties survived. His evidence is that all lights went out with the explosion – Oldhams lamps were brought into use – orders passed to remain seated, when oil fuel was knee high, orders were then given to evacuate. After that order he presumably lost consciousness, as he can remember nothing. It may be that there was a short interval between the explosion and the time when the Gunroom flat filled with smoke, and during this interval someone rescued two from the Main W/T Office and shut down the manhole while someone else shut down the remainder of the 4-inch Magazine's Crew who were in the trunk, but this interval is problematical as the door in the flat nearest the explosion was blown open and the deck beyond up to the deckhead.

That there was no fire was most fortunate. Had the oil fuel that was thrown into the flats and damaged compartments caught fire the situation would have been seriously aggravated. There were several reports of fire, but none was found.

The safety arrangements of 4-inch time fuze and the protection afforded by the bottle rack stowage proved most satisfactory. In some cases where the metal containers had been squeezed almost flat the shell had forced its way out of the container, completely wrecking the nose fuze.

The value of the prone position was well borne out in 'Y' flat. Two ratings here, lying flat, were thrown bodily up to the deckhead which they actually hit without receiving damage. On the other hand four Army Officers who died of head injuries are understood to have been sitting at the time of the explosion playing cards, in spite of the fact that they had been instructed previously to lay on the deck.

The consequences resulting from the fact that an Engine Room Artificer had gone down to the Port outer stern gland compartment just before the explosion leaving the manhole door to the Midshipmen's Chest Flat open when the ship was struck that oil fuel flooded up into the gunroom flat. Great difficulty was experienced in trying to make the manhole watertight as the door was badly distorted. It may be, however, that the open manhole acted as a vent and prevented serious damage to the parent armoured hatch and surrounded deck.

Gas masks were found to give adequate protection until the flats had been ventilated. At first, a few of the repair parties and rescue parties became temporary casualties themselves through slipping and falling where the oil fuel was deep. This put the gas mask containers out of action and initially it was not possible to work with unaided breathing.

In the Gunroom flat and 'X' and 'Y' turrets, lighting was extinguished which should have remained effective according to intact circuits. Shattered fittings, bulbs and filaments seem to have caused this failure. Also in Gunroom and 'X' flats when new circuits were rigged, these were rendered partially ineffective due to bulbs being fitted with oil covered hands. Oldhams lamps were not powerful enough to work by, especially when covered in oil fuel. Yard arm groups and reflectors were the only effective illuminant.

With regard to the Medical side, the most useful fact elicited concerned the siting of the forward distributing station. Originally this had been in a very inaccessible and badly arranged place on the lower deck.

After due consideration, this had been moved up to the deck above, contrary to accepted practice.

As events turned out, the change proved right. Had the Distributing Station been on the lower level, it would have been impossible to give adequate attention to such a large number of casualties with the after station out of action.

RECOMMENDATION SUGGESTED IN VIEW OF EXPERIENCE GAINED:

Watertight Hatches: Fire and repair parties should be warned to exercise great vigilance when volunteer rescue parties are working in the vicinity of damaged and flooded compartments. Their zeal is liable to exceed their knowledge of the situation with the result that they may try to open up hatches which must remain closed for the safety of the ship.

Communication doors: It is essential that they should all conform rigidly to standard dimensions so as to be readily interchangeable.
Portable Pumps and Suction Hoses: Allowance to ships should be increased. Had further damage been sustained, requiring the

employment of portable pumps, the number available (3) would have been quite inadequate.

Miner's Lamps: Some type of electric miners' lamp with head harness should be provided for Fire and Repair Parties. It is essential to have two hands available for work, and for support when necessary.

Torches: All torches in use in the ship should be fitted with lanyards. A number of torches not so fitted were borrowed during rescue work and were quickly lost in the oil fuel.

Air Test Plugs: These should be fitted with butterfly nuts so that they can be worked without a spanner. This would greatly simplify their quick operation in difficult conditions when the life of trapped personnel is at stake.

Portable Pump Connections: A greater number of portable pump starting resistance terminal connections should be provided throughout the ship. At least one in each lower deck compartment.

Emergency Ring Main: It is considered that a Centre Line Emergency Systems:

(a) (Watertight) with suitable switchgear fitted on the Platform Deck, would be a great advantage over the present permanently wired Emergency Ring Main System.

(b) The existing Emergency Ring Main, at present follows the permanent Ring Main through all compartments, therefore any damage occurring, immediately affects the Emergency System.

(c) The Centre Line System could be so arranged as to take one or more dynamos sub-divided or complete through switchgear operated by hand or hand or at the Main Control Board. Supplies then could be taken from this system to various branch breaker compartments, fuse boards fitted in the same compartments as the Centre Line System, and to verticals at present fitted to the lower deck.

Electrical Vertical Supplies: Further vertical supplies to be fitted from the lower deck to the upper deck in order to by-pass damaged and partial flooded compartments, thereby avoiding runs of cable through hatches and doors.

Model Ring Main:

(a) In view of the extensive flooding due to the explosion it may be necessary to abandon the main control position forthwith. Therefore, it is necessary to abandon the main control position forthwith. Therefore it is proposed that a hand-operated Model Ring Main may be fitted in the secondary position i.e. the workshop flat, and would be operated in conjunction with the Main Control Board.

(b) In the event of abandoning the Main Control Position to the

Secondary Position, the exact state of the Ring Main would be available.

Warning Telephone System:

(a) The warning telephone system failed through the flooding of the Main W/T Office, and in view of previous reports, i.e., Damage Control Handbook 1941, and it is considered that this system should be duplicated. One situated forward and one aft, controlled by a change over switch, fitted in the Damage Control Headquarters.

(b) Also change over switch fitted in the sound producing room to incorporate the public address system into the warning telephone system.

Fuse Boards:

(a) At present, 12 in number fuse boards are allowed, these are fitted in various compartments, breaker rooms, engine and boiler rooms, main W/T office and low power room, all compartments being on the platform deck.

(b) It is suggested that a further supply of 12 in number, required to be fitted on the lower deck, would meet all requirements of lighting and power.

Electrical Stores: That all electrical stores should be de-centralised. During the recent damage, No. 5 central store flooded, and all electrical stores, i.e. lamps, torches, batteries, cables etc, were destroyed causing extreme inconvenience to rescue work and damage repair.

Electrical Repair Boxes: Electrical repair boxes, 3 in number to be increased by at least 100%.

Steering Motors Supply:

(a) The steering motors supply as fitted are:

Port ring main extension to branch breakers XII, C2 and XII, C1 for the forward steering compartment, and Starboard ring main extension XI, C2 and XI, C1 for the after steering compartment.

(b) It is proposed that change over switches normal and emergency, i.e., a supply from Port to Starboard or vice-versa be fitted one in each compartment. These could be operated in the event of any damage to the ring main, thereby ensuring an immediate supply of power to the steering motors.

Appendix III

Lessons learned during Operation *Pedestal*, 2-16 August 1942
(ADM 199/1242)

One lesson learnt from *Pedestal* was that there should be provision of fully standardised Fighter Direction equipment in all aircraft carriers, capital ships and cruisers – the experience of *Pedestal* lent urgency to fitting of such kit.

During *Pedestal* the Anti-submarine measures taken were reasonably successful. On only one occasion did a U-boat (*U 73*) penetrate the screen and get in a successful attack. The result was the loss of HMS *Eagle*. At the time of her loss *Eagle* was conforming to movements of the convoy which was using the very simple zig zag Number 10. It is considered that the anti-U-boat security of Force F would have been increased had the more complicated zig zags been used and varied frequently and had the heavy ships zigzagged independently at higher speed. It is not known however, to what extent such action would have been compatible with the requirements for defence against air attack, but judged by the results, the air menace, though more serious for the convoy than U-boat attack, was less serious for the escort and covering force.

The torpedoing of *Nigeria, Cairo* and SS *Ohio* took place at a time when the convoy and escorts were disorganised for various reasons and in this the submarine almost certainly fired from outside of the screen such as it was. In the case of the torpedoing of *Kenya* the submarine was seen just before the attack and the cruiser was unfortunate in not avoiding the whole salvo. As it was, her turn to comb the tracks saved her from all but one torpedo which exploded under the fore-foot.

The disorganisation following the dusk attack and the lack of destroyers made it virtually impossible to round up the convoy during the night and it was therefore a relatively easy prey to E-boats.

The outstanding feature of this operation was that the four heavy air attacks, by a total of 120 aircraft, achieved so little while the convoy

216

was fully escorted. The only damage done to the convoy was *Deucalion* near-missed and reduced in speed for a time, and to the escort, *Foresight* damaged by a torpedo and *Indomitable* by bombs.

The successful defence was partly due to the improved AA armament of the merchant ships, all of whom carried Oerlikons, while tracer ammunition provides an excellent deterrent to close and accurate air attack.

Few of the warships engaged had previous experience of heavy scale air attacks, and on the whole their AA fire control equipment was out of date. None of the ships were fitted with any of the following:

Joystick control of HA Directors
A.B.Us for firing RDF barrage
Accurate deflection units
R.P.C. for either 4-inch guns or pom pom mountings
Beam switching (permits identification of the correct target for the guns concerned) for RDF equipment (fitted in *Charybdis*)

Even so, the effect of the AA fire put up must make the German and Italian air forces begin to realise that air attack in daylight is becoming less and less profitable. Their 'interest' in air attack by night will correspondingly increase and it is essential that the fleet should be equipped without delay to deal with night air attack.

Contributory factors toward the comparative immunity of the convoy were:

The unusually large proportion of fighters in the aircraft carriers.
The good Fighter Direction

The large number of screening destroyers, which enabled an all-round screen to be used, this preventing the torpedo aircraft from finding an easy way to attack the convoy.

When the fleet contains several units capable of engaging aircraft formations at long range, there appears to be a need for a Fleet Air Defence Officer to co-ordinate the long range gunfire of the fleet with fighter defence, thus ensuring that no enemy formation is left unfired at.

If the torpedo bombers had dropped their torpedoes at ranges under 1000 yards they would have been more effective and more of them would have been shot down. However, they were not willing to face the close range gunfire and so were ineffective. The fleet did well with their limited equipment.

In spite of the failure of the convoy to reach the expected dawn position on D.4 and the fact that both fighter direction ships had been put out of action, Spitfires extended their cover to a distance of 173 miles from Malta – a very commendable achievement.

Appendix IV

Commander Robb's report on the damage caused to
HMS *Manchester* on 13 August 1942

Ship's side penetrated abreast the After Engine Room, approx.
station 170 starboard or possibly a little aft of this.
Triangular rent in lower (armoured) deck over the After Engine
Room abreast the RDF generators.
X.7, X.5, Y.1 oil fuel tanks damaged and flooded.
Port and starboard Inner Main Engines (and After Engine Room)
out of action due to damage and flooding.
Starboard Outer Main Engine out of action, presumably due to a
broken shaft.
No. 4 dynamo out of action due to flooding and/or damage.
Electric power failed to all services aft including: steering gear, 'X'
& 'Y' turrets, after air compressors, after 50 ton pump.
Both After Engine Room Fire and Bilge pumps flooded.
After a short interval, electric power failed to the circulating
pumps of both diesel dynamos.
Fire main fractured in Office Flat about 170 S.
Main suction and oil fuel suction fractured in After Engine Room.
Machinery damage in After Engine Room not ascertainable.
Compartments flooded included:
Outer bottom: compartments previously containing oil but made
open to the sea X.5, X.7 and Y.1 oil fuel tanks; starboard W.T.
compartment abreast after Engine Room and presumably W.T.
compartment 155 – 159 starboard.
Hold: After Engine Room, 4-inch magazine, shaft passage,
plummer block compartment and gland compartment. 179 – 198
starboard. Shaft passage 137 – 155 starboard under diesel room.
Slow flooding, probably controllable by ship's pumps, probably took
place in all remaining shaft passages, plummer block compartments
and gland compartments through shaft bulkhead glands.
Platform deck: Gunner's and Paymaster's (clothing) stores 179 –
198 starboard.

Main W.T. office (slow flooding from 4-inch magazine or plummer block compartment through splits in deck – probably controllable with ship's pumps.
Starboard cable passage abreast After Engine Room.
Forward Engine Room:
Port shaft doing 'Full Ahead'

The immediate effects of the explosion were:
Loud knocking of starboard outer shaft which was stopped on orders of Cdr (E)
Starboard inner shaft observed to have stopped
Stoppage of Port Main Circulator causing condenser or turbine relief valve to lift, giving a cloud of steam over the port side of the engine room. Steam shut off to Port Outer Engine temporarily, until the circulator was restarted but the order to stop all shafts was received about this time. The engine was subsequently tried under steam and was correct.

Appendix V

Effect of the Explosion on the Ship on 13 August 1942

The Court reconstruction of the narrative of the loss of *Manchester* in ADM 156/210 summarises the damage caused by the explosion:

As to the hull and adjacent compartments: Ship's side penetrated in the neighbourhood of 175 station (i.e. in the vicinity of the after end of the after Engine Room. Platform deck immediately abaft Engine Room split in two places.
Compartments flooded:
Following compartments flooded rapidly (i.e. were open to the sea):
After Engine Room
4-inch Magazine
Starboard Shaft Passage 127 – 155
Starboard Watertight Compartment abreast After Engine Room (155 – 179)
Starboard Plummer Block Compartment (186 - 190)
Starboard Gland Compartment (186 – 190)
Starboard Cable Passage abreast After Engine Room (155 – 179)
Armament Office (179 – 198)
Soap and Tobacco Store (179 – 198)
Clothing Issue Room (179 – 198)
X.5, X.7 and Y.1 Oil Fuel Tanks
Following compartments flooded slowly and could not be controlled:
Port Shaft Passage (127 – 155)
Port Plummer Block Compartment (186 – 190)
Plummer Block Compartments (Port and Starboard (198 – 202))
Gland Compartments (Port and Starboard (213 – 218))
Main W/T Office
The effect of this flooding was that the ship quickly listed 10.5° to 11° to starboard.
As to the main and auxiliary machinery:

After Engine Room: Flooded thereby putting out of action port and starboard inner shafts. The starboard inner shaft was probably damaged.

After Boiler Room: Controllable leaks. Fires put out due to sea water in oil fuel.

Forward Engine Room:
Starboard Outer shaft damaged and useless, minor defects and leaks which were very soon rectified. Port outer turbine and shaft in working order, but port circulator tripped.

Forward Boiler Room: Full head of steam of 340 lbs at all times maintained in both boilers.

Fire Main: Fractured in the Office Flat about station 170 starboard. No. 4 Steam Dynamo situated in the After Engine Room was put out of action by flooding. The remaining three dynamos were not affected.

Ring Main: Power failed on after sections of the ring main to port and starboard.

Armament:
Main armament (6-inch): Main armament was undamaged mechanically except that power was not available to train 'X' and 'Y' turrets. Structure to 'X' Turret possibly affected by the explosion and possibly rendered temporarily unavailable owing to fumes. There was a temporary failure of electric power to 'A' and 'B' turrets.

High Angle Armament: (4-inch)
High Angle armament was mechanically undamaged. Ammunition supply was limited to the 350 rounds outside the 4-inch magazine.

Short Range Weapons:
Pom Poms and Oerlikon guns were correct except that Numbers 3 and 5 Oerlikons were temporarily unusable due to oil fuel on the deck.

Gunnery Control:
Fore DCT was mechanically sound and in order. After DCT was damaged by the explosion and had no electric power.

The Starboard and Port High Angle Directors were mechanically sound but the Starboard and After HA.DCTs reported difficulty in training.

Fire Control Communications in the fore part of the ship, in all probability remained intact, but some damage must have occurred to the circuits leading aft.

Torpedoes and Paravanes:
All torpedo armament was mechanically correct, except the

training gear of the starboard tubes was slightly buckled. There is no evidence as to state of the paravanes which remained streamed.

Internal Communications:
The ship's main telephone exchange switchboard was undamaged, but a certain number of lines were put out of action mainly in the after part of the ship.
Damage Control Headquarters remained in communication with the Bridge.
Warning telephone system was put out of action.
Sound Reproduction Equipment remained in action.

External Communications:
Loud Hailing Equipment: Remained in working order.
The Main Office was partially flooded.
The Second Office remained in order.
The Auxiliary Office remained in order.
The Remote Control Office remained in order.
V/S Equipment remained in working order.

Navigational:
The After Master Gyro was put out of action.
The Fore Master Gyro and Pelorus remained in order.
The Echo Sounding Gear was put out of order.
The steering gear and motors were mechanically sound, but power failed to the steering motors.

R.D.F. Equipment:
All gunnery R.D.F. Sets remained serviceable except Type 284 in which a fuse was blown, but immediately replaced. Type 279 was probably put out of action owing to destruction of generators. Type 273 remained in action.

Appendix VI

HMS *Manchester* Roll of Honour, 13 August 1942

Coyle, James H.	Stoker
Dunning, Thomas W. F.	Petty Officer
Frankland, Leonard M.	Sub-Lieutenant (E)
Godden, Leslie J.	Acting Leading Stoker
Hodgkinson, Francis R.	Stoker 1st Class
Noble, William H.	Stoker 1st Class
Powis, William A.	Acting Stoker Petty Officer
Smith, Charles F.	Chief Mechanic
Toogood, William	Acting ERA 4th Class
Whitehead, Ronald G.	Able Seaman
Turner, Bert	Stoker

Bibliography

PRIMARY SOURCES

Admiralty Records; Documents held in The National Archives, Kew, London

ADM 1/9360	6-inch cruiser with triple turrets: legend and design 1933.
ADM 1/9365	M Class Cruisers: catapult and aircraft arrangements.
ADM 156/209	Items to be investigated by Court of Enquiry into the scuttling of HMS *Manchester*.
ADM 156/209	Report of Court of Inquiry into the loss of HMS *Manchester* 17.9.42.
ADM 156/209	HMS *Manchester*: Report of Loss, 13/8/42 from Captain H. Drew RN.
ADM 156/209	Captain Drew, Lieutenant Commander Duff, Lieutenant Duff, Sub-Lieutenant Tabor, Warrant Officer Reddy and Petty Officer Phillips, Courts Martial 2-20/2/43.
ADM 156/209	Minutes of proceedings of Court-Martial held at Admiralty House, Portsmouth, to enquire into the loss of HMS *Manchester* under Section 92 of the Naval Discipline Act.
ADM 156/210	Court Reconstruction of the Narrative of the loss of HMS *Manchester*.
ADM 156/210	Minutes of Proceedings of Court Martial held at Admiralty House, Portsmouth to enquire into the loss of HMS *Manchester* under Section 92 of the Naval Discipline Act.
ADM 199/385	18th Cruiser Squadron, War Diary 1.3.1940–31.12.1940.
ADM 199/396	Home Fleet War Diaries 1.1.1941 – 31.12.1941.
ADM 199/415	Mediterranean Command: War Diaries, 1941.
ADM 199/657	Force H: Reports of Proceedings, 1941.
ADM 199/830	Report of Proceedings on Operation *Substance*.
ADM 199/1242	Operation *Pedestal* 2-16 August 1942.
ADM 234/444	HM Ships Damaged or Sunk by Enemy Action 3rd Sept 1939 – 2nd Sept 1945.

Author's Archive

Director of Naval Construction Damage Report DNC 4B/R81 (Copy No.2) HMS MANCHESTER TORPEDO DAMAGE 23.7.1941.

Director of Naval Construction Damage Report DNC 4B/R120 (Copy No.18) HMS LIVERPOOL TORPEDO DAMAGE 16.6.42.

SECONDARY SOURCES

Official Reports and Histories

British Mining Operations 1939-1945 Volume 1, Naval Staff History BR 1736(56)(1), MoD 1973.
Submarines Volume II: Operations in the Mediterranean, Naval Staff History BR 1736(52)(2) Second World War, Historical Section Admiralty, 1955 (MLRS Books).

HMSO Publications

Roskill, Captain S.W., *The War at Sea 1939-1945 Volume I: The Defensive* (HMSO, 1954).
Roskill, Captain S.W., *The War at Sea 1939-1945 Volume II: The Period of Balance* (HMSO, 1956)

Articles

Matt Outram, 'Sleeping Giant', *Diver*, November 2009.

Studies

Austin, Douglas, *Churchill and Malta's War 1939-1943* (Amberley Publishing, 2010).
Bagnasco Erminio *I MAS e le motosiluranti italiane 1906-1968* (Roma: Ufficio Storico della Marina Militare, 2nd Ed. 1968).
Barnett, Corelli, *Engage the Enemy More Closely: The Royal Navy in the Second World War* (Hodder & Stoughton, 1991).
Brescia, Maurizio, *Mussolini's Navy: A Reference Guide to the Regia Marina 1930-1945*, (Seaforth, 2012).
Brown, David K. (Editor), *The Design and Construction of British Warships 1939-1945: Volume 1, Major Surface Warships* (Conway Maritime Press, 1995).
_____, *Nelson to Vanguard: Warship Design and Development 1923–1945* (Chatham Publishing, 2000).
Campbell, John, *Naval Weapons of World War Two* (Conway Maritime Press, 1985).
Crabb, Brian James, *In Harm's Way: The Story of HMS Kenya, A Second World War Cruiser* (Paul Watkins, 1998).
van Crefeld, Martin, *Supplying War* (Cambridge University Press, 1977).
Cunningham, Admiral of the Fleet Viscount A.B., *A Sailor's Odyssey* (Hutchison & Co., 1951).
English, John, *The Hunts* (World Ship Society, 1987).
_____, *Amazon to Ivanhoe* (World Ship Society, 1993).
_____, *Afridi to Nizam: British Fleet Destroyers 1937–43* (World Ship Society, 2001).
_____, John, *Obdurate to Daring: British Fleet Destroyers 1941–45* (World Ship Society, 2008).
Faulknor, Marcus, *War at Sea: A Naval Atlas 1939-1945* (Seaforth, 2012).
Friedman, Norman, *British Cruisers: Two World Wars and After* (Seaforth Publishing, 2010).
Galea, Frederick R., *Call-Out: A Wartime Diary of Air/Sea Rescue Operations at Malta* (Malta At War Publications, 2002).
Greene, Jack and Massignani, Alessandro, *The Naval War in the Mediterranean 1940-1943* (Chatham Publishing, 1998).
Haines, Gregory *Cruiser at War* (Ian Allan, 1978).
Haarr, Geirr H., *The German Invasion of Norway April 1940* (Seaforth Publishing, 2009).
_____, *The Battle for Norway April – June 1940* (Seaforth Publishing, 2010).
_____, *The Gathering Storm: The Naval War in Northern Europe September 1939 – April 1940* (Seaforth Publishing 2013).

Hague, Arnold, *The Allied Convoy System 1939-1945: Its Organization, Defence and Operation* (Chatham Publishing, 2000).

Holland, James, *Fortress Malta: An Island Under Siege 1940 – 1943* (Orion Books Ltd, 2003).

Holman, Gordon, *The King's Cruisers* (Hodder & Stoughton, 1947).

Ireland, Bernard, *The War in the Mediterranean* (Pen & Sword, 2004).

Marder, A.J. Jacobsen, M., and Horsfield, J., *Old Friends New Enemies: The Royal Navy and the Imperial Japanese Navy, the Pacific War 1942-1945* (Oxford University Press, 1990).

Mattasini, F., *La Battagliam Aeronavale di Mezz'Agosto* (Edizoni dell'Ateneo e Bizzari, Roma, 1985).

Mitchell, W.H., and Sawyer, L.A., *The Empire Ships* 2nd Edition (Lloyds of London Press Ltd, 1990).

Mizzi, John A., *Operation Pedestal: The Story of the Santa Marija Convoy* (Midsea Books Ltd, 2012).

O'Hara, Vincent P., *Struggle for the Middle Sea: The Great Navies at War in the Mediterranean Theater 1940-1945* (Naval Institute Press, 2009).

_____, *In Passage Perilous: Malta and the Convoy Battles of June 1942* (Indiana University Press, 2013).

Pearson, Michael, *The Ohio and Malta: The Legendary Tanker that Refused to Die* (Pen & Sword, 2004).

Raven, Alan, and Roberts, John, *British Cruisers of World of War Two* (Arms and Armour Press, 1980).

Rohwer Jurgen, *Chronology of the War at Sea 1939-1945: The Naval History of World War Two* (Chatham, 2005).

Spong, H.C. and Osborne, R., *Shaw, Savill & Albion: A Fleet History* (World Ship Society, 2011).

Spooner, Tony, *Supreme Gallantry: Malta's Role in the Allied Victory 1939-1945* (John Murray, 1996).

Van Crefeld, Martin, *Supplying War* (Cambridge University Press, 1977).

Woodman, Richard, *Malta Convoys 1940-1943* (John Murray, 2000).

Websites

http://2ndhmsmanchesterassoc.org.uk.

http://divernet.com/Wrecks/159173/diving_for_justice.

http://en.Wikipedia.org/wki/HMS_Manchester_(15)

http://msptv.co.uk/index.php/programmes/running-the-gauntlet/

www.naval-history.net.

http://telegraph.co.uk/news/uknews/1404472/Disgraced-war-commander-innocent.html

http://www.unithistories.com/officers/RNofficersH.3html

http://wartimememoriesproject.com/ww2/ships/manchester.php#djenson

Notes

Introduction: 'Not the Royal Navy's Finest Moment'

1 Captain S.W. Roskill DSC, RN, *History of the Second World War: The War at Sea Volume II*, *The period of Balance* p.433, (HMSO, 1956), p.433.

2 *Manchester - Diving For Justice*, 'Divernet', http://divernet.com/Wrecks/159173/ diving_for_justice.

3 *Running the Gauntlet*, Crispin Sadler, quoted on: http://msptv.co.uk/index.php/programmes/ running-the-gauntlet/

4 Neil Tweedie, *Disgraced War-Commander 'Innocent'*, 15 August 2002, quoted on: http:// telegraph.co.uk/news/uknews/1404472/Disgraced-war-commander-innocent.html

5 http://2ndhmsmanchesterassoc.org.uk.

6 http://2ndhmsmanchesterassoc.org.uk.

7 http://en.Wikipedia.org/wki/HMS_Manchester_(15)

8 Ordinary Seaman Ronald Hindmarsh, quoted on: http://wartimememoriesproject.com/ww2/ ships/manchester.php#djenson

Chapter 1. The Watery Grave

1 Matt Outram, 'Sleeping Giant', *Diver*, November 2009.

Chapter 2. A Ship is Born

1 Alan Raven and John Roberts, *British Cruisers of World of War Two* (Arms and Armour Press, 1980) p.172.

2 ADM 1/9360, *6-inch Cruiser with Triple Turrets: Legend and Design 1933*, the National Archives, Kew; Alan Raven and John Roberts, p.173.

3 ADM 1/9365, *M Class Cruisers: Catapult and Aircraft Arrangements*, the National Archives, Kew.

4 D.K. Brown, *Nelson to Vanguard: Warship Design and Development 1923–1945* (Chatham Publishing, 2000), p.75. In note 43, David Brown states that 'there is a small piece of paper in the cover with a sketch of the funnels and Henderson's writing says make it like this'.

5 D.K. Brown (Editor), *The Design and Construction of British Warships 1939–1945: Volume 1 Major Surface Warships* (Conway Maritime Press, 1995), pp.106-107.

6 Alan Raven and John Roberts, *British Cruisers of World War Two* (1980), pp.174-175.

7 Sir Charles Jefferies, '*O.E.G'.: A Biography of Sir Oliver Goonetilleke* (London,1969) p.47, quoted by A.J. Marder, M. Jacobsen and J. Horsfield in *Old Friends New Enemies: The Royal Navy and the Imperial Japanese Navy, the Pacific War 1942–1945* (Oxford University Press, 1990), p.7.

8 Gregory Haines, *Cruiser at War* (Ian Allan, 1978) p.61.

Chapter 3: War

1   Gregory Haines, *Cruiser at War* (1978), p.61.
2   ADM 199/385, *18th Cruiser Squadron, War Diary 1.3.1940–31.12.1940*, the National Archives, Kew.
3   ibid, p.4.
4   A certificate specifying the contents of a neutral ship's cargo issued in time of war by a blockading power and exempting a non-contraband consignment from seizure or search.
5   ADM 199/385, *18th Cruiser Squadron, War Diary 1.3.1940–31.12.1940*, p.5.
6   ibid. p.6.
7   ibid. p.11.
8   ibid. p.12.
9   ibid, p.13.
10 ibid. p.14.
11 ibid. p.17.
12 ON and HN convoys operated during 1939-1940 and were outward to Norway and homeward from Norway respectively. This series of convoys escorted the Norwegian trade from the east coast Scottish port of Methil to and from the limit of Norwegian territorial waters.
13 Operation *Wilfred*: The minelayer *Teviotbank* left Scapa Flow on 5 April 1940 escorted by the destroyers *Inglefield*, *Isis*, *Imogen* and *Ilex* en route for Stadtlandet to lay the southernmost of the *Wilfred* minefields. Four minelaying destroyers, *Esk*, *Ivanhoe*, *Icarus* and *Impulsive*, each carrying sixty mines were en route for Vestfjord. The operation was cancelled in the evening of 7 April.
14 Operation *R4*: The 1st Cruiser Squadron (*Devonshire*, *Berwick*, *York* and *Glasgow*) and eight destroyers were at Rosyth on 7 April embarking troops and equipment for Bergen and Stavanger.
15 ADM 199/385, *18th Cruiser Squadron, War Diary 1.3.1940–31.12.1940*, p.21.
16 ibid. p.24.
17 Captain S.W. Roskill DSC, RN, *History of the Second World War: The War at Sea Volume I* (Her Majesty's Stationery Office, 1954), p.186.
18 ADM 199/385, *18th Cruiser Squadron, War Diary 1.3.1940–31.12.1940*, pp.42-9.
19 ibid. pp.52-60.
20 ibid. pp.61-5.
21 ibid. pp.66-70.
22 ibid. p.85.
23 ibid .p.96.
24 ibid. p.104.
25 ibid. p.107.
26 ibid. p.108.
27 The Director of Naval Construction, Sir Stanley Goodall, noted that 'these Southamptons are a groggy lot' as well as observing that there were 'bad design troubles with *Manchester*'. Quoted by D.K. Brown in *Nelson to Vanguard*, p.204.

Chapter 4: Captain Drew

1   ADM 199/385, *18th Cruiser Squadron, War Diary 1.3.1940–31.12.1940*, pp.150-4.
2   ibid. p.154.
3   ibid. p.155.
4   ADM 199/396, *Home Fleet War Diaries 1.1.1941 – 31.12.1941*, p.4
5   *British Mining Operations 1939-1945 Volume 1*, Naval Staff History BR 1736(56)(1), MoD, 1973, p.138.

Chapter 5: Operation *Substance*

1   ADM 199/415, *Mediterranean Command: War Diaries, 1941*, p.41.

2   Cunningham, Admiral of the Fleet Viscount AB, *A Sailor's Odyssey* (Hutchison & Co., 1951), pp.404-5.

3   'Club Run' was an informal name for aircraft supply operations to Malta during 1940-1942 covered by Force H based at Gibraltar.

4   The two operations undertaken during 26 June to 1 July were code-named *Railway I* (two Hurricanes) and *Railway II* (thirty-five Hurricanes).

5   ADM 199/657, *Force H: Reports of Proceedings, 1941*, pp.136-8.

6   ibid. p.124.

7   ibid. p.133.

8   ibid. pp.126-7.

9   ibid. p.128.

10   ibid. p.128.

11   ibid. p.130.

12   ibid. p.132.

13   ibid. p.133.

14   ibid. p.134.

15   ibid. p.135.

16   *Arethusa* was camouflaged in Mountbatten pink from mid-1939 to mid-1941.

17   The Osprey-class sloop HMS *Cormorant* was reduced to harbour service in 1889 and commissioned on 5 November 1889 as a tender to the composite gunboat *Goshawk*. The Gibraltar base was moved ashore and renamed *Rooke* on 1 July1946. *Cormorant* was broken up in 1949.

18   ADM 199/657, p.136.

19   ibid. pp.138-9.

20   ibid. p.79.

21   ADM 199/415, *Mediterranean Command: War Diaries, 1941*, p.81.

22   ibid. p.83.

23   *Submarines Volume II: Operations in the Mediterranean*, Naval Staff History BR 1736(52)(2) Second World War, Historical Section Admiralty 1955 (MLRS Books), pp.44-5.

Chapter 6: Back Home

1   ADM 199/830, *Report of Proceedings on Operation Substance from Flag Officer Commanding 18th Cruiser Squadron to Flag Officer commanding Force H*, pp.64-7.

2   Many British fleet destroyers were fitted with a pair of davits on the quarterdeck to enable them to deploy minesweeping gear. TSDS: Two Speed Destroyer Sweep.

3   *Diana*, which was to have been Mussolini's State Yacht, was commissioned on 12 November 1940 and was soon employed as a fast transport.

4   Motoscafo Turismo boats were 6.15m long and carried a 300kg explosive charge. They were derivatives of an existing design of fast sporting motor boat. They were also known as Barchini Explosivi (explosive motor boats).

5   MAS 451 and 452 had been built in 1938 as experimental diesel-engine craft based on the 500-class hulls. Their engines were unsuccessful and they were later fitted with Isotta Frashini petrol engines. Both were lost on the night of 25/26 July 1941.

6   The Motoscafo Turismo Lento was a SLC carrier.

7   Siluri a Lenta Corsa was also known as 'maiali' (pig).

8   A new steel bridge linking St Elmo to the breakwater opened on 25 July 2012.

9   Frederick R. Galea, *Call-Out: A Wartime Diary of Air/Sea Rescue Operations at Malta* (Malta At War Publications, 2002), p.71.

10   ADM 199/657, p.142.

11   ibid. p.149.

12   *HMS Manchester Torpedo Damage 23.7.41*, Director of Naval Construction Damage Report Ref. DNC 4B/R81.

13   ADM 199/396, *Home Fleet: War Diaries 1.1.41 – 31.12.41*, p.146.

14   ADM 199/657, p.166.

15   *British Mining Operations*, p.158.

Chapter 7: Operation Pedestal

1   Correlli Barnett, *Engage the Enemy More Closely: The Royal Navy in the Second World War* (Hodder & Stoughton, 1991).

2   Martin van Crefeld, *Supplying War* (Cambridge University Press, 1977), p.199.

3   ADM 199/1242 *Operation Pedestal 2-16 August 1942, HMS* Ashanti *Report of Proceedings*.

4   ADM 199/1242 *Operation Pedestal 2-16 August 1942, Appendix B: Detaching of Force 'X' Until Rejoining Force 'A'* [actually Force 'Z'].

5   ibid.

6   A similar incident occurred on 15 September 1942 the Japanese submarine *I-19* fired a spread of six torpedoes at an approaching United States Navy task force. Three hit the aircraft carrier USS *Wasp* which sank after being devastated by internal explosions. A fourth torpedo hit the destroyer USS *O'Brien* while a fifth hit the battleship USS *North Carolina*.

7   ADM 199/1242, *Operation Pedestal 2-16 August 1942, Reports of Proceedings of HMS Ashanti*, p.2.

8   ibid.

9   This Italian report is somewhat confused. Thus, it correctly identifies a Tribal class destroyer (*Ashanti*) ahead of the second cruiser (the damaged *Kenya*) and then goes on to state that this latter ship was the one attacked. In fact it was the *Manchester* (the lead cruiser) which was attacked and hit by one torpedo fired from *MS 16*.

10   Francesco Mattesini, *La Battaglia Aeronavale di Mezzo Agosto*, Translated by Andrew Smith, (Edizioni dell' Ateneo, Roma, 1986).

11   ADM 199/1242, *Operation Pedestal 2-16 August 1942, Reports of Proceedings of HMS Eskimo*, p.1.

12   ibid; Fortunately, Rear Admiral Parona's mission to attack the *Pedestal* convoy early on the morning of 13 August was cancelled at 23.30 hours the previous day. Had the sortie been allowed to proceed there can be no doubt that the remnants of Force X would have encountered an Italian force which was far superior in fighting strength. The cancellation of Parona's operation probably cost the Axis their best chance of annihilating the surviving merchant ships and thereby forcing the besieged island to surrender because of starvation. Most sources explain this decision as being the result of Italo-German disagreements over air cover. Andrew Smith (personal communication with the author) points out that when the cruiser operation was launched certain risks to Parona's ships were deemed to be unacceptable. These were (a) a night battle with British ships (b) a day battle with British ships unless the Italian force was superior in strength and (c) coming within range of Malta's strike aircraft unless an adequate fighter escort was provided. The Italians were concerned that tactical surprise had been lost and did not know that at 07.00 hours on 13 August Force X had been reduced to one damaged 6-inch gun cruiser, one 4.5-inch gun AA cruiser and nine destroyers. Andrew Smith believes that, in the final analysis, it was the threat posed by British surface ships that caused the operation to be cancelled.

Chapter 8: Torpedo Strike!

1   Royal Navy ships kept zone time, and the zone that each vessel was in was marked in the log on a daily basis: Z(ero) = Greenwich Mean Time (known as 'Zulu Time'). Zone divisions were 15° of longitude, Z extending 7.5° either side of the Greenwich meridian. Zones A to M (omitting J) extended eastwards, Zones N to Y extended westwards. In the non-suffix system employed by RN vessels, Z –n = GMT and Z -2 means zone time is 2 hours ahead of Greenwich Mean Time. FDSN54/2000 Naval Historical Branch Ministry of Defence 28/03/00.

2   Extracts from Erminio Bagnasco, *I MAS e le motosiluranti italiane 1906-1968* [*Italian MAS and motosiluranti 1906-1968*] (Roma: Ufficio Storico della Marina Militare, 2nd Ed. 1968), pp.440-3 (ships' histories of *MS 16* and *MS 22*). Translated by Andrew Smith.

3   ADM 156/209, *Report of Court of Inquiry into the loss of HMS* Manchester *17.9.42,* pp.19-20.

4   ibid. p.43.

5   ibid. p.21.

6   ibid. p.42.

7   ADM 156/210, *Court Reconstruction of the Narrative of the Loss of HMS* Manchester, pp.554-75.

8   Gordon Holman, *The King's Cruisers* (Hodder & Stoughton, 1947), pp.175-6.

9   ADM 156/209, *Report of Court of Inquiry into the loss of HMS* Manchester *17.9.42*, p.39.

10 ibid, pp.35-6.

11 ADM 156/210, *Minutes of Proceedings of Court Martial held at Admiralty House, Portsmouth to Enquire into the Loss of HMS* Manchester *Under Section 92 of the Naval Discipline Act*, pp.307-8.

12 ADM 156/209, *Report of Court of Inquiry into the Loss of HMS* Manchester *17.9.42*, p.38.

13 ibid. p.49.

14 ibid. p.46.

15 ibid, p.34

16 ibid. p.30.

17 ADM 156/210, *Court Reconstruction of the Narrative of the loss of HMS* Manchester, p.565.

18 ADM 156/209, *Report of Court of Inquiry into the loss of HMS* Manchester *17.9.42*, p.16.

19 Ordinary Seaman Roland Hindmarsh, quoted on: http://wartimememoriesproject.com/ww2/ships/manchester.php#djenson

20 ADM 156/209, *Report of Court of Inquiry into the Loss of HMS* Manchester, *17.9.42*, p.49.

21 ADM 156/210, *Court Reconstruction of the Narrative of the Loss of HMS* Manchester, p.562.

22 ADM 156/209, *Report of Court of Inquiry into the Loss of HMS* Manchester *17.9.42*, p.46.

23 ibid, p.37.

24 ibid. p.50.

25 ADM 156/210, *Court Reconstruction of the Narrative of the Loss of HMS* Manchester, p.563.

26 ADM 156/209, *Report of Court of Inquiry into the Loss of HMS* Manchester *17.9.42*, p.52-3.

27 ibid. p.54.

28 ibid, pp.26-7.

29 ADM 156/210, *Court Reconstruction of the Narrative of the Loss of HMS* Manchester, p.563.

30 ADM 156/209, *Report of Court of Inquiry into the loss of HMS* Manchester *17.9.42*, pp.17-8.

31 ibid. p.23.

32 ADM 156/210, *Court Reconstruction of the Narrative of the Loss of HMS* Manchester, pp.563-4.

33 ADM 156/209, *Court Reconstruction of the Narrative of the Loss of HMS* Manchester, p.58.

Chapter 9: Scuttled

1   ADM 156/210, *Minutes of Proceedings of Court Martial held at Admiralty House, Portsmouth to Enquire into the Loss of HMS* Manchester *Under Section 92 of the Naval Discipline Act*, pp.271-83.

2   ibid. pp.284-92.
3   ADM 156/210, *Court Reconstruction of the Narrative of the Loss of HMS* Manchester, pp.568-9.
4   ADM 156/209, *Report of Court of Inquiry into the Loss of HMS* Manchester *17.9.42*, p.63.
5   ibid. p.61.
6   ibid.
7   ADM 156/210, *Court Reconstruction of the Narrative of the Loss of HMS* Manchester, p.574.
8   ADM 156/209, *Report of Court of Inquiry into the Loss of HMS* Manchester *17.9.42*, p.62.
9   ibid. pp.72-4.
10 ADM 156/210, *Court Reconstruction of the Narrative of the Loss of HMS* Manchester, p.575.

Chapter 10: Board of Inquiry

1   ADM 156/209, *Items to be Investigated by Court of Enquiry into the Scuttling of HMS* Manchester, p.2.
2   ibid. p.3.
3   ibid. p.5.
4   ibid. p.6.
5   ibid. p.1.
6   ADM 156/209, *Report of Court of Inquiry into the Loss of HMS* Manchester *17.9.42*, p.9.
7   See Chapter 13 for the reports of some of those who were either transferred to HMS *Pathfinder* or rescued by HMS *Eskimo* or HMS *Somali* and returned to the United Kingdom in late August 1942.
8   ibid. p.67.
9   ibid. p.69
10 ibid. p.22.
11 ibid. p.64
12 ibid. pp.4-8.
13 ADM 156/209, *Items to be Investigated by Court of Enquiry into the Scuttling of HMS* Manchester, p.1.
14 ibid. p.2.
15 ibid.

Chapter 11: Court Martial

1   ADM 156/209, *Minutes of Proceedings of Court-Martial held at Admiralty House, Portsmouth, to Enquire into the Loss of HMS* Manchester *Under Section 92 of the Naval Discipline Act*, p.3.
2   ibid. p.75.
3   ibid. p.3.
4   ibid. p.12.
5   ibid.
6   ibid. p.13.
7   ibid. p.16.
8   ibid. p.9.
9   ibid. p.22.
10 ibid.
11 ibid. p.23.
12 ibid.
13 ibid.
14 ibid. p.32.
15 ibid. pp.11-7.

16   The three originated from Captain Drew asking a leading question and then using the question as the answer.

17   ADM 156/209, *HMS* Manchester: *Report of Loss, 13/8/42 from Captain H. Drew RN*, p.10, and *Minutes of Proceedings of Court-Martial held at Admiralty House, Portsmouth, to Enquire into the Loss of HMS* Manchester *Under Section 92 of the Naval Discipline Act*, p.26.

18   ADM 156/209, *HMS* Manchester: *Report of Loss, 13/8/42 from Captain H. Drew RN*, p.11, and *Minutes of Proceedings of Court-Martial held at Admiralty House, Portsmouth, to Enquire into the Loss of HMS* Manchester *Under Section 92 of the Naval Discipline Act*, p.18-9.

19   ADM 156/209, *Minutes of Proceedings of Court-Martial held at Admiralty House, Portsmouth, to Enquire into the Loss of HMS* Manchester *Under Section 92 of the Naval Discipline Act*, p.47.

Chapter 12: Captain Drew's Evidence

1   ADM 156/209, *Minutes of Proceedings of Court-Martial held at Admiralty House, Portsmouth, to Enquire into the Loss of HMS* Manchester *Under Section 92 of the Naval Discipline Act*, p.60.
2   ibid. pp.61-2.
3   ibid. p.63.
4   ibid. p.65.
5   ibid. pp.66-8.
6   ibid. pp.69-70.
7   ibid. pp.70-1.
8   ibid. p.72.
9   ibid. pp.78-9.
10   ibid. pp.82-4.
11   ibid. pp.84-5.
12   ibid. p.87.
13   ibid. pp.89-90.
14   ibid. pp.91-2.
15   ibid. p.93.
16   ibid. pp.94-6.
17   ibid. p.98.

Chapter 13: Evidence of Key Witnesses

1   ADM 156/209, *Minutes of Proceedings of Court-Martial held at Admiralty House, Portsmouth, to Enquire into the Loss of HMS Manchester Under Section 92 of the Naval Discipline*, p.113.
2   ibid. pp.115-6.
3   ibid. p.118.
4   ibid. p.121.
5   ibid. p.122.
6   ibid. p.129.
7   ibid.
8   ibid.
9   ibid. p.130.
10   ibid. p.133.
11   ibid. p.134.
12   ibid. p.139.
13   ibid. p.143.
14   ibid. p.150.
15   ibid. p.157.

16   ibid. pp.162-5.
17   ibid. p.170.
18   ibid.
19   ibid. pp.170-1.
20   ibid. pp.172-3.
21   ibid. pp.173-4.
22   ibid. p.174.
23   ibid.
24   ibid. p.186.
25   ibid. p.187.
26   ADM 156/210, *Minutes of Proceedings of Court-Martial held at Admiralty House, Portsmouth, to Enquire into the Loss of HMS Manchester Under Section 92 of the Naval Discipline*, p.210.
27   ibid. p.219.
28   ibid. p.218.
29   ibid. p.220.

Chapter 14: The Damning Evidence

1   ADM 156/210, *Minutes of Proceedings of Court-Martial held at Admiralty House, Portsmouth, to Enquire into the Loss of HMS Manchester Under Section 92 of the Naval Discipline*, pp.294-5.
2   ibid. p.296.
3   ibid. pp.296-7.
4   ibid. pp.298-300.
5   ibid. pp.300-1.
6   ibid. p.302.
7   ibid. p.304.
8   ibid. pp.304-5.
9   ibid. pp.307-9.
10   ibid. p.326.
11   ibid. p.319.
12   ibid. p.410.
13   ibid. pp.415-6.
14   ibid. p.421.
15   ibid. pp.424-6.
16   ibid. p.429.
17   ibid. p.430.
18   ibid. p.432.
19   ibid. p.438.
20   ibid. p.440.
21   ibid. pp.478-9.
22   ibid. pp.501-6.
23   ibid. p.509.
24   ibid. pp.515-6.
25   ibid. p.516.
26   ibid. p.517.
27   ibid.
28   ibid.
29   ibid. p.518.
30   ibid. p.519.

31   ibid. pp.532-3.
32   ibid. p.534.

Chapter 15: The Verdict

1   ADM 156/210, *Minutes of Proceedings of Court-Martial held at Admiralty House, Portsmouth, to Enquire into the Loss of HMS Manchester Under Section 92 of the Naval Discipline*, pp.537-575.
2   ibid. pp.578-9.
3   ibid. p.580.
4   ibid.
5   ibid. p.583.
6   ibid. p.588.
7   ibid. p.590.
8   ibid. p.593.
9   ibid. p.595.
10   ibid. p.598.
11   ADM 156/209, *Captain Drew, Lieutenant Commander Duff, Lieutenant Duff, Sub-Lieutenant Tabor, Warrant Officer Reddy and Petty Officer Phillips, Courts Martial 2-20/2/43*, pp.12-3.
12   ibid. pp.14-5.
13   ibid. pp.1-2.
14   ibid. pp.3-4.
15   ibid. pp.5-6.
16   ibid. p.6.
17   ibid.
18   ibid.
19   http://www.unithistories.com/officers/RNofficersH.3html

Chapter 16: England Expects

1   ADM 156/210, *Minutes of Proceedings of Court-Martial held at Admiralty House, Portsmouth, to Enquire into the Loss of HMS Manchester Under Section 92 of the Naval Discipline*, p.563.
2   ibid. p.562.
3   ibid. p.493.
4   ibid. pp.339-340.
5   ibid. p.302.
6   ibid. p.496.
7   ibid. p.569.
8   ibid. pp.571-3.
9   Mattasini, F., *La Battagliam Aeronavale di Mezz'Agosto*, Edizoni dell'Ateneo e Bizzari, Roma, 1985, pp.348-350, translated by Andrew Smith, personal communication of his translation of Italian sources.
10   Jurgen Rohwer, *Chronology of the War at Sea 1939-1945: The Naval History of World War Two*, p.186.
11   ADM 234/444, *HM Ships Damaged or Sunk by Enemy Action 3rd Sept 1939 – 2nd Sept 1945*, p.80.
12   ibid. p.82.
13   ibid. p.85.
14   ADM 156/209, *Captain Drew, Lieutenant Commander Duff, Lieutenant Duff, Sub-Lieutenant Tabor, Warrant Officer Reddy and Petty Officer Phillips, Courts Martial 2-20/2/4*, pp.1-4.

15   Rear Admiral Roger Morris RN Retired, personal communication.

16   As a junior officer Rear Admiral Roger Morris was present at the post-war grounding of the survey ship *Cook* in Fiji. He saw at first-hand how decisive firm leadership by his captain was in the whole business of extricating the ship from what could well, under less energetic direction from the top, have resulted in the ship's loss.

17   ADM 156/209, *Minutes of Proceedings of Court-Martial held at Admiralty House, Portsmouth, to Enquire into the Loss of HMS Manchester Under Section 92 of the Naval Discipline*, p.94.

18   ADM 156/209, *Captain Drew, Lieutenant Commander Duff, Lieutenant Duff, Sub-Lieutenant Tabor, Warrant Officer Reddy and Petty Officer Phillips, Courts Martial 2-20/2/4*, p.15.

Index